INEBRANLABLE

DEVON AND CORNWALL RECORD SOCIETY

New Series, Volume 49

Issued to members for the year 2006

In association with The Somerset Record Society

DEVON AND CORNWALL RECORD SOCIETY

New Series, Volume 49

THE ACLAND FAMILY: MAPS AND SURVEYS 1720–1840

Edited with an Introduction by

Mary R. Ravenhill and Margery M. Rowe

Exeter

2006

ISBN 0 901853 49 6

Designed and typeset by Mike Dobson, Quince Typesetting
Times New Roman 9/12

Printed and bound in Great Britain
by Short Run Press Ltd, Exeter

Front cover and back covers: Detail from the map of Heale and Tower Hill in Jacobstow, Cornwall taken from the *Atlas of the Manors of Efford and Thurlibeer* by S.T. Coldridge, Exeter, 1828. (By kind permission of the owner)

Frontispiece: Part of the Ordnance Surveyor's Drawing sheet 40, dated 1801. Scale as original, 3" to one mile. (By courtesy of the British Library Board)

End Papers: Front: Acland coat of arms from an estate atlas of 1828 (see Illustration 1); part of the Ordnance Survey Maps, scale 6" to one mile. Killerton, originally surveyed 1886–7, revised in 1904
Back: Part of the Ordnance Survey Maps, scale 6" to one mile. Holnicote, originally surveyed in 1888, revised in 1928.

Contents

Acknowledgements

In 2002 the Devon and Cornwall Record Society published our volumes on *Devon Maps and Map-Makers to 1840*. The limits thus imposed meant that maps of estates owned by the great Devon families in other counties could not be included, nor could the work of some of our important surveyors and map-makers be fully explored. The Acland estates, lying as they do in Somerset and Cornwall as well as in Devon, provided an opportunity to develop and extend our earlier study. We are grateful therefore to the Devon and Cornwall Record Society and their General Editor, Professor Andrew Thorpe, who agreed to publish this third volume on maps, and to Dr Todd Gray who agreed to act as Editor for us for another book. We have been pleased to publish this volume in association with the Somerset Record Society. The documents we have included have come from a variety of sources and we are grateful to their owners for allowing reproduction. Each is named in the List of Illustrations.

Successful research depends on the help and advice of many people and it is always a pleasure to express our thanks to them. The Acland estates were given to the National Trust in 1944 and we have received assistance from many of their staff; in particular, Shirley Blaylock, Hugh Mellor, Isabel Richardson and David Whitworth. Carolyn Keep of the Devon Gardens Trust also provided information about Killerton. Acland papers have been deposited in two West Country Record Offices (Devon and Somerset) and the Archivists there have patiently dealt with our many requests; their help has been invaluable. John Draisey at Exeter, Tim Wormleighton at Barnstaple, Anne Morgan at Plymouth, Paul Brough at Truro and Tom Mayberry in Taunton all deserve special mention. We would also wish to thank Colin Edwards, formerly of the Cornwall Record Office, and Sue Berry of the Somerset Record Office. Christine North and Dr Robert Dunning have assisted in the identification of the place-names mentioned in the Surveys of Manors in Cornwall and Somerset and we are grateful for their expertise. Archivists at the Record Offices in Aberdeen and Hampshire have taken much trouble to answer our letters of enquiry in considerable detail. Peter Waite, Tony Rowse, Richard Applegate, and Lucy Browne of the West-country Studies Library in Exeter and David Bromwich of the Somerset Local Studies Library in Taunton have all assisted us and we are most grateful to them.

The discovery of a little-known atlas of Cornish estates owned by the Aclands led to a very happy co-operation with Bryan Dudley Stamp of Ebbingford Manor and Philippa Fitzpatrick, former Archivist to the Bude and Stratton Council, who were helpful in sorting out the affairs of the Bude Canal.

We owe a constant debt of gratitude to Professor Roger Kain of Exeter University who has always encouraged us and given us the benefit of his wide knowledge of the history of cartography. With Professor Harold Fox he supported our successful applic-ation to the Marc Fitch Fund which has made possible the inclusion of the illustrations of many maps. Peter Barber, April Carlucci, and Kimberly Kowal of the British Library, Map Library, made possible the reproduction of the Surveyors' Drawings of 1801 which provide an interesting addition to the maps of Killerton. The high quality of the illustrations is the work of Andrew Teed and Barry Phillips of the Photographic Unit of the School of Geography and Archaeology, University of Exeter, and Peter Collings of the Reprographics Department, Somerset Record Office; the maps were drawn by Helen Jones and we are most appreciative of all their work. For the typesetting and many helpful suggestions for the arrangement of the text we wish to thank Dr Mike Dobson and for the final appearance of this volume we would like to express our appreciation of the work of the Short Run Press, Exeter, in particular Andrew Gliddon. In conclusion, we must record our thanks to our Editor, Dr Todd Gray, who has followed the progress of this venture from the beginning and has made many helpful suggestions.

It is inevitable in any description of maps and surveys that some errors and discrepancies will occur and these are of course our responsibility, which we are more than ready to recognise and accept.

Mary R Ravenhill   *Margery M Rowe*

Candlemas 2006

The Editors and the Society acknowledge with thanks financial assistance from the Marc Fitch Fund towards the cost of this volume.

Illustrations and Maps

Maps

Abbreviations

AL	Alexander Law	NDRO	North Devon Record Office
b.	born	*OED*	*A New English Dictionary on historical principles* edited by James H. Murray (Oxford, 1888)
bap.	baptised		
BMI	Burnet Morris Index (in Westcountry Studies Library)	O.S.	Ordnance Survey
c.	circa	OUP	Oxford University Press
CRO	Cornwall Record Office	PB	Charles Prideaux Brune
d.	died	PRO	Public Record Office
DCNQ	*Devon and Cornwall Notes and Queries*	PWDRO	Plymouth and West Devon Record Office
DCRS	Devon and Cornwall Record Society	*SM*	*Sherborne Mercury*
DRO	Devon Record Office	SRO	Somerset Record Office
EFP	*Exeter Flying Post*	TDA	Sir Thomas Dyke Acland, 10th Baronet
JPA	John Palmer Acland	WCL	Westcountry Studies Library
n.d.	undated		

Sources for Genealogical Table (opposite):

J. L. Vivian, *The Visitation of the County of Devon* (Exeter, 1895), page 5

Richard Ballard, *The Priory Church of St Andrew Stogursey* (Exeter, 1992), p. 39

Richard Crisp, *Abstracts of Somersetshire Wills*, second series (privately printed, 1888)

Anne Acland, *A Devon Family* (Chichester, 1981), end paper

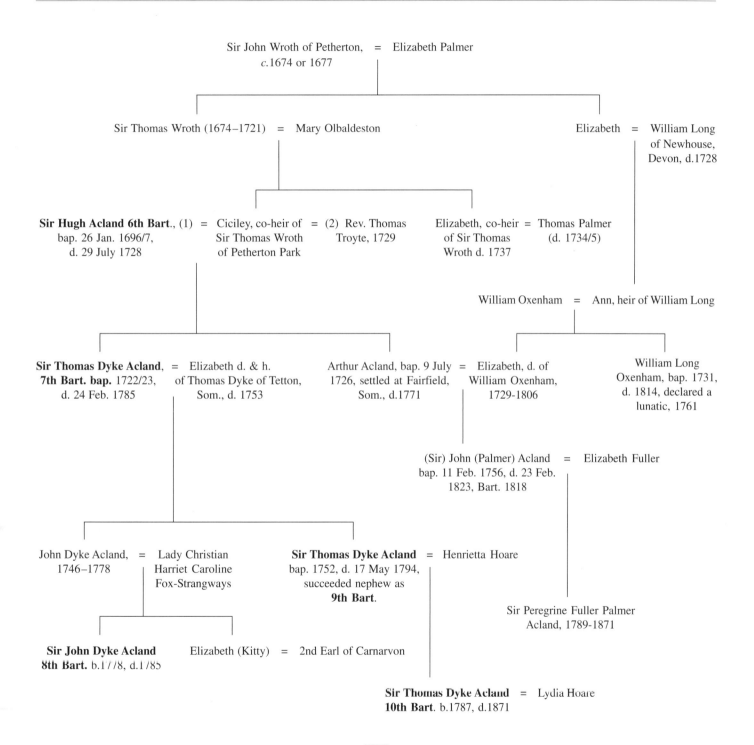

Sir John Wroth of Petherton, = Elizabeth Palmer
*c.*1674 or 1677

Sir Thomas Wroth (1674–1721) = Mary Olbaldeston

Elizabeth = William Long
of Newhouse,
Devon, d.1728

Sir Hugh Acland 6th Bart., (1) = Ciciley, co-heir of = (2) Rev. Thomas
bap. 26 Jan. 1696/7,   Sir Thomas Wroth   Troyte, 1729
d. 29 July 1728   of Petherton Park

Elizabeth, co-heir = Thomas Palmer
of Sir Thomas   (d. 1734/5)
Wroth d. 1737

William Oxenham = Ann, heir of William Long

Sir Thomas Dyke Acland, = Elizabeth d. & h.
7th Bart. bap. 1722/23,   of Thomas Dyke of Tetton,
d. 24 Feb. 1785   Som., d. 1753

Arthur Acland, bap. 9 July = Elizabeth, d. of
1726, settled at Fairfield,   William Oxenham,
Som., d.1771   1729-1806

William Long
Oxenham, bap. 1731,
d. 1814, declared a
lunatic, 1761

(Sir) John (Palmer) Acland = Elizabeth Fuller
bap. 11 Feb. 1756, d. 23 Feb.
1823, Bart. 1818

John Dyke Acland, = Lady Christian
1746–1778   Harriet Caroline
Fox-Strangways

Sir Thomas Dyke Acland = Henrietta Hoare
bap. 1752, d. 17 May 1794,
succeeded nephew as
9th Bart.

Sir Peregrine Fuller Palmer
Acland, 1789-1871

Sir John Dyke Acland
8th Bart. b.1778, d.1785

Elizabeth (Kitty) = 2nd Earl of Carnarvon

Sir Thomas Dyke Acland = Lydia Hoare
10th Bart. b.1787, d.1871

Devon parishes in which the Aclands held land

List of Devon parishes in which the Aclands held land

• Parishes with maps(s) described in this volume

1 Hartland	37 Stoodleigh
2 Berrynarbor	38 Bampton
3 Marwood	39 Loxbeare •
4 East Down	40 Washfield •
5 Parracombe	41 Tiverton •
6 Bratton Fleming	42 Hatherleigh
7 Barnstaple •	43 Northlew
8 Goodleigh	44 Inwardleigh
9 Charles and High Bray •	45 Bickleigh
10 Landkey •	46 Thorverton
11 Bishop's Tawton •	47 Rewe
12 Swimbridge •	48 Silverton
13 East and West Buckland •	49 South Tawton
14 North Molton •	50 Colebrooke •
15 Huntshaw	51 Crediton •
16 Great Torrington	52 Newton St Cyres
17 St Giles in the Wood •	53 Broadclyst •
18 Little Torrington •	54 Huxham
19 Peters Marland	55 Poltimore
20 Beaford •	56 Tedburn St Mary
21 Chittlehampton	57 Alphington
22 South Molton •	58 Exeter
23 Bishop's Nympton	59 Tavistock
24 George Nympton •	60 Manaton •
25 King's Nympton •	61 Ilsington •
26 Romansleigh •	62 Ashburton •
27 Roseash	63 Chudleigh •
28 Knowstone	64 Kenn •
29 East Anstey	65 Exminster •
30 Ashreigney	66 Kenton •
31 Chulmleigh •	67 Mamhead •
32 East Worlington	68 Widworthy
33 Creacombe	69 Seaton
34 Witheridge	70 Clyst Honiton
35 Rackenford •	71 Cheriton Fitzpaine •
36 Chawleigh •	72 Cullompton •

• Parishes with maps(s) described in this volume

1 Exmoor •
2 Porlock •
3 Luccombe and Stoke Pero •
4 Exford •
5 Winsford •
6 Hawkridge
7 Dulverton •
8 Brushford
9 Selworthy •
10 Minehead •
11 Wootton Courtney •
12 Cutcombe •
13 Timberscombe •

14 Dunster •
15 Carhampton •
16 Withycombe
17 St Decumans (part of Watchet &Williton)
18 Old Cleeve
19 Bicknoller
20 Crowcombe
21 Kilve and Kilton •
22 Stringston •
23 Stogursey •
24 Holford •
25 Nether Stowey •

26 Over Stowey •
27 Pawlett
28 Huntspill (East & West) •
29 Bridgwater
30 Broomfield
31 North Petherton •
32 Kingston St Mary
33 Hillfarrance (part of Oake)
34 Durston
35 Lyng •
36 Aller •
37 Meare •
38 Glastonbury •

Western Somerset parishes in which the Aclands held land

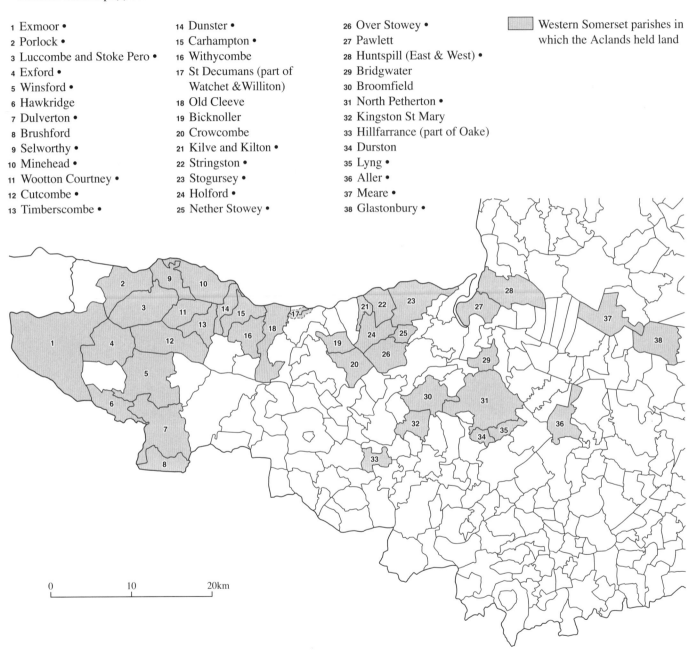

0   10   20km

Map 3 List of Cornish parishes in which the Aclands held land

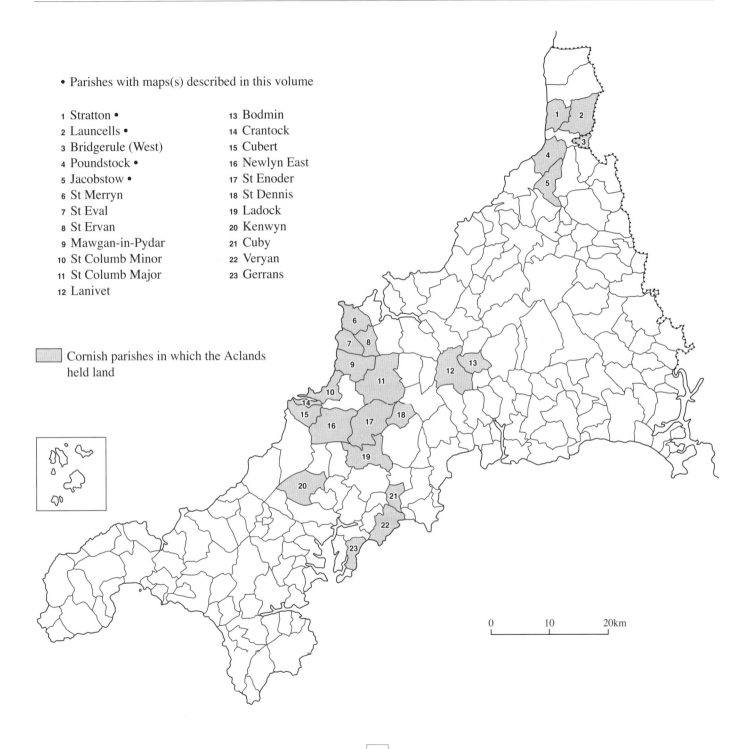

• Parishes with maps(s) described in this volume

1 Stratton •
2 Launcells •
3 Bridgerule (West)
4 Poundstock •
5 Jacobstow •
6 St Merryn
7 St Eval
8 St Ervan
9 Mawgan-in-Pydar
10 St Columb Minor
11 St Columb Major
12 Lanivet

13 Bodmin
14 Crantock
15 Cubert
16 Newlyn East
17 St Enoder
18 St Dennis
19 Ladock
20 Kenwyn
21 Cuby
22 Veryan
23 Gerrans

Cornish parishes in which the Aclands
held land

Introduction

1. The Acland Family

Maps and surveys

The period with which this volume is concerned, the eighteenth and early nineteenth centuries, was one of particular change relating to map-making and this is reflected in the record of the maps and surveys of the Acland estates. The publication in 1699 of Joel Gascoyne's near one inch to the mile map of Cornwall was no doubt the herald in South West England of what has been described as the 'cartographic revolution' of the eighteenth century.[1] For the time this was a large scale and Gascoyne's map was followed by Thomas Martyn's Cornwall in 1748 and Benjamin Donn's map of Devon in 1765, the first to win the prestigious award of the Royal Society for the Encouragement of Arts, Manufactures and Commerce for 'an actual survey of a county or counties'.[2] Among the 253 subscribers was Sir Thomas Dyke Acland[3] who, with many others in the county of Devon, may have come to realise the potential value of maps. However, the one-inch scale was too small to provide more than a framework on which some larger-scale maps could, if it was thought useful, be based. The many larger-scale maps commissioned by local landowners, surveyed and drawn, for the most part, by local map-makers mirrored the sudden increase in map-making elsewhere in the country. In Devon, between 1750 and 1800 some 700 have been located. The influence of the Ordnance Survey one inch to the mile map of Devon published in 1809 can be detected on some of the Acland maps drawn after that date. Even though sale of the O.S. map was prohibited between 1811 and 1816 there is evidence that 'Mudge's Map' had been acquired by the surveyors at Holnicote (see below p. 19). The conventional signs introduced by the draughtsmen in the Tower of London were on occasions adopted by contemporary map-makers and can be found on some Acland maps.[4] However, the tithe and enclosure maps, followed by the larger scale O.S. maps, meant that landowners did not need to rely on personal commissions to record their properties, and so few are found in the Acland archives for the period after 1840.[5] Therefore, the final date of 1840 chosen for this volume better reflects developments in mapping than important events in the history of the Acland family. Sir Thomas Dyke Acland, the 10th Bart, who commissioned so many of the maps and surveys described in this study, lived until 1871. The initial date of 1720 for this volume had

---

[1.] Quoted by Catherine Delano-Smith & Roger J.P. Kain, *English Maps A History* (London, The British Library, 1999), 81.

[2.] For a detailed account of this enterprise see W.L.D. Ravenhill, *A Map of the County of Devon* (DCRS and the University of Exeter, 1965).

[3.] A copy is in the Acland Archive at DRO, 1148M add 23/Z4.

[4.] See the drawings by Rodney Fry in J.B. Harley and Yolande O'Donoghue, *The Old Series Ordnance Survey Maps of England and Wales* (Harry Margary, 1977), Fig. 8.

[5.] Tithe numbers are used for fields on the map drawn for Sir Thomas Dyke Acland of lands in the parishes of Swimbridge and Landkey by A. Rowe of Barnstaple in 1847 (DRO, 1148M add13/E1) and there are copies of the tithe maps of Broadclyst (DRO, 1148M add3/APB1), Charles (DRO, 1926B/A/P/2/1) and High Bray (DRO, 1926B Series II Box 119) in the Acland archives.

the advantage that a cluster of surveys of Somerset estates, made shortly before these properties came into Acland hands as a result of the marriage of Sir Hugh Acland and Cecily Wroth, could be included.

Surveys and maps have long been important tools in the efficient management of landed estates. The surveys, compiled from written records and oral testimonies, defined the terms on which land was held, named individuals who were tenants or lessees and described the area concerned and its value, usually arranged under manors. From the middle of the sixteenth century the new environment of changing land ownership, rising land values and advancing agricultural practices, coupled with the development of accurate field surveys, meant that maps showing the location of those landholdings and details of the terrain could add a graphic dimension to the original written survey. In time the two processes came to be closely associated, appearing either in single volumes, estate atlases, or in the case of large areas as single maps accompanied by a written survey of the same date and usually by the same surveyor. It was John Richards, a local man, who played a part in making Devon landowners aware of the importance of these developments. In the years 1730 and 1739 he published *The Gentleman's Steward*[6] in which he described at length 'the usefulness of Surveys and correct Maps of Gentlemen's Estates; the Lord may, at any time as it were, look over his Demesnes, and not go out of his Mansion-house . . . In short the Map is no other than the Lands in Miniature; and if it be accurately done, the Scale and Compasses will tell the Length of any Hedge, or the Distance between any two Places on the Estate, by applying the same to the Map, as well as by the Chain by an actual Mensuration from Place to Place in the Field.'[7] With the map the 'Survey-Book will, at one View, discover the Situation, the Tenure, the term granted out, with details of tenants, their rents, the value etc, with such other Remarks as a judicious Surveyor thinks proper to insert'. He concluded that this information is of value to the Lord, 'especially when neither himself nor his Steward live on the Spot.'[8] It is this fusion of the written and land surveys and their use in land management which is characteristic of the maps and surveys of the Acland estates. Indeed, most of the maps are annotated in pencil or ink showing changes in the properties which occurred over time, thus bearing witness to the continuing use of the maps and surveys in the stewardship of the estates.

The general increase in map consciousness in the mid-eighteenth century reflected not only the landowner's desire to record details of his own estates but his interest in what was happening elsewhere by way of agricultural improvements, landscaping of parks and re-building of houses. This is borne out by maps in the Acland family archives which are discussed and listed in this volume and also in the family collections of other landowners in Devon. For example, the Courtenay archives provide a fairly early example of the genre in that an atlas of the Manors of Powderham and Kenton was produced for Sir William Courtenay by Robert Whittlesey in 1723. Whittlesey was a professional surveyor who worked nationally but no other examples of his work have been found in Devon. More typical in terms of date and the surveyors employed were the maps produced by William Doidge for the Cliffords at Ugbrooke in the 1740s and the maps of Tavistock and area drawn for the Russells, Dukes of Bedford, by John Wynne in the 1750s. Both Doidge and Wynne were local surveyors, although Wynne appears to have been born in Bedfordshire and came south to act as agent for the Bedford's Devon estates. The Aclands' preference was evidently for surveyors who lived close to the estates when the earliest mapping of these was undertaken in 1756–7.[9]

[6] John Richards, *The Gentleman's Steward and Tenants of Manors Instructed* (London, 1730), reprinted with *Annuities on Lives* (London, 1739). For information on John Richards and his contribution to mapping in Devon see Mary R. Ravenhill and Margery M. Rowe, eds, *Devon Maps and Map-makers* (DCRS, Exeter, 2000, 2002) Appendix A.

[7] Richards, 136.

[8] Richards, 146.

[9] In fact the earliest map in the Acland archives is a manuscript diagrammatic plan of Exmoor, drawn about 1700, but this does not relate specifically to the Acland estates. It is included in the list of maps for the sake of completeness.

The Acland estates

Robert Fraser, writing in 1794, noted that 'the freehold property of the County of Devon is also very much divided . . . a few families excepted there are no very great proprietors'.[10] The Aclands must be included amongst these exceptions; unlike the Courtenays, the Russells and the Petres, they never profited directly from the spoils of the Dissolution of the Monasteries, nevertheless by the early nineteenth century they had accumulated an estate of some 40,000 acres in Devon, Somerset and Cornwall. A claim made in the late-eighteenth century that it was possible to travel over Acland lands all the way from the English Channel to the Bristol Channel was only a slight exaggeration. The Aclands' wealth equalled that of a lesser peer[11] but unlike the families of Fortescue, Russell and Petre, their lands lay almost entirely in the West Country and especially in Devon and Somerset.

Much has been written on the dynastic history of the Acland family.[12] A simplified genealogical table appears on page xi but the purpose of this study is to concentrate more on the acquisition of their estates which may have been a factor in the generation of maps and surveys. Athough large collections of Acland papers survive in both the Devon and Somerset Record Offices[13] which relate to the two main branches of the family, there is no continuous series of estate accounts for the pre 1816 period and there are significant gaps in the survival of title deeds.[14] Therefore other types of document have to be used to build up a more accurate picture of when properties were acquired and how they were managed. The maps and surveys described in this volume shed light on these two aspects and the letters of the Aclands and one of their surveyors, Alexander Law, give an insight into the day-to-day administration of this large West Country estate.

All manuscript maps before and up to 1840 which were made for the Aclands or for previous owners of properties which they subsequently acquired have been listed in chronological order; some of the atlases also contain surveys, which are described with the map listing. A list of surveys of Acland properties, but with no maps attached, is also given, and three surveys of estates, for Devon in 1726, some Somerset manors in 1746–7 and Cornish properties *c*.1802 have been abstracted.

The growth of the estates

The Aclands were first recorded as holding land near Barnstaple in 1155, flourished quietly in the medieval period and were able to produce male heirs to make fortuitous marriages and thus add to their estates. Some indication of this may be seen in the Acland coat-of-arms, registered in the Heralds' Visitation of 1620 where the arms of the Leighs, the Hackworthys and the Mallets (Sir Arthur Acland married the heiress of the Mallets of Wooley thus securing the Manors of Wooley and Nimet St George), are incorporated. In the eighteenth century two Acland marriages in particular added to the family's prosperity: that of Sir Hugh Acland to Cecily Wroth, daughter and co-heiress of Sir Thomas Wroth of Petherton Park in Somerset in 1721 brought into the Acland family's possession some 2300 acres of land near Bridgwater, including the Manors of Newton Roth, Newton Regis and North Petherton, and a cash endowment of £12,000.[15] In 1745 Hugh's son, Thomas (the 7th Bart), married Elizabeth Dyke of Tetton, near Taunton. This marriage brought three separate new estates in Somerset to the Acland family, based on the houses of Holnicote and Pixton in the north west of the county and Tetton near Taunton. The land extended into 24 parishes and

[10.] R. Fraser, *General View of the County of Devon*, (London, 1794), 17.

[11.] J. Porter, 'The Development of Rural Society' in *The Agrarian History of England and Wales, 1750–1850*, G.E. Mingay, ed. (Cambridge, 1989), 836.

[12.] See, for example, Anne Acland, *A Devon Family* (London and Chichester, 1981), Rev. John Collinson, *The History of Somersetshire in Three Volumes* (Bath, 1791) and J.L. Vivian, *The Visitations of the County of Devon* (Exeter, 1895).

[13.] DRO, 1148M and adds; SRO, DD/AH (Acland Hood collection).

[14.] Letter from Sir Richard Acland to the Deputy County Archivist, Miss M.E. Cash, dated 17 August 1962 in DRO Deposit file. Sir Richard stated that some documents had perished in Anstey and Thompson's solicitors' office in Southernhay, Exeter, during the blitz in 1942.

[15.] For Marriage Settlement between Sir Hugh Acland, 6th Bart, of Columb John and Cecily Wroth dated 1721 see DRO, 1148M add/4/8.

included the Manors of Holnicote (acquired by the Dykes from the Arundells) and Bossington which passed to Sir Thomas.[16] The Manors of Lyng and Aller had been awarded to Thomas Palmer and Elizabeth his wife under a Wroth family settlement but later came into the Acland family.

A third large addition to the Acland estates occurred in the first few years of the nineteenth century when the 10th Bart succeeded to lands formerly of the Arundell family. Eight Cornish manors (Trerise alias Trerice, Tresillian, Goviley, Penstrase Moor, Cragantallan, Degembris, Ebbingford alias Efford and Thurlibeer) were devised to Sir Thomas Acland with the Manor of East Luckham in Somerset and the Manor of Stockley Luckham in Devon at that time, he being the heir of the last Lord Arundell who had died in 1768. Margaret Acland, granddaughter of the 1st Bart, had married John, 2nd Lord Arundell in the mid-seventeenth century. However in 1768 the estates were settled on William Wentworth of Henbury in Dorset as the heir of Elizabeth, the sister of Thomas Wentworth, Earl of Strafford, who had married the 4th Lord Arundell in 1722. William died in 1775 and the estates were then inherited by his son, Thomas Frederick Wentworth. Thomas Frederick became Earl of Strafford in 1791 but died without issue in 1799. The inheritance passed to his sister, Augusta Ann who had married Hatfield Kaye. She died without issue in 1802 which was when the Arundell estates came into the possession of the Acland family.

Throughout the period under review and earlier the Aclands purchased properties. The Devon Manor of Hacche was acquired sometime before 1726, the Manor of Loxbeare in 1723 and the Manor of Broadclyst sometime after 1808. In Somerset Sir Thomas Dyke Acland bought the Manor of Blackford from Sir Charles Whitworth about 1776. In Devon the two main Acland residences had been purchased, Columbjohn by Sir John Acland in the sixteenth century and Killerton from the Drewes in the early seventeenth century. In the nineteenth century farms were

bought to consolidate existing estates, such as Coomroy in Broadclyst, bought by Hugh Acland in 1805[17] but which had been mapped in 1762 when the property belonged to the Exeter City Chamber as Trustees of the St John's Hospital Charity. Higher Newland Farm in the same parish was purchased by the Aclands in 1838 but had been for sale three years earlier.[18] The map of this farm included in the list in this volume, undated but endorsed by Thomas Hawkes in 1825[19] relates to both Higher and Lower Newland Farms but does not give any indication of the ownership of these properties at that date. Another map of both farms in the Acland collection but its date of 1842 places it outside the scope of this volume.[20]

The Palmer Aclands, resident at Fairfield in Somerset, came into an inheritance in Devon early in the nineteenth century. This passed to them under a Marriage Settlement of Arthur Acland and Elizabeth Oxenham. Arthur was the son of Sir Hugh Acland and Cecily Wroth and the nephew of Thomas Palmer who had married Elizabeth Wroth. Arthur's son, Sir John Palmer Acland took on both family names on his elevation to the baronetcy in 1818. Elizabeth Oxenham was the heiress of the Long(e) and Oxenham family estates in Devon. These were in the parishes of Ashburton, Exminster, Mamhead, Kenton, Kenn, Chudleigh, Ilsington, Manaton, Crediton and Colebrooke and according to Alexander Law's survey of 1805 the estate extended to over 3000 acres and was valued at £1487. 16s. 9½d.[21] Evidently this was not a Survey of the entire estate, for in 1807, the year in which John Acland was given 'custody' of William Long Oxenham, 'a lunatic', Alexander Law surveyed the Oxenham properties at South Tawton and High Bray. The Oxenhams had possessed the estate at South Tawton from at least the time of Henry III. According to Lysons, writing in 1822,[22] the mansion had long been inhabited as a farmhouse and it was then the joint property of Thomas Acland and his sister, the wife of Hugh Hoare. The surveys of lands in South Tawton and High Bray were extremely

16. For Marriage Settlement of Sir Thomas Dyke Acland, 7th Bart and Elizabeth Dyke, 1744 see DRO, 1148M add/4/1.

17. DRO, 1148M add/1//T8/81–82.

18. DRO, 56/4/9, printed Particulars of Sale dated 23 October 1835, Lot 7. The map of the premises was made by William Dawson.

19. SRO, DD/WY/Box 121.

20. DRO, 1148M add/10/5/5.

21. SRO, DD/AH/Box 14/5.

22. Daniel and Samuel Lysons, *Magna Britannia Volume the Sixth containing Devonshire Parts I and II* (London, 1822), 484.

detailed and followed the same form as the 1805 survey although because of the absence of referential letters it is assumed that no maps were drawn.

The Aclands had held estates in the parish of High Bray since the 1550s.[23] The parish is not specified in the 1726 Survey although Little Bray in the parish of Charles is listed. An Agreement concerning the jointure of Mary Acland in 1516 to entail lands on her son Arthur mentioned estates in Charles, Little Bray and High Bray.[24] In the nineteenth century, High Bray was the collective name given to the Aclands' North Devon estates[25] and this can lead to confusion. Kedworthy in High Bray (see Map 31) was not assigned to Thomas Palmer Acland of Charles by Richard Bryan of West Down and others until 1832[26] which may provide a possible date for the map.[27] The collections of deeds and other documents in the Acland archives provide evidence of the family's consolidation of estates where possible;[28] however, the yield from lands such as those bordering on Exmoor was poor and there appears to have been no direct drive to effect this nor to reorganize the tenancies when the purchases had been made.

Three surveys (1726, 1746–7 and *c*.1802)

The three surveys of Acland lands which have been abstracted in this volume provide lists of the family's main estates. The first two, that of 1726 of the main Devon holdings and the 1746–7 survey which relates to the Somerset lands shortly after the marriage of Sir Thomas Dyke Acland to Elizabeth Dyke in 1745, both pre-date any maps of the family's estates. The third, which is dated *c*.1802 is valuable in giving an indication of the Arundell

family properties which came into the Aclands' hands in the early nineteenth century.

The 1726 survey[29] was made only five years after Sir Hugh Acland's marriage to Cecily Wroth and just two years before his death. It is described as 'Taken from former Surveys and Rent Rolls and Counterparts of Leases . . . by Mr Thomas Knott Steward' and it lists lands in 40 Devon parishes in the Manors of Riverton, Hackworthy, Nimet St George, South Molton, Hacche, Romansleigh, Woolleigh Omer and Hunshaw, Essebeare alias Aishbeere, Loxbeare, Leigh and Collom:john. Killerton, the main seat of the Aclands and Killerton Frances are not included but the table of contents to the volume has a note 'Kildrington alias Killerton Manor vide Kill. Rent Book' and a similar note for Killerton Frances. The document begins with a description of the 'farme of Akelane' in Landkey parish, the main Acland residence in Devon before the purchases of Columbjohn and Killerton. Akelane contained 200 acres and was let to Edward Ratcliffe for a term of 14 years from 28 March 1718 at a rent of £79. Part was leased by him to Gregory Davy but actually tenanted by Samuel Wreford. The term of years on the lease was determinable on 3 lives, in this case people aged from 11 to 35 and the heriot (£5), payable when the lease fell in, is also specified. The expectation was that the lease would then be negotiated for a 'consideration' and probably kept in the same family with new members of that family being put in as 'the lives'.

The practice of issuing leases for lives was common in the eighteenth century and continued well into the nineteenth century in the South West. The valuation of the property depended upon the lives in being (hence the different valuations for any one tenement which are given in the survey). John Richards[30]

23. Anne Acland, *The Acland Family* (Chichester, 1981), 3.
24. DRO, 1148M/ Marriage Settlements.
25. Anne Acland, 139.
26. DRO, 1148M add/1/T6/64–66.
27. DRO, 1148M add/10/3/1. A map of Gratton in High Bray (DRO, 1148M add/10/3/2) made for the owner, Richard Harding, in 1803–4 shows Thomas Palmer Acland as a 'peripheral owner' of properties but Sir Peregrine Acland

did not purchase Gratton until 1869 (1148M add/1/T6/40) and so the map is not included in this volume.
28. DRO, 1148M/Box 21 (iv)/10, letter from Charles Chilcott dated 1823 advising the purchase of lands in Winsford, Somerset.
29. DRO, 1148M add/6/11. Abstracted as 'Survey 1' in this volume.
30. Richards, xxv.

discussed the valuation of leases for lives and the drawbacks of the system:

> I don't know of any thing (like a national Scheme as yet published for adjusting the Values of Leases on the several Tenures in Use amongst us . . . For although several Persons have with good Success endeavour'd to obviate Part of the Difficulties; yet the Application of their Precepts . . . does still remain a Task insuperable to the Generality of People whom they concern; the Gentleman's Steward and Tenants being (for the most part of them at least) as much in the dark as ever.

He continued:

> Where an Estate hath been occupied by the Lesssee for a great many Years, and the Lease comes to be filled or renewed, the yearly Value, by which the filling up or renewing is generally adjusted, is taken from the Landlord's Rent-Roll, made perhaps a hundred years before. Now in that Interval the Estate may have been improv'd by good Husbandry, or impoverish'd by the contrary to a very great Degree; from whence it comes to pass, that

the present yearly Value by which, and which only, the Value of the subsequent Tenure is to be had, is far different from that in the Rent-Roll.[31]

Richards described the types of leases then prevalent: a lease for a long term, say, 200 years; leases for a term of years absolute; copyhold lands; leases for a term of years, determinable on the death of one, two or three persons. It is into this latter category that most of the tenures of premises listed in the surveys fall. He also has a section on 'Reversions'.[32] He described this as the right to an estate which is to take place after the determination of a term of years or lives during which it is held by some former grant. There are instances of reversionary leases in these surveys.

The survey contains a wealth of information on the division of lands within the eleven manors. It records the dates when the original leases had been made to tenants and almost half of these had been made before 1700 (115) with only 30 made after 1720, so more could have been expected to expire during the next few years after 1726, giving the chance of a renegotiation of the rent. In about 10 per cent of the entries the yearly value has not been inserted but nevertheless, the totals are impressive, as may be seen from the following table:

Devon Manors: Annual Values of Estates in 1726

Manor	Rents	High and conventionary rents	Rents payable from the Manor
Riverton	£111 1s	£28 2s.10d	£17 18s.4d
Hackworthy	£65 18s	£14 19s.7d	£1 5s.7d
Nimet St George	£153 10s	19s.2¾d (+£100 for Advowson)	13s
South Molton	£384 19s	£44 0s.3d	11s
Hacche	£364	£14 11s.4d	4s
Romansleigh	£187	6s.10d	7s.2d ('lost out of mind')
Woolleigh, Omer and Hunshaw	£250 6s	£50 16s.10d	£1 17s.4d
Essebeare alias Aishbeere	£237 15s	£11 4s.10d	£1 1s.1d
Leigh	£232 10s	nil	£13 8s.8d
Loxbeare	£187 1s.	6d	nil
Collom:john	£169 10s	£7 6s.6d	nil
Total	**£2345 9s**	**£272 9s.8¾d**	**£37 6s.2d**

[31.] Richards, xxix.

[32.] Richards, 26.

Thus in 1726 Sir Hugh Acland was receiving an annual income of just over £2580 per annum from his Devon manors alone. As a comparison in 1747 the annual value of Sir William Courtenay's Devon estates was assessed at £2597 16s.10d.

The Steward of Sir Hugh's lands must have been a man of some status, as signified by the title 'Mr'. A Thomas Knott is recorded in the Survey as living in South Molton and it is not unexpected that the Aclands, who later used local men to map their estates, would have employed someone who lived locally and was familiar with the lands he was valuing and recording. There is no doubt that in his survey he created a most useful record of Sir Hugh's lands but with hindsight one can say that this would have been even more so had there been an accompanying map. Some acreages are given in the survey and often there is an indication of land use, but the exact location of many of the lands cannot now be identified because of the practice of naming a tenement after its tenant. Yet in the 1720s it is probable that there was no local map-maker available. As already mentioned, Sir William Courtenay had used Robert Whittlesey, a professional surveyor who worked nationally, to map and survey his Manors of Kenton and Powderham in 1723.[33] John Richards, following in the footsteps of Ralph Agas and others who were writing in the seventeenth century, advocated the production of a map to accompany the written survey:

> The only Objection that can be made against surveying and mapping Estates, is that of the Expence that attends it; and this will, I believe on mature Consideration, be thought much over-balanced by the Benefit that will accrue thereby: But, if any Gentleman still thinks otherwise, let him look back into the Accounts and Transactions of his Predecessors, and see whether he cannot discover in every 7 years, some Fraud or Destruction committed by Tenants &c. which might have been prevented by the Assistance of such a Map, purchased at half the Expence.[34]

John Richards' first extant map, of Wood in Bishopsteignton, is dated 1732.[35]

In 1757, 31 years after Thomas Knott's survey, some of the Acland estates were surveyed for Sir Hugh Acland's son, Sir Thomas Dyke Acland, by John Bowring of Chulmleigh. He produced maps to accompany the written survey or terrier and this atlas is discussed at greater length on page 11. Unfortunately, it is incomplete: however a partial set of maps and terriers survives for the Manors of Riverton, Hacche, George Nympton (alias Nimet St George), South Molton and Romansleigh. No maps accompany another survey of Acland lands made in 1765 which is in the same volume as that of 1726 and this has the same coverage as the 1726 survey. In 1756 Thomas Hodge included not only maps and written surveys of the Manors of Leigh and Loxbeare in his atlas but also remarks on some of the problems attached to certain tenements and how matters might be rectified.

The survey made in 1746–7 (with some later additions)[36] just post-dates the marriage of Sir Thomas Acland and Elizabeth Dyke in 1745 and describes lands in Somerset which formed part of the marriage settlement. It lists estates in the Manors of Avil, Bossington, Wilmersham and West Luckham, West Luckham, Holnicote and Exbridge Ryphay which lie in 18 Somerset parishes and land in the parish of Bampton in Devon.

The Manor of Avil, originally a Domesday manor, was acquired from the Blackford family by the Dykes shortly before or in 1744 as 'W.B. ar[miger]' grants leases of tenements there between 1698 and 1730. Elizabeth Dyke (widow) and Elizabeth Dyke, spinster, grant six leases of premises there in 1744 and Sir Thomas Dyke Acland is the lessor of properties there from 1745 onwards. The yearly value of the tenements is stated in only four of the 56 listed (total £61) and indeed throughout the survey only about 50 per cent of these values are given, which is surprising as the lands were so newly acquired by the Aclands. Of the three surveys under discussion in this section, this is the only one to have a separate column for 'Remarks' in which the duties of grinding at the lord's mill, providing labour for cleaning

33. Powderham Archive.
34. Richards, 146.

35. DRO, 1039M/E18a.
36. DRO, 1148M add/6/20. Abstracted as 'Survey 2' in this volume.

out the mill leat at Whitsun and 'the keeping of hounds' (sometimes a spaniel or beagle is specified), presumably for stag hunting on Exmoor, are stated. Another duty, that of entertaining the Steward and four horses, was also placed upon the tenants of Overborough in Avil.

In the Manor of Bossington, another acquisition by the Dykes from the Blackfords, no less than 12 tenements were charged with keeping hounds, all these leases being granted either by the Dykes or the Aclands. Yearly values for premises in Bossington amounted to £265 but were given in only 29 out of 33 entries.

The Manors of Wilmersham and West Luckham and West Luckham also came to the Dykes from the Blackfords. In the first manor yearly values are given in only two of the seven entries and in the second, in only 16 out of 48 cases, so the totals of £21 and £207.17s are very much an under-recording. Holnicote was much the largest and wealthiest of the manors listed in the survey. Yearly values are not recorded in 18 out of the 50 entries but even so, the total is £358.11s. The duty of grinding at the lord's mill is mentioned in 22 cases, sending a man to work on the mill leat in 23 cases and keeping hounds in 12 instances, the latter all in leases granted by the Dykes or Aclands between 1744 and 1749. The last manor, that of Exbridge Ryphay, another former Blackford family possession, lists 17 tenements. Yearly values are not stated in four of these but the total is £131.18s. Two premises are charged with keeping

hounds, both leases being granted by Sir Thomas Dyke Acland.

Few acreages of tenements are given in this survey. In some cases attempts are made to describe the exact location of the property, for example, a dwellinghouse 'near the highway from a village called Stream to Watchet' in the Manor of Avil and 'late Ellis's potatoe garden in Horner Green near the gate leading in[to] the meadow belonging to Horner Farm' in West Luckham Manor but where the place-names do not now survive, it is difficult to plot the situation of the lands described, for no accompanying maps have been found for the 1746–7 survey. The Manors of Holnicote, Bossington, West Luckham and Wilmersham and West Luckham were mapped and surveyed between 1809–1812. The Manor of Avil was mapped in 1810.

The third survey abstracted in this volume is undated but must have been made c.1802.[37] Information added in a later hand in the Survey includes details of leases made by Mrs Augusta Kaye up to April 1802. As has been mentioned (p. 4) Mrs Kaye inherited the Arundell estates on the death of her brother, Thomas Frederick Wentworth, Earl of Strafford, in 1799 and on her death in 1802 the properties passed to Sir Thomas Dyke Acland, the 10th Bart. These extensive lands, consisting of eight manors in Cornwall, one in Somerset and one in Devon are all recorded in this Survey and some idea of the relative values of the manors may be seen from the following table.

Arundell Manors: Annual Values of Estates c.1802

Manor	Rents	High rents	Total	Total in *c.*1770 rental
CORNWALL				
Trerise	£14 0s.4d.	9s.0d.	£14 9s.4d.	
Tresillian	£26 9s.6d.		£26 9s.6d.	
Goviley	£25 14s.4d.	£1 2s.10d.	£26 17s.2d.	
Penstrase Moor	£9 19s.0d.		£9 19s.0d.	
Cragantallan	£14 8s.8d.	17s.0d.	£15 5s.8d.	£404 15s.
Degembris	£28 6s.8d.	£3 8s.10d.	£31 15s.6d.	£563 14s.8d.
Thurlibeer	£43 15s.8d.	11s. *and	£44 6s.8d.*	£636*
		*and 1lb of cummin seed		

[37.] DRO, 1148M add/6/13. Abstracted as 'Survey 3' in this volume.

Manor	Rents	High rents	Total	Total in *c.*1770 rental
Ebbingford alias Efford	£27 6s.4d.	£1 12s.10½d.	£28 19s.2½d.	£570 4s.
SOMERSET				
East Luckham	£29 15s.4½d.	15s.6½d.	£30 10s.11d.	£1483 15s.03½d.
DEVON				
Stockley Luckham	£15 7s.8d.	£3 12s.11d.	£19 0s.7d.	
Total	**£235 3s.6½d.**	**£12 10s.0d.**	**£247 13s.6½d.**	

It is difficult to reconcile the amounts given in the last column of the above table with those totalled for the *c.*1802 Survey. The survey or rental of *c.*1770[38] covers just four of the Cornish manors which are present in the *c.*1802 Survey (Cragantallan, Degembris, Ebbingford alias Efford and Thurlibeer) and the Manor of East Luckham in Somerset. It is described as both 'A Rentall of the Arundell Estate' and 'A Survey of the Manor of East Luckham' but the kind of information given under both headings is much the same, recording only the names of the tenements and tenants and the rent payable. The document is not dated but it has been assumed by the staff of the Devon Record Office to be about 1770, shortly after the death of the last Lord Arundell in 1768. 'Lady Arundell of Long hern' is listed as a tenant in Lanivet, the rent being paid by Mr Lovelace of Redruth, her Steward. Also mentioned is the Reverend John Trevenon who was Patron of the Rectory of Cardinham when a John Penrose was instituted there in 1777 and this lends credence to a date in the 1770s. However, some of the notes are in a later hand and mention 'Mrs Kaye's book' and so presumably date from the period 1799–1802. The 1770s' figures must be valuations of the premises and not rents as they are so much higher than the rents given in the *c.*1802 Survey, but they are considerably lower than the fines exacted for new leases where these are specified. It

seems that the contemporary descriptions of 'rental' and 'survey' should be treated with some caution.

The *c.*1802 Survey provides evidence that a review of properties was taking place during the period of the Kaye family ownership (1799–1802) as leases for no less than 90 out of the 210 tenements listed under the Cornish manors were renegotiated and for 27 out of 76 in the Somerset manor of East Luckham. New leases are not mentioned for the Devon Manor of Stockley Luckham.

No accompanying maps have been found for this Survey. David Palmer had mapped the Devon Manor of Stockley Luckham *c.*1791 and the Somerset Manor of East Luckham was mapped and surveyed in 1809–12 by Alexander Law and Messrs Bradley and Summers.[39] There is an early nineteenth-century survey of lands in the parishes of Luccombe and Selworthy,[40] a rental of Efford and Thurlibeer dating from 1820[41] and the last two manors were mapped and surveyed by Samuel Coldridge in 1828.[42] David Palmer had mapped lands in the Manor of Thurlibeer in the 1790s.[43] No maps of the Manors of Cragantallan, Degembris, Goviley, Penstrase Moor, Trerise and Tresillian have been located.

As tools of estate management, surveys were concerned not only with the monetary value of tenements but also the corroboration at a certain date of the number of lives still in existence on the premises as specified in a particular lease. The Aclands' survey

[38] DRO, 1148M/Box 9/2.
[39] DRO, 1148M add/10/7 and DRO, 1148M add/ 9/6/24.
[40] DRO, 1148M add/6/15.
[41] DRO, 1148M add/6/12.
[42] Document in Private Hands.
[43] DRO, 1148M add/10/19.

of Devon estates in 1726 describes its information as taken from former surveys, rent rolls and *counterpart leases* and the descriptions of property in the survey such as messuages, quillets, burgages, etc. reflect those appearing in the leases. As is to be expected, most of the premises listed in the surveys were located in small villages or in rural areas but the details given for property in towns follow the same pattern. For instance in 1726 a messuage in South Molton is described as 'late the sign of the Bell' and the Town Hall and shops, cellars [storehouses] and chambers belonging were leased to the Mayor and Burgesses of South Molton and valued at £8 a year.

Of the three surveys abstracted in this volume, that for Somerset dated 1746–7, provides most detail of the life and economy of the manors listed, as many occupations of tenants and lessees are given. Added information on the accompanying rights enjoyed by individual tenants also helps to build up a picture of the daily activities in a rural settlement. In the Manor of Avil, premises tenanted by Abraham Blackmore by right of Rebecca, his second wife, carried with it the right to have stones from Kitswall Common for building and repairing and water from Avil ground 'in a friendly manner'. Robert Griffith held a messuage and rights in a limekiln on Bossington beach with the right to lay stones and culm on the beach while the kiln was in use without obstructing the passage there. The survey of the Manor of West Luckham gives details of a fulling mill with the use of a furnace and tenants having the right to depasture sheep, bullocks and horses on the hills of West Luckham: 'late Goss's vineyard' is also mentioned. In the Manor of Holnicote some tenants had the right to cut turf, pull heath on Cloutisham Common and 'to take all sear wood from time to time in coppice wood happening or falling out', probably for fire wood. Two gifts by the Acland family are also described: Margaret Gorton of Tetton, spinster, was the lessee of property in Brushford parish 'in consideration of her faithfull service done and performed for Lady Acland' and Robert Heard of Dulverton held messuages called North Coombe in Dulverton, a gift of Sir Thomas Dyke Acland.

The *c.*1802 survey of chiefly Cornish manors provides a contrast to the Somerset survey of 1746–7 in that few occupations of lessees and tenants are supplied. However, acreages for individual tenements are given for four Cornish manors and the document provides useful information on the location of eight manors in Cornwall and the names of inhabitants living in those manors. Post 1700 surveys are a much under-rated source for family and social historians: they often provide the names of a large proportion of the inhabitants of a village at a date before the availability of land tax records.

2. Maps and Surveys, 1750–1808

The Devon estates

The earliest maps with accompanying surveys of the Acland estates date from 1756–7 and were the work of two local surveyors. Although slightly the later of the two groups, i.e. 1757, the maps and surveys produced by John Bowring[44] will be discussed initially, as these relate to the nucleus of the Acland lands in mid and north Devon described *in toto* in the 1726 Survey. Many of John Bowring's maps and surveys survive, albeit damaged by damp, for the Manors of Romansleigh, Hacche, South Molton, George Nympton [alias Nimet St George], and Riverton.[45] There are five maps and terriers of the Manor of Romansleigh, described as I–V, the first of these being a general map; a map of the Manor of South Molton (no. VII) which is now in South Molton Museum; a map and terrier of the Manor of Hacche and Snurridge in South Molton and West Brayley Barton in East Buckland which is now to be found in the Fortescue family archives[46]; a terrier for map no. X but not the map itself; maps and terriers for Hacche (no. XI) and for George Nympton (nos XIV–XVI); a map only for Riverton Manor (no. XVIII); one map of street properties in Barnstaple[47] and one map without a title. To sum up, there are at least nine maps and at least seven terriers missing and of those extant, two had strayed from the Acland collection into other archives, possibly when the properties depicted on the maps were sold by the Aclands.

The maps are coloured and on parchment but are too large ever to have been bound into one volume. Most scales are stated (often 1"=4 chains, 1:3168), the orientation is given and all the maps have decorative cartouches. The terriers give the names of tenants and tenements, field names with land use and content, value and the conditions on which the land was held. In its entirety, and we can only guess at its completeness, it must have been an impressive piece of work by a local surveyor. It is unfortunate that no supporting documentation has been found as to why it was commissioned at that date and what it cost.

The first-known maps of the Killerton estate are dated 1756.[48] Twelve maps were bound together in an atlas 40cms x 62.5cms with no general title; however each map bears its own title and eight (nine with an inset map) include the surveyor's name or initials, Thomas Hodge. He was a native of nearby Silverton, baptised 1714/15 and probably employed because he was a man familiar with the area. Only two other maps of estates in Devon by Hodge have survived, the earlier dated 1752 was of the Glebe land of Silverton[49] and the other, of 1764, was of lands in East Portlemouth in the possession of Blundell's School.[50] The 12 maps in the 1756 Atlas therefore represent the most significant contribution made by this surveyor to the cartography of Devon in the mid-eighteenth century.

The area covered in the Atlas is considerable, amounting to 1321 acres, 3 roods, and 11 perches in those parts of the estate close to Killerton and 1205 acres, 2 roods and 18 perches in the nearby parishes making a total of some 2527 acres, 1 rood and 29 perches. The first map, a general map of the Manor of Killerton and Columbjohn is followed by three larger-scale maps of areas close to Killerton itself. The remaining eight show land in the manors or parishes of Leigh, Essebeare, Rackenford, Loxbeare and Tiverton and these differ in their content and general

---

[44.] Not a great deal is known of John Bowring. He is described as 'of Chulmleigh' and according to an entry in the International Genealogical Index was born in 1690. There is a reference to a Will of John Bowring dated 1774 which may be his (the original does not survive). He produced an atlas of 12 maps for the Feoffees of the Long Bridge at Bideford in 1745 and he is possibly the author of a map of the Manor of Aller in Somerset which was drawn for Arthur Acland, Esq., in 1761 (SRO, DD/

SAS/W51).

[45.] DRO, 1148M add/6/11.

[46.] DRO, 1262M/E22/44, originally number IX in the Bowring atlas.

[47.] DRO, 1148M add/10/1a.

[48.] DRO, 1148M add23/E1.

[49.] DRO, 3359A & add/PBI.

[50.] Blundell's School Archive.

emphasis from the other examples. An initial appraisal of their quality might perhaps suggest that the maps were of doubtful value because the penmanship and application of colour gives an impression of an unpractised hand at work. However a closer study suggests that this is not a fair assumption. Comparison of the roads with those on Benjamin Donn's map of 1765 and more particularly with the O.S. map of 1809 shows that Hodge had made a competent survey. Any assessment of the accuracy of the other basic elements of the survey, namely the field boundaries, is less straightforward. In the immediate vicinity of Killerton House some small fields have been amalgamated into larger units but outside the park itself and in the more distant parishes the general alignment can be traced with some confidence.

The information provided on the maps and in the Rental which follows shows quite clearly the purpose behind their making. In the case of the four 'Killerton' maps the fields have an alpha-numeric reference to tables giving their names and content. Frequently the land use and quality is implied where the words such as orchard, meadow, moor, or waste follow the actual field name. Various annotations entered over time indicate that these were working estate documents. This is quite clearly shown in the succeeding maps of land held in more distant parishes. Fields there are named with letters suggesting land use – **T**, Tillage, **P**, Pasture, **M**, Moorish, **F**, Furze and in some cases the letters **N S E W** show the aspect. This is sometimes also described in notes beside the map; '. . . very good land remarkable for being the best Barly (sic) Land in all Loxbeare Situate on ye Side of Hill – South, South West and South East Aspect', and '. . . three small Ten.ts prettily situated in ye South Side of an Hill of an easy Ascent'. The additional information about relief implies an appreciation of the difficulties of cultivation in this particular landscape. Barley is the crop mentioned above all others. This detailed assessment of the land in these Manors is supplemented by descriptions of some of the buildings; Leigh Mill '(frequently

in want of slates)', the house on Ford tenement '(wch is but an indifferent one)', and 'Loxbeare Barton consists of a very good Stone built House with all other Necessarys wanted in Husbandry'. The Rentals which follow again emphasise that this is a management document. Details of leases etc are on slips of paper inserted through slits cut in each page making changes in the entries simple to register. The latest date entered is 1760 – some four years after the maps were drawn.

Other maps commissioned in the lifetime of the 7th Bart show in considerable detail areas of land not included in the Hodge atlas. A map of 1766 by John Case[51] demonstrates the constant interest in developing the potential of the Killerton estate. It was to identify 'the Intended new Cut from the Leather Mill above Etherly Bridge to water ye Meadows and turn an Engine'.[52] One rather interesting feature is the fenced coniferous copse in a meander of the Culm which could represent investment in a future resource. A note added below the title suggests that the leat would water between 58 to 70 acres and thus would increase both yield and income for the estate. The quality of the draughtsmanship and the manner in which the details are portrayed mark a considerable advance on the work of Thomas Hodge. Relief is shown by hill shading coloured in ochre and brown; this feature is important in the context of the area mapped and for the construction of the intended leat which is shown by a double ink line. The contrast between the flood plain of the river Culm and the cultivated fields, shown in yellow-brown with pecked lines, marks the limit of the water meadows. Other details complete what is a comprehensive plan of this part of the Killerton estate. Case differentiates between deciduous and coniferous trees, marks the fences and gates and shows the four-arched Etherly Bridge in elevation. The map alone conveys the information required and thus there is less need for verbal descriptions to be added on the margins of the map, a clear contrast to the maps in the Hodge atlas.

[51.] DRO, 1148M add/10/5/1.

[52.] A leather mill (used for grinding the bark for use in tanning) was located at Broadclyst as early as 1699 when it was in the occupation of John Martyn. The Aclands acquired Etherly Mills from John Knight of Broadclyst by a

Quitclaim of 1763. See A.H. Shorter, 'The Tanning Industry in Devon and Cornwall, 1550–1850', *DCNQ* XXV (1952), 10–11; DRO, 1148M add/l/T8/93.

Only half of the map of 1775 by Matthew Blackamore has survived.[53] This shows the buildings at Etherly Bridge (now Ellerhayes Bridge) in greater detail than on the earlier example and more of the estate to the east. Originally this map would have been a large one, some 104cms square, and thus it would also have encompassed Killerton House, possibly included some of the early improvements made by John Veitch, and certainly have indicated any changes introduced as a result of the suggestions made on the Case map.[54] There are records of two payments made to Matthew Blackamore. The first appears in the Account Book for 24 May 1775 'pd. Mr Blackamore in pt for maping 10.10.0' and on 3 Oct 1775 'pd Blackamore in pt 05.05.0.'[55]

William Hole was a prolific map-maker: 30 examples of his work have been found in Devon alone. His map of 1774 of land which was part of the Manor of Langacre in Broadclyst accompanies a deed of 29 March in that year from Trustees, of whom Sir Thomas Dyke Acland (the 7th Bart) was one, to Sir John Davie of Creedy and Catherine his wife.[56] The trust had been set up as part of the marriage settlement of Sir John and his wife in 1763 and in 1774 the property was mortgaged to Edward Shute of Exeter. It was subsequently sold to the 7th Bart and the purchase money is itemised in the Acland accounts for 1774: 'Drew payment to Sir John Davie 112.0.0.' and 'to be vested in the Stocks on account of my purchase with Sir John Davie 734.0.0.'[57] There are payments for the Manor of Langacre in the accounts in the 1830s and in 1839 the property was re-mortgaged.

The practice of including a map with a title deed (William Hole's map is joined at the foot with the other parchment membranes) was fairly common at the end of the eighteenth century where a complicated transaction of property required large parchment sheets. It also enabled all parties to the deed to have copies of the map, so that there could be no dispute over the boundaries of the property described. It is interesting that Alexander Law, the Acland's surveyor at a later date, advertised in 1805 that he had been admitted a member of Gray's Inn 'whereby he is enabled to draw leases, covenants and all other instruments under seal',[58] which seems to imply that he could do more than simply draw maps to accompany deeds. However, it seems unlikely that William Hole also penned the deed relating to Langacre.

The Aclands continued to acquire plots of land elsewhere in Devon in the late-eighteenth and early-nineteenth centuries. A late eighteenth-century map of the Manor of Stockley Luckham, described as 'The Fee of which is in Earl Strafford' relates to land in the parish of Cheriton Fitzpaine.[59] Unfortunately the map is in poor condition and the map-maker's name is not given. However, on stylistic grounds it can be attributed to David Palmer with some certainty. The reason for making this map may have been a change in ownership. The Cheriton Fitzpaine Land Tax Assessments establish the owner of the parcels of land shown on the map to have been the Earl of Strafford in 1797 and Augusta Key (or Kay) in 1800. By 1802 the property had passed into the ownership of Sir Thomas Dyke Acland, Augusta Kay (nee Wentworth) having died without issue. Thomas Frederick Wentworth became Earl of Strafford in 1791 and died in 1799; therefore the map must have been drawn between those dates. It is interesting that the map-maker, David Palmer, produced a map of Thurlibeer Manor in Cornwall,[60] also part of the Arundell estate, which Manor was subsequently inherited by the Aclands.

One of the larger acquisitions by the Aclands was the Manor and Lordship of Broadclyst alias Cliston. The agreement for sale was dated 1808 but the actual conveyance was not made until January 1811.[61] This was from Mrs Levina Luther and

---

53. DRO, 1148M add/10/5/2.
54. The Surveyors' drawings on a scale of 3 miles to one inch, prepared for the O.S. map published in 1809, do not show either the leat or the 'plantation' and so it would seem that Case's suggestions had not been implemented.
55. DRO, 1148M General A/C 1.
56. DRO, 1148M add/l/T8/168. *Devon Place-Names* describes Langacre as 'lost' and last noted in the PRO Recovery Roll in 1779; certainly it is not marked on O.S. maps and so Hole's map is particularly valuable in establishing its location.
57. DRO, 1148M General A/C 1.
58. *EFP*, 7 November 1805.
59. DRO, 1148M add/10/7.
60. DRO, 1148M add/10/19.
61. DRO, 1148M add/l/T8/44-46.

other surviving legatees of the will of the Rt. Hon. Humphry Morice. The Aclands paid £56,025 and £30,000 of this was to be secured on mortgage. Humphry Morice had died in 1784 and the Steward, William Hole, had administered the estate in the interim period. Almost certainly, the large untitled map of Broadclyst which exists in the Acland archives[62] was surveyed and drawn at Hole's instigation prior to the sale. The map covers a large part of the parish of Broadclyst but not Killerton which was a separate manor. It is the work of Robert Ballment who acted as Steward to the Fortescues at Castle Hill, following William Hole in the post. Evidence of Hole and Ballment's co-operation in the administration of the Broadclyst estates exists in documents of 1793–4 concerning the lease of a plot of ground in the parish to John Winter on which to build a house.[63] The memorandum is attested by Robert Ballment and he supplies a small sketch. The Lease of 10 April 1794 is signed, sealed and delivered in the presence of William Hole and Robert Ballment 'Clerk to Mr Hole'.[64] A printed Survey of the Manor of Cliston entitled 'A Survey of the Manor and Hundred of Cliston in the Parish of Broadclist, and County of Devon, the Property of the Right Honourable Humphry Morice, deceased, from an Actual View of the Premises, Taken in the Year 1801, by William Hole' was printed by W. Syle of Barnstaple, 1802 and presumably acted as Sale Particulars.[65] An advertisement in the *Sherborne Mercury* of 26 July 1802 for the sale of the Manor states that 1550 acres are rich arable, meadow and pasture land and 546 acres are common grounds, very capable of improvement. The gross value is given as about £2200 per annum in demesne and set to good tenants at clear annual rents, about £360 a year held by leases determinable on the death of one life each, about £880 a year held by leases determinable on the deaths of two lives each and about £1070 a year more held by leases determinable on the deaths of three lives each, some of them very old. The rest is made up in a fee-farm rent and ten chief rents. For a Survey, and particulars of the Manor, application could be made to a firm in Gray's Inn 'where a very large and correct map of this extensive and compact manor may be viewed until the 10th day of August next, after which it will be removed to Phillip's Hotel in Exeter.[66] Particulars may also be acquired on application to Richard Clarke, Esq. at Newport, Isle of Wight. the York Hotel in Bath, the King's Arms Inn, Plymouth, William Hole, Esq., Barnstaple, and from Mr Silvester Rookes in Broadclyst 'who will shew the said manor and lands to any person inclined to purchase the same.'[67]

John Veitch and Killerton Park

John Veitch and the contribution he made to the development of Killerton and its Park must be considered in any study of the Acland estates in spite of the fact that no maps or plans can be directly attributed to him.

The peripatetic and convivial social round of the 7th Bart made him aware of the architectural improvements made by his friends and the desirability of enhancing those changes with the planned development not only of the immediate surroundings of a new house but also of the more distant landscape. In 1769, following the recommendation of friends, an approach was made to James Lee, Nurseryman of the Vineyard Nursery in Hammersmith which led to the arrival at Killerton of John Veitch, then 18 years of age. In the next 50 years he was to play a vital role in the design and development of the gardens close to the house and the Park beyond. Veitch himself made no cartographic record of these improvements but letters and accounts go some way to document the changes which took place principally in the lifetimes of the 7th and 10th Barts.[68] However, contemporary maps by other surveyors show the work which was accomplished.

---

[62]. *DRO*, 1148M add/10/5/3.

[63]. *DRO*, 1148M add/2/L15/47 and unnumbered documents between this and L15/48.

[64]. *DRO*, 1148M add/2/L15/48.

[65]. *DRO*, 1148M add 7 (unlisted).

[66]. James Phillips was the Proprietor of The Hotel, now the Royal Clarence Hotel, in Cathedral Yard, Exeter, from 1799 to 1813.

[67]. *SM*, 26 July 1802, col. 2c.

[68]. Sue Shephard, *Seeds of Fortune* (Bloomsbury Publishing Plc, London, 2002), gives a vivid account of the early life of John Veitch, his arrival at Killerton and the establishment of the nursery which bore his name;
    Shirley Heriz-Smith, *The House of Veitch A Horticultural Record* (Diss, 2002).

From 1770 when John Veitch first came to Killerton until the death of the 7th Bart in 1785 the Park gradually came to assume its present form. Five hundred acres were enclosed and the Exeter to Cullompton road to the east of Killerton House was moved. Annotations on the Hodge map, possibly in Sir Thomas Acland's hand, noted that certain areas now belonged to him and were 'in the Park' and the lines of the new road pencilled in are the only cartographic evidence found to date. These annotations must have been entered before 1780; the stable block, built over the old road, was completed in that year and the accounts for 1781/2 signed by Sir Thomas Acland and Batten, the estate Agent, mention payments for 'filling up the old road'.[69] The 1756 Hodge map was thus still in use some 24 years after it had been drawn. (There was no need to replace a good estate atlas!) The Surveyors' Drawings of 1801, on a scale of 3" to one mile, record these changes. They show the fields near Etherly Bridge taken into the Park, the fence to the north which marks the separation of the Park from the water meadows beside the Culm. On the west the path to Columbjohn Chapel and the fields through which it passes are much the same as on the Hodge map.

When, in 1808, the 10th Bart attained his majority and decided to live at Killerton he demanded John Veitch's full attention and developments there gathered momentum. Although Veitch was not a landscape designer by profession he shared their ability to understand the importance of the visual appearance of the plantings proposed, the significance of relief, together with some skill in putting such ideas on paper. Surviving letters from Veitch to the 10th Bart reveal something of their plans. Plantings of trees and the layout of the gardens close to the house are covered in detail but more important in the cartographic context is the discussion relative to the boundary of the Park close to Columb-john Chapel. Veitch is critical of Sir Thomas's wish to take ground near there into the park because he feels that Sir Thomas has 'not considered that you will disjoint Culm John Barton of 300 l [£300] a year if you proceeded, as without the Dry Ground it will not be worth Topwills [the tenant] while to rent it

afterwards as he will have no dry ground for his sheep in winter when the marshes is covered with water – & too wet for sheep – as he always lets (?) up the Grass in the dry fields for his Ewes & Lambs & other Sheep in the winter But if you will let it be done, *as I marked it out* you will Improve both Farms and also the Park appearance, and I can continue to conceal the Park fence by sinking it, and where the Road to the Chappell is to Cross it, put a plantation with a Cottage & & keep the Gate but so as no trace of the boundary may appear'.[70] Lines pencilled on the Hodge map of Killerton Dolberry suggesting an alteration to the field boundaries may perhaps refer to the problems in this area, but in any event these changes do not appear on either the Surveyors Drawings or later maps.

Veitch's comments appear in a letter dated 14 December 1808 and should be considered beside the road map of 1812 and the later map of the 'Manors of Broadclyst and Aishclyst'. The former, attached to a Declaration by Sir Thomas Dyke Acland concerning the ownership of the land through which the new and old roads was to pass (see p. 21), shows where the road between Columbjohn and Killerton was to be closed and the new road to replace it was to be made. It was to follow the field boundaries to the south; the suggested line was adopted and these changes are quite clear on the second map.

Later maps, endorsed *William Gilpin*, introduced the 'pictur-esque' approach to landscape design to Killerton.[71] William Sawrey Gilpin (1762–1843) took up landscape gardening late in life following a career as a painter and drawing master at the Royal Military College.[72] By the 1820s he was employed by the gentry and the aristocracy as 'a kind of gentleman adviser . . . steering the ideas of his employer and assisting with staking out plantations and drives'. He was involved only with the disposition of the external scenery of a country residence; cultivation of plant species and the act of gardening was not his concern. The National Trust Guide to Killerton House states that Gilpin was a friend of the family and that he was responsible for the appear-ance of the fields between the house and Columbjohn but omits

---

69. DRO, 1148M General Accounts/Batten, 1781–2.
70. DRO, 1148M Box 11(i)27.
71. DRO, 1148M add/10/5/15.

72. Sophieke Piebenga, 'William Sawrey Gilpin (1762–1843): Picturesque Improver' *Garden History* Vol. 22 Number 2 (Winter, 1994), 175–96 and the contribution to the *Oxford Dictionary of National Biography*.

any supporting documentary evidence. To date the editors have found no connection between the Aclands and Gilpin other than these maps which most probably date from 1820–30. There are two, one of the area close to Killerton House and the stables, the other of Columbjohn Chapel and Mill. At first sight each map appears to show a perspective view of tree plantings but these are more than 'views' as they are based on a measured plan on a scale of 1 inch to 65 feet. Existing roads, a sunk fence, a proposed new approach road and drive leading to Killerton House, together with detailed drawing of mixed woodland and individual trees shows the hand of the landscape designer and artist. It would seem that few, if any, of the suggested developments were incorporated into the Park. In fact the description of Killerton House by English Heritage states that Gilpin's plans were not implemented.[73]

It was Veitch and his son James who were responsible for continued work in developing the Park but the elder Veitch's appointment as head Steward in 1779 meant that his interests were not confined to Killerton.[74] In 1808 soon after Alexander Law had been given 'full direction to Survey Plan and value the whole of his [Sir Thomas Acland's] Property' it was Veitch to whom Law was eventually referred for information regarding the 'Particulars' of the estates.

The Somerset estates

The Somerset lands which came to the main branch of the Acland family on the marriages of Sir Hugh Acland to Cecily Wroth in 1721 and Sir Thomas Acland (the 7th Bart) to Elizabeth Dyke in 1745 have been discussed on page 3. Cecily Wroth's sister, Elizabeth, co-heiress, had married Thomas Palmer and in 1723 Articles of Agreement for the division of Sir Thomas Wroth's properties were drawn up between the Palmer and Acland families.[75] The subsequent Deed of Partition dated the same year

allocated the Manors of Lyng, Aller Court and Aller and Oath and lands in Woolmersdon and North Petherton to Thomas Palmer and Elizabeth his wife.[76] They died without issue and the estates passed to Thomas's brother, Peregrine, who died in 1762, when the inheritance passed to Arthur Acland (a younger son of Sir Hugh Acland and Cecily) and Elizabeth his wife.[77] However, from the survey and map evidence discussed below, it appears that Arthur Acland had an interest in the Manors of Lyng and Aller as early as 1752. He had settled at Fairfield in the north of the county of Somerset in the parish of Stogursey. It seems that he followed the example of his elder brother, Thomas, in commissioning maps to be made of some of his properties, the earliest being the Manors of Lyng and Aller, but both of these post-date the surveys.

Surveys of Lyng and the Manor of Auler (alias Aller) are included in a volume with parchment covers entitled 'Mannors of Chedmeade Banckland & Buckland Soror 1752 & 1755'. The heading describes the properties as formerly in the tenure of Sir Coplestone Bampfylde Bart, afterwards of Thomas Wroth Bart deceased and now of Arthur Acland by the right of Elizabeth, his wife.[78] The Steward who made the Survey is named as Jer. [Jeremiah] Dewdney. The demesne lands of Lyng are described as a messuage, barn, barton and farm of Lyng, commonly called Lyng Court, and totalled 278 acres. The lands were rented out in three parcels bringing in a rent of £251.19s.6d. A rent of £9.5s.4½d was reserved for the Manor 'lately parcell of a Monastry or Priory of Athelney purchased of and from the right Honble Francis Lord Hawley'.

The Survey of the Manor of Auler gives tenants' names, tenements, tenures, rents, heriots, yearly value and lives in being. It lists some 20 tenements, many of which are on 'middle moore'. Some are described as near Auler Decoy, Auler Moore Wall, abutting against Stathdrove, in broad or great drove, abutting against Marshbrookdrove, and a meadow (3½a.) in Auler Moore

---

[73.] English Heritage, Register of Parks and Gardens of special historic interest in England, addition to the website.

[74.] Arthur Dyke Acland, *Memoirs and Letters of Sir Thomas Dyke Acland* (London, for private circulation, 1902), 17, quoting a letter from Veitch dated 1809 in which he was advising against the proposed fencing and

planting in Selworthy Coombe.

[75.] SRO, DD/AH/51/10.

[76.] SRO, DD/AH/1/3/9.

[77.] John Collinson, *The History of Somersetshire* (Bath, 1791), i, 255–6.

[78.] SRO, DD/AH/65/15.

at a place called Church drove. The total yearly value of the properties is £132.10s. Some of the estates may be identified on a map dated 1761 of 'Aller Manor in the County of Somerset the Lands of Arthur Acland Esq.' which shows in some attractively-coloured detail the fields, gardens, drove roads, an orchard, and a 'Decoy' with ducks, in addition to the church, drawn in elevation, and the names of peripheral owners.[79] The map-maker is not named but the style of the cartouche allows a tentative association with John Bowring, whose name appears on Sir Thomas Acland's atlas of Chulmleigh lands. Possibly also about 1761, but certainly some time before 1767, a map was drawn of 'Ling Farm an Estate of Arthur Acland Esq. T.H. Fecit'.[80] The features shown give a comprehensive picture of the rivers and ponds in blue, fields outlined with green hedge symbols, with a numeric reference to a list giving field names and content. Tree symbols, the 'rick yard', the 'Common Meadow' and the 'Smith's Shop' together with the roads and buildings complete the information recorded on the map. Additions in a later hand on the body of the map show that this was again a working document. The surveyor is not named directly but enough information is provided to identify him. The statement 'T.H. Fecit' also appears on six maps in the atlas of estate maps drawn for Sir Thomas Dyke Acland in 1756 by Thomas Hodge. In addition, the title cartouche on the large map of Killerton in that atlas is identical to that on this map with its scroll and flower decoration and a diaper pattern included in the voids at the base. The Aclands held Lyng and Aller until 1834 when the lands were sold by auction on 16th August by the Trustees of the late Sir John Palmer Acland, Bart.[81]

The later and larger estate atlas with the title 'A Plan of the Manor of Fairfield the Seat of Arthr Acland Esq.r . . .' is dated 1767.[82] The atlas included 17 unnumbered maps of lands in six other Manors found in various parishes in addition to Stogursey.[83]

Each map is titled and apart from the 'Plan of Aller Allotment in King's Sedgmoor' (Map 14) the atlas is the work of William Fairchild.[84] However, in the title to 'A Plan of Ling Farm' (Map 8) Fairchild acknowledges his debt to 'T.H.' from whom this map was copied. The maps show rivers, some relief, fields outlined in various colours with land use distinguished; tree symbols indicate orchards but for woods the trees are merely shown in 'clumps'; land belonging to others is named in a cursive script with roads, buildings in plan and peripheral owners and estates named completing the information. Each map is preceded, and where necessary succeeded, by pages containing the written survey which includes information supplementing that shown on the maps: the names of tenants and their farms, the content in 'Computed' and 'Measured Acres'. Land use and 'Yearly Values' complete the written information providing a detailed and comprehensive survey of the Somerset estates at this date belonging to the younger branch of the Acland family.

Fairchild's atlas was followed in 1795 by another, similarly comprehensive, showing lands in the 'Manors of Fairfield and Durborow with the detached Estates in the several Parishes of Stogursey, Littlestoke Stringston Holford & Kilton in the County of Somerset belonging to John Acland Esq. by C. Chilcott Land Surveyor'.[85] This atlas was also intended for estate management in the present and in the future; one page headed 'Remarks' stated '1806 Many new purchases & exchanges having been made by the aforesaid Jno Acland Esqr since this Survey was made & arranged in 1795; it is therefore entered and corrected down to the present year 1806 Chas Chilcott'. In fact there is evidence that the information was updated even after 1806. The 20 maps in the volume are accompanied by pages of 'Reference' listing the field names, content in computed and statute measure and land use or 'Qual[ity]' as Chilcott describes it. Letters exchanged in 1819 and 1820 between Alexander Law, John

79. SRO, DD/SAS/W51.
80. SRO, DD/AH/65/13c.2252.
81. SRO, DD/AH/65/16.
82. SRO, DD/AH/66/11.
83. Manors of Durborow, Curril, Bankland, Buckland, Huntspill Verney, Woolmerston. Parishes of Durborow, Holford, Ling, North Petherton, Mear

(sic), Glastonbury, Nether and Over Stowey.
84. William Fairchild, 1743–84, (Bendall, F 016), worked principally in eastern England. In Somerset he also worked for the Slade family whose estate was contiguous with the Acland's.
85. SRO, DD/AH/65/12; John Acland inherited his father's estates in 1771.

Acland and Chilcott show that these maps continued in use long after their original drafting.[86]

John Acland, Alexander Law and the Devon estates of the Oxenham family

The Acland interest in the Oxenham estates in Devon followed the marriage of Arthur Acland to Elizabeth Oxenham in 1752.[87] It seems that her brother, William Long Oxenham (bap. 1731), was of unsound mind for in 1761 control of the affairs of 'William Long Oxenham of Newhouse Mamhead was granted to John Short Esqr of Bickham.'[88] It was customary at this date for the estates of 'lunatics' to be granted to 'committees', frequently the next of kin, who were given the power to act independently in the management and disposition of property.[89] Arthur Acland died in 1771 and after his wife's death in 1806[90] the interest in the Oxenham estates passed to John Acland as his uncle's heir. Direct responsibility was transferred to him the following year when he was given 'custody of William Long Oxenham, a lunatic.'[91] The grant was dated 8 April 1807, sureties being given by John Acland, Thomas Palmer Acland of Little Bray and George Short of Bickham House. William Long Oxenham died in December 1814 and was buried at Kenn in January 1815.[92] However, some years before his mother's death in 1806 John Acland was taking an active interest in the Devon estates, initiating surveys and the compilation of an estate atlas. It is through the letters of Alexander Law, eventually Acland's Agent, that John Acland's commitment to his duty of care for his uncle's estate, admittedly one conditioned by self interest, can be fully appreciated.

In 1804 Law had engaged the services of a young man 'regularly bred to surveying' and reported that he was 'surveying the greater part of the Oxenham property for which I am concerned'.[93] The estate atlas completed in the following year[94] was the result of this survey and it bears the annotation in ink, 'Mr Acland', on one of the early pages. The inclusion in pencil of 'Mr Acland' on the title page only serves to emphasise John Acland's participation in the affairs of this estate. The atlas covered lands in the 'Long Estate situated in the Parishes of Mamhead, Kenton, Chudleigh Ilsington, Ashburton Manaton Crediton & Colebook (sic) in the County of Devon Property of William Long Oxenham Esqr'. The title goes on to state that the maps were 'Copied from different Surveyors Maps & Valued in 1805 by Alexr Law'. However, each map has included in its individual title the statement that it was 'taken in 1805' implying that it was surveyed at that date, and on only one (Kenn) is the additional comment that surveys of 1796 were incorporated.

The seven maps of the atlas were bound into a leather-covered volume tooled in gold with a title page decorated with delicately-drawn leaves entwined around a mirror frame in which the title is inscribed. The maps are good examples of Alexander Law's surveying and penmanship identifying clearly rivers, relief, fields, woods, orchards, avenues and isolated trees. An alphanumeric reference in each field applies to lists on the facing pages providing the names of the 'parcels', fields, land use, content and total content. Other important details included were the roads, buildings, names of peripheral owners and estates. The scales used vary between six and 16 chains to the inch, with direction indicated by eight-point compass roses. At the end of the volume an Abstract gives the High and Chief Rents payable to the Long estate followed by two pages with the names of occupiers, tenements, terms of Lives, content, etc. The statute

86. SRO, DD/AH Box 11/15/1–4 Bundle 2, Letter 4 Dec. 1819, AL to JPA; Bundle 3, Letters 19 and 20 April 1820, AL to JPA.
87. For Marriage Settlement see SRO, DD/AH/54/6/2.
88. DRO, 53/6 Box 39.
89. PRO, Lunacy Inquisitions 1627–1932, C211; PRO, WLO DY/224/5.
90. R.W. Dunning, ed., *The Victoria County History of the County of Somerset*, VI, (London, 1992), 57.
91. SRO, DD/AH/ 43/2/15.

92. SRO, DD/AH/42/13/7.
93. CRO, PB/6/8.
94. SRO, DD/AH/Box 14.5.

As has been noted in the List of Abbreviations, Sir Thomas Dyke Acland, 10th Bart, John Palmer Acland, Alexander Law and Charles Prideaux Brune are hereafter referred to as TDA, JPA, AL, PB respectively.

measure of the whole estate was 3290 acres 1 rood 14 perches and its value as assessed by Alexander Law in 1804 was £1487.16s.9½d.

This atlas remained the sole cartographic record of the Oxenham estates throughout the early years of the nineteenth century. Its detailed description of the extent of the property and of the tenants clearly provided much information needed for efficient and effective management.

3. MAPS AND SURVEYS, 1808–1840

The Devon and Somerset estates

This period was dominated by the 10th Bart who, after attaining his majority in 1808, took a keen interest in his estates, involving himself personally in their management.

It was at this time that Alexander Law played an increasingly active part surveying and mapping the Acland estates not only for Thomas Dyke Acland, the 10th Bart, but also for John (Palmer) Acland for whom he also acted as agent. The earliest references to involvement in the Acland affairs date from 1802 when Law wrote from Killerton to the Rev. Charles Prideaux Brune of Place Court Padstow mentioning that he was doing business for the Acland family.[95] It was, however, not until six years later that Alexander Law began to play a significant part in the survey and mapping of Sir Thomas Acland's estates, especially those at Holnicote and Killerton. In January 1808 he was at Killerton 'at the request of Sir Thomas Acland who hath given me full direction to Survey Plan and value the whole of his Property' and by March he had been at Killerton for a fortnight to 'put that business in such train as can with safety be proceeded on in my absence.'[96] It is clear that much of the field surveying was carried out by William Summers of Ashill and William Shillibeer of Walkhampton and that the fair mapping was the work of Thomas Bradley, Alexander Law's nephew[97] with William Summers. The names of Bradley and Summers are included, albeit after that of Alexander Law, on the title page of the surviving atlas of the Holnicote estates.[98] The part played by William Shillibeer is not acknowledged in the atlas but is made known in a letter from Summers to John Day in which he states that Shillibeer was paid in October 1811 for 'sketching the adjoining Country on the Holnicote map'.[99] This no doubt followed Law's agreement in November of the previous year that 'the whole of your [TDA's] Lands at and near Holnicote and those at or near Winsford' should be put 'on One General Map'.[100] Mention is also made of the purchase of Mudge's map, that is the O.S. map on the scale of 1" to one mile published in October 1809; there is evidence of its influence on some of the maps in the atlas but in any event it would have proved a useful starting point in surveying the area.

The atlas itself is a fine leather-bound volume (22cms x 27cms) tooled in gold with brass clasps. The title on the cover is in gold on red leather, 'Part of the Manor of Holnicote The Manors of Bossington Wilmersham West Luckham Stoke Pero

---

95. CRO, PB/6/6, letter 30 May 1802, AL to PB.
96. SRO, DD/AH/Box 24/FT9/1–2, Bundle 1, Letter 14 March 1808, Al to JPA.
97. DRO, 96M Box 27/12.
98. DRO, 1148M add/9/6/24

99. DRO, 1148M add/36/241, Letter 10 Jan. 1817, William Summers to [John Day].
100. DRO, 1148M add/36/144, Letter 5 Nov. 1810, Letter AL to TDA. The general map referred to has not survived in the Acland archive. The general map in the Holnicote Atlas does not extend to Winsford.

East Luckham & Blackford Also the Barton of East Luckham & Eastcotts & Goodwins Lands'. A title page contains the same information with additional details of the parishes concerned and the statement that it was 'Surveyed and Mapped in 1809 & 1812, By Alexr Law & Messrs Bradley & Summers'. A general map of the whole area is followed by eight maps showing the constituent manors in more detail. Each of these, except the last, is followed by lists giving the names of the various 'Parcels', their land use and content. An Abstract names tenants, gives terms of leases and property values which are stated to have been estimated by A. Law with, in some cases, the date of 1809 included.

The quality of the field surveying is reflected in the work of the draughtsmen making the fair copy. This is very fine with relief shown by hill shading, fields outlined with precision, washed in colour and outlined in deeper shades. Tree symbols mark woods, orchards, plantations and, with stippling, waste; roads are shown, fenced and unfenced with buildings in plan; settlements, principal features, together with some archaeological sites, are named. A title cartouche is present on all but one map; there is a common style but this is not typical of Law's other work and so reinforces the impression given in the correspondence that Bradley and Summers were the draughtsmen.

The letters exchanged between Sir Thomas Dyke Acland and Alexander Law in 1808[101] and the existence of the 1809–10 Survey of the Manor of Hacche make it clear that the survey and mapping of Holnicote was to be accompanied by a similar programme for the Acland lands at Killerton and Broadclyst. Later correspondence confirms that this was accomplished,[102] but no maps have survived. Letters from William Summers to Sir Thomas and John Day, the Agent, dated 1813–1817, provide a possible explanation.[103] There appears to have been considerable friction in the relationship between Alexander Law and William Summers. In the letter of April 15th 1813 Summers wrote to Sir Thomas Acland:

> On the completion of the outdoor Surveys of your Property I went into partnership (sic) with Mr Bradley and the fair mapping of the estates was given up to us by Mr Law – Since which we parted before the Broadclist Lands being quite finished; & by the most scandalous treatment have now a great balance due to me from Bradley on account of your work; to secure a part of which I was under the necessity of taking into my possession the rough and fair Maps of the Lands in Broadclist Ashclyst & Killerton – The Book is now ready for your inspection . . . A statement of my account together with the Book, I will do myself the honour to present to you at any time your leisure may admit of, & at any place you may appoint . . .[104]

This and three other letters surviving in the Acland archive in the Devon Record Office do more than confirm the way in which the survey and mapping was organised; they explain the causes of the trouble between Alexander Law and his assistant. (see letters transcribed from the Acland archive in Section III of this volume.)

While Summers was engaged in the 'out door' surveying at Holnicote and Killerton, Alexander Law and Thomas Bradley were involved in mapping other Acland properties at Wooleigh Barton (1809)[105] in Devon and North Petherton (1809)[106] and the Manor of Avil near Dunster (1810)[107] in Somerset. The Manor of Wooleigh included land in several parishes; Beaford, St Giles in the Wood and Little Torrington. The map, originally on rollers, was a large one 190.5cms x 140.5cms and the use of an alphanumeric reference in the fields must have referred to a Survey Book which unfortunately has not been found. However, it is

101. SRO, DD/AH Box 24/FT9/1–2, Bundle 1, Letters 28 Jan. 1808, 14 March 1808, AL to JPA.
102. DRO, 1148M add/36/181, Letter 15 April 1813, William Summers to TDA.
103. DRO, 1148M add/36/181, Letters 15 April 1813, /227, 4 Nov. 1816, /241, 10 Jan. 1817, /244, 19 Jan. 1817, William Summers to TDA and John Day.
104. See above, note 103.
105. DRO, 1148M add/10/1b.
106. DRO, 1148M add/10/23a, DRO, 1148M add/10/10/28 and DRO, 1148M add/11/1.
107. DRO, 1148M add/10/20.

the survey and maps of Petherton Park which together reveal more of what may well have been the pattern of recording these three properties. A large map and a reduced copy wth a Survey Book relating to it have survived in the Acland archives. The larger 'Map of Petherton Park and the Manor and tithes of Newton=Roth & Regis . . . by Alexander Law and Assistants' includes a 'Table of Particulars' listing details of the tenants, tenements with their content together those lands which were titheable but not belonging to the Manor of Newton Roth. The smaller map has no 'Table of Particulars'; these details, much elaborated, are to be found in the Survey Book. This, leather-bound, tooled in gold with a delicately-ornamented title page, names Alexander Law and Thomas Bradley as being responsible for the map as well as the Survey and Valuation. There is one curious discrepancy; the smaller map has Petherton Park outlined in yellow with an alpha-numeric field-reference system which is not included in the Survey Book, the only information entered being the total content of Petherton Park, a considerable 1234 acres. The larger map, originally on rollers, may well have been used in the estate office and the smaller one with the elegant Survey Book in Killerton library. The Manor of Avil, like Wool-eigh Barton, included land in more than one parish; Dunster, Carhampton and Timberscombe. Unfortunately there are only two sheets in a readable condition of what must have been a very large map, also on rollers, possibly 176cms x 137cms. An alpha-numeric reference system again points to the existence of a survey book as was the case with Wooleigh Barton but it too has not been found and so our information is incomplete.[108]

Two maps in the Devon Record Office,[109] one of which is a copy of the other, may well be the only survivors of the Killerton and Ashclyst surveys. They show the 'Plan of the intended new road at Killerton' and although neither map includes the name of the maker the style and hand of one of the two implies it was Alexander Law. The map is attached to an Agreement whereby Sir Thomas Dyke Acland exchanged the land required for the new road with that presently occupied by the old road from Columbjohn to Killerton. This was described as 'frequently impassable on account of floods'; the new road followed the field boundaries to the south and joined that from Hatchleigh to Killerton at Danes Wood. The detail shown of field boundaries and settlements is considerable, and was probably derived from an earlier survey such as that undertaken by Thomas Bradley and William Summers, but now 'lost'. The date on the Agreement of 23 March 1812 makes it possible to assign a date sometime after 1812 to a map of the Manors of Killerton and Aishclyst now in the Somerset Record Office.[110] It includes the old road then 'stopped up' and the new road to the south and is a comprehensive survey of the Manors showing relief, rivers, fields with an alpha-numeric reference to a Survey Book (not found), orchards and woods, roads and settlements. The boundaries of the fields separating the two properties are also shown in detail together with rivers, streams, roads and settlements but little else. It is interesting to note the use of conventional signs used by the Ordnance Survey draughtsmen on the 1809 map of Devon.[111] The heavy and light lines of the river banks, the fence symbols below Dolberry Hill and those protecting the path from Killerton House to Columbjohn Chapel together with those on the boundary of the Park to the east, tree symbols with the slight shadows on the east and the indication of open woodland and rough pasture can all be recognised.

A collection of 13 maps,[112] undated and with no surveyor named, poses some interesting questions. The maps, eight of estates in the Manors of Leigh and Loxbeare and five of properties in mid Devon around Riverton, George Nympton and Romans-leigh, are closely related to maps in the Hodge Atlas of 1756 and the Bowring Atlas of 1757. Those of the Manors of Leigh and Loxbeare were copied (probably traced) from the originals with most of the detailed information included even to its place-ment. Some additional material was added, usually fields being numbered in red. The maps of the mid-Devon estates bear a less

108. The evidence of the original presence of rollers on the maps of Wooleigh Barton and Avil and the absence of Survey Books would reinforce the thesis that the Petherton Park maps and survey represent the contemporary pattern of recording estates.

109. DRO, DQS 113A/34/1 and 1148M add/21/3/1.
110. SRO, DD/SAS/c1540/12/1.
111. See p. 1.
112. DRO, 1926B/A/E2/12.

close resemblance to Bowring's work even though they are clearly derived from it. A Survey Book,[113] with entries in the same hand, refers to each of the maps. Three pieces of evidence imply that this mapping exercise was undertaken certainly after 1804[114] and most probably between 1810 and 1813. A Survey of the Manor of Hacche[115] by Alexander Law was completed in 1810 and a letter sent by him to the 10th Bart on 25 February 1813 suggested the sale of scattered holdings in South Molton town.[116] At the same time Law stressed the desirability of a second survey to be paid for by 'those Gentlemen who hath obtain'd your promis'd accomodation (sic)'. The word 'Lot' pencilled in on the General Map of Leigh and Loxbeare perhaps indicates that the maps were used in connection with the sale. An entry in the Accounts submitted by J. Carew to Sir Thomas Dyke Acland dated 1819 details expenses for 'Selling land in Essebeare, House in Barnstaple, Loxbeare.'[117] The date of the accounts does not necessarily refer to the date of the transactions; all accounts seem to have covered a considerable period.

The Cornish estates

It was not until 1802 that the Aclands acquired their estates in Cornwall. Eight Cornish manors (Trerise, Tresillian, Goviley, Penstrase Moor, Cragantallan, Degembris, Ebbingford alias Efford and Thurlibeer) were devised to Sir Thomas Acland, 10th Bart, as part of the Arundell inheritance. These Cornish estates in no way equalled in value the lands the family held in Somerset and Devon. An account of 1811 gives the income of lands in Somerset as £3220.19s.3d., as £5448.0s.0¾d for Devon and for Cornwall only £624.18s.9d.[118] Like many other landowners in the South West the Aclands depended upon the lands which were let out on leases for lives and this is evident in the surveys

of all their lands but the Cornish properties included a fair proportion of moorland which was let at a lower rent. Penstrase Moor Manor included mining activity but it was not until the 1820s when Bude was developed as a resort that the income from the Cornish properties saw an increase in rents.

With the exception of the Manor of Thurlibeer, which was mapped for Thomas Frederick Wentworth before 1791,[119] no maps have been found for the Aclands' Cornish properties before 1802. Indeed, with the exception of the maps of Bude discussed below, detailed knowledge of the estates has to be obtained from surveys rather than maps. There is a reference in the Acland accounts for 4 May 1815 'Paid Mr Hayward in Truro in part for his Bill for surveying and mapping Garras Barton and Penstrace Moor £40' but this map does not appear to have survived.[120] There is a Survey for the Manors of Cragantallan, Degembris, Ebbingford alias Efford and Thurlibeer dated c.1770 which is discussed in this Introduction on pages 9 and a Survey of all eight Cornish Manors which dates from the time of the Aclands' acquisition. This is printed as 'Survey 3' in this volume with some discussion of its content on pages 8–9.

The manors varied in size and in value: 55 tenements are listed for Ebbingford while there were only 13 in Cragantallan, the others mustering between 18 (both Trerise and Tresillian), Goviley (21), Degembris (23), and Thurlibeer and Penstrase Moor both with 31. During the Wentworth ownership the Elizabethan mansion of Trerice was let out to tenants. It is not included in the c.1802 Survey although Trerice Mill was let with just over six acres to John Varco at a rent of £2. The Aclands held Trerice until 1915 when it was sold. The Manor Farm of 500 acres was bought by Cornwall County Council in 1919.[121] The Acland family visited Cornwall in the summer months usually staying in Bude; Trerice was always a problem because

[113.] DRO, 1148M add/6/11.

[114.] The map of Riverton is drawn on paper with a watermark of 1804.

[115.] DRO, 1926B/A/E1/95.

[116.] DRO, 1148M/add36/171, Letter 25 Feb. 1813, AL to TDA.

[117.] DRO, 1148M General Accounts, J Carew with Sir Thomas Dyke Acland from 1816 to Aug. 1828.

[118.] DRO, 1148M/General Accounts, 1811.

[119.] DRO, 1148M add/10/19.

[120.] DRO, 1148M/ General Accounts, 1815. John Hayward's activity in mapping Cornish mining areas is evidenced by his map of the Manor of Tolgullow alias St Day in 1809 (NDRO, B170/94).

[121.] The National Trust, *Trerice Cornwall*, 1981. Early documents refer to the name as *Trerise*: both spellings of the name are found in this volume.

of the distance.[122] In 1815 it was reported that Mr Acland's steward had offered stone from Trerice Quarry towards the building of a schoolroom in Newlyn.[123]

Few references to the Manor of Tresillian have been found apart from the *c.*1802 Survey. A copy of a letter in the Acland archives to Mr Day dated 19 October 1827 mentions the 10th Bart's estates at Treluckey Major, Pencoose and Resparva, all of which were in the Manor of Goviley[124] and a letter of Edward Collins states that Sir Thomas Dyke Acland is thinking of disposing of the same manor.[125] Penstrase Moor Manor was still owned by the Aclands in the 1870s as Sir Thomas was leasing property there in 1873 and 1876.[126] Letters about streaming and mining mention Penstrase Moor in 1823.[127]

The Manor of Degembris was purchased by the Arundells in the seventeenth century after being forfeited by Francis Tregian. The Aclands held it from 1802 until 1915 when it was sold. Cragantallan was inherited by Sir John Arundell in the fifteenth century on the death of John Durrant and Ebbingford alias Efford and Thurlibeer came to Sir John Arundell of Trerice (*c.*1370–1448) on his marriage to Joan, daughter and heir of John Durrant of Cragantallan.[128]

Among the properties, originally held by the Arundells of Trerice, which came to Sir Thomas Dyke Acland in 1802, it was the manors of Efford and Thurlibeer which were to become especially important. This was because of a revival of interest in the construction of a canal designed to link Bude with the Tamar Manure Navigation canal.[129] There had been an earlier proposal in 1774 for a canal to link Bude with the Tamar at Calstock which was not successful. A more modest scheme was put forward in 1793 which was supported by the principal landowners in the area, Sir William Molesworth, Sir John Call, Denys Rolle and the Cohams. However, it was not until 1817 that the project went ahead. James Green and Thomas Shearm were invited to survey a line from Bude Harbour to Holsworthy and their Report provided an estimate 'for improving Bude Harbour & of cutting the Canal nearly to Okehampton, with lateral branches, is about 120,000£ & if it be carried to Launceston, so as to connect it with the Tamar about 30,000£ more'.[130] A company was formed in which Sir Thomas was an important shareholder for he was the owner of much of the land through which the canal would pass. In 1819 an Act of Parliament gave the Company the power to raise the money needed to finance the construction of the canal; it was opened in July 1823.

Of necessity maps of the area were important and several have survived in the Acland archive together with letters reporting on the detailed plans and the progress of the enterprise. However, when these maps are considered one which passed to the Aclands on the acquisition of the manors of Efford and Thurlibeer must be examined first. This predates the canal, and most probably is not later than 1791.[131] It is by David Palmer and is 'A Plan of the Manor of Thurlibeer in the County of Cornwall The property of Fred.k T.s Wentworth Esqr Survey'd & Delineated by David Palmer'.[132] It is an estate map typical of the late-eighteenth century with details of rivers, fields, woods, roads, buildings, peripheral owners and estates, supplemented by a summarised list of landholdings with their content, and identified numerically to the map. Features of the canal were added later and show in considerable detail the associated works and buildings. Of particular importance is the Thurlibeer Inclined Plane, three pits, including one halfway up the Plane, the Reservoir, Waste Drain and the Aqueduct. Other new works were bridges with their approach paths, towing paths and wharves beside the canal and laybys in the canal itself. Green had proposed that the width of the canal to the foot of the first inclined plane

122. Anne Acland, *The Acland Family*, 139.
123. CRO, J/3/2/364. We are indebted to Colin Edwards for this reference.
124. DRO, 1148M add/36/362.
125. DRO, 1148M add/36/441.
126. CRO, AD 241/2–3.
127. DRO, 1148M/Box 21(iv)/14.
128. We are indebted to Bryan Dudley Stamp for information on these Cornish manors.
129. The sea sand from the beach at Bude is composed almost entirely of shells which had long been used as a fertilizer instead of lime. See G.B. Worgan, *A General View of the Agriculture of Cornwall* (1811), 126.
130. DRO, 1148M add36/316, Letter 18 April 1818, John Carew to TDA..
131. Frederick Thomas Wentworth became Earl of Strafford in 1791.
132. DRO, 1148M add/10/19.

should be 37ft 6in at the surface and 4ft 6in deep. This would enable barges of 40 tons, which had taken up sand at low water, to enter the first lock at flood tide, and after passing two further locks to reach the inclined plane. He made other suggestions to protect the harbour which included the building of a breakwater between the mainland and Chapel Rocks, and in addition, the construction of a sea lock at the entrance to the canal.[133] These proposals were shown in detail on various maps, some printed and some in manuscript with Reference Books to accompany them.[134] One of these maps is no doubt the 'model'[135] referred to in a letter from G. B. Kingdon to Sir Thomas Acland dated 18 April 1818 in which he said 'Mr Green, the engineer, read his Report . . . He also exhibited an admirable Model, on a large Scale . . .'.[136] Another suitable candidate would be the large map on parchment in the Bude Museum entitled 'Map of the Proposed Lines of Canal, from Bude-Haven into the Interior of Cornwall and Devon, Surveyed under the direction of James Green, Civil Engineer by Thomas Shearm, Land Surveyor, 1817.' This map shows in considerable detail the hinterland in the two counties through which the canal would pass and which it would serve. On this map of 1817 all the works indicated existed as proposals only but they can be identified on later maps drawn after the completion of the canal in 1823.

A map of 1824 by Thomas Shearm[137] with the title 'Bude Canal Sketch Map from Bude to Heale Bridge Incline Plane 1824 (No. 1)' amplifies the details added to the Palmer map. The cliffs, the high and low water marks, the breakwater, the sandy beach, the river with its old and new courses are all clearly marked and supplement the earlier information about the canal. The sea lock, and intended entrance lock, swivel bridge, the towing paths, the rail road with its extension to the sea sand and the various wharves including the 'Private Wharf of Sir Thomas Dyke Acland' and the 'Company's Wharf' are all distinguished. The Marhamchurch Incline Plane is shown but not the details of its ancilliary works although these were added to the Palmer Map of Thurlibeer. Quarries, owned by Sir Thomas and G.B. Kingdon, provided the stone required for the breakwater and harbour works, and these are shown on the map. The fields adjoining the canal with their content and owners are listed in a void of the map. This map, described in the title as No.1, was probably one of a series similar to the nine maps also by Thomas Shearm held in the Cornwall Record Office.[138] They are dated 1826, are on the same scale, four chains to the inch, provide the same information but with the whole canal surveyed details are available as far as Shernick Bridge which marks the limit of the Acland interest.

An estate atlas of 1828 by Samuel T. Coldridge, 'Landsurveyor and General Draftsman' of Exeter[139] is primarily concerned with lands belonging to the Manors of Efford and Thurlibeer. The Bude Canal from the sea lock to Shernick Bridge passes through these manors and the inclusion of the waterway with the various works, roads and buildings associated with it adds much of interest and value.

The Atlas, a leather-bound volume 20.5cms x 28.5cms is entitled 'Maps and Particulars of the Manors of Efford and Thurlibeer in the Parishes of Stratton, Jacobstowe, Poundstock and Launcells Cornwall The Property of Sir T:D: Acland Bart:' This is preceded by the Acland coat of arms, richly coloured with some gold decoration.. There are five maps, three of which are folded into the volume, the remaining two interleaved with the text which lists the various tenements, their map references and total content.[140] These lists are followed by 'The Aggregate' of the manors dealing with the tenants, the area of the land in statute and customary measure, terms on which the land was

---

133. Helen Harris & Monica Ellis, *The Bude Canal* (Newton Abbot, 1972), 28.
134. Notebooks, Reference Books and accompanying plans: DRO, DP 36; CRO, QS/PDH/1/1,2; QS/PDH/1/3/1,2.
135. Shorter Oxford Dictionary, Vol. I (Oxford, Reprinted 1964), 1268, 'model' a delineation of a ground plan.
136. DRO, 1148M add/36/315.

137. DRO, 1148M add/10/15/1.
138. CRO, DC/NC 15/ 37–45. Maps 37, 38, and 39 cover areas where there was an Acland interest.
139. Ravenhill and Rowe, *Devon Maps and Map-makers* Vol. 2, 392, A 54. Bendall, *Dictionary*, 106, C 325.1
140. The atlas is in private hands and we are grateful to the owner for allowing us to make this close study.

held, rents etc, in fact all the information required for management of the estate.[141] Two statements affecting the canal are of interest; 'Lands taken for the Bude Canal including that part of the harbour which lies between the old and new river courses 10a.3r.0p.(9a.0r.5p.)' and 'Land sold to the Canal Co. 27a.0r.0p. (22a.2r.30p.)'.

Each map has its title in a cartouche varying from a simple medallion for the 'Lands near the Town of Stratton', and 'West Down' with 'The Two Penleans' to 'Heale and Tower Hill' where a fold of inscribed fabric hangs from the branch of a tree. 'The Manor of Thurlibeer' and 'Lands at Efford and Lunstone' appear on large boulders. Each map shows the hand of a skilled draughtsman and is carefully coloured to show the principal features clearly. Rivers, relief, land holdings, woodland, rivers, roads and buildings are all easy to identify, and the way in which Coldridge has shown the rocks below the cliffs on the shore is especially to be noted. Details of the canal and its associated works are all present, and to the south where the canal passes through detached areas of Sir Thomas's land their relationship with the principal part of the manor of Thurlibeer is clearly shown by the continuation of the roads from one area to the other. Scales vary between eight, nine or nine point five chains to the inch. Each map has direction indicated but particular mention must be made of the decoration on two of them; Efford and Lunstone has an anchor and two masts, one flying a narrow pennant; Thurlibeer has an interesting collection of agricultural implements: a seed-sowing device, a scythe, a sickle, a pitchfork and a sheaf of corn. Prince of Wales feathers decorate two of the other maps.

A later map of 1833 with the title of 'A Design for laying out certain ground for Building at Bude-Haven, Cornwall: The Property of Sir Thos Dyke Acland, Bart. George Wightwick Archt.'[142] reflects what must have been the increasing prosperity of Bude following the opening of the canal. There is no indication of scale or direction but the former must have been generous for the detail shown is considerable. In addition to the information provided of the physical landscape and of the canal as far as 2 basons and a lock, the plans of the buildings, either already built or planned are the most important features on the map. Labourers' cottages (?shown in yellow on the 1826 Shearm map), and houses beside the Falcon Inn are described as 'built'. Houses, not yet built, are drawn in plan on numbered plots. Trees shown behind the Falcon Inn and the planned houses and marked as 'Plantation' would have formed an important shelter belt against the prevailing winds. Efford Cottage, refurbished by George Wightwick on the base of old fish cellars at the mouth of the river is also designated as 'built'. This was to be the summer cottage of the Acland family. One large house coloured grey, also described as 'built', is of general interest. It was erected in 1830 on land leased from Sir Thomas by Mr (later Sir) Goldsworthy Gurney, an engineer of distinction. He believed that building on sand was possible provided that a concrete raft was constructed first. Time has proved him right.

These developments were restricted to land close to the river and the canal for Sir Thomas was warned in 1826 of possible trouble if there was building on North Down.[143] However, although in 1831 Carew, the Agent, was writing from Wellington discussing leases for the buildings to be erected, Wightwick's map shows that there was to be no encroachment on North Down.[144] The Acland family maintained an interest there and Efford Down as it became known was preserved as open land until the 1940s when it was handed over to the Town Council on a long lease.

[141.] There are 60 tenements entered for Efford and 27 for Thurlibeer. The content of the Manor of Efford is '611a. 1r. 2 (statute) or 513a. 2r. 28p (customary)' and of the Manor of Thurlibeer 1418a. 3r. 12p. (1192a. 1r. 15p.)'.

[142.] DRO, 1148M/Box 20/7.
[143.] DRO, 1148M add/36 373, Letter 1 April 1826, John Carew to TDA.
[144.] DRO, 1148M add/36 445, Letter 23 Feb. 1831, John Carew to TDA.

4. The Stewards, Agents and Surveyors

In the eighteenth century, and more particularly after 1750, three groups of men practising different professions emerged as being collectively responsible for the efficient management and administration of large landed estates: the stewards, the agents and the surveyors. Over time their individual duties and responsibilities became more complex in response to changes in ownership following the Dissolution of the Monasteries, the growth of large, often scattered landholdings, the introduction of new methods in agriculture and the emergence of a large body of men skilled in the techniques of land surveying, measuring and plotting.

The Steward

The importance of the land steward in the management of large estates in the eighteenth and early nineteenth centuries has long been accepted. Their responsibilities were many, caring for the immediate domestic needs of the household and the estate and although they served no formal apprenticeship 'they usually commanded a very wide and divers body of knowledge useful to the running of an estate, and had the ability as well as the delegated authority to mobilise the skills of other professional men'.[145] Stewards came from a variety of backgrounds and frequently profited from their former experience to pursue other activities, a practice permitted by their employers, sometimes with positive encouragement, for it was often to their advantage. This was the case with the 7th Bart and John Veitch. After his appointment as Steward in 1779 Veitch was allowed and indeed encouraged to establish a nursery on Acland land at Budlake. However, it must be admitted that these independent ventures inevitably depended on the interest of the landowner, his status and inclination and the location of his estates.

The Agent

The agent, almost always an attorney, dealt with the administration of the estate as the landowner's man of business. He kept the estate accounts, paid salaries, arranged the setting of farms, the drawing of leases, and saw that the terms were generally observed. Agents were responsible for rent collection, for 'plantations' (i.e. afforestation) and when the landowner was absent in London kept him supplied with bills of exchange and local information.[146] The most comprehensive statement of an agent's duties in the early nineteenth century is to be found in a letter of advice to his employer from one such man who felt he would soon have to relinquish his post. 'It cannot in the common and ordinary course of events be many years longer that I can continue in this service, and therefore, I would recommend you to look out some person who not only understands your Rents, holding your Courts, which by the bye is but a small part of the Business of an Agent, but the nature and management of Lands Woods and Buildings and Tenants suitable to the Farms which in my oppinion (sic) as difficult a part as any to find out, and to secure that Person'.[147]

To all intents and purposes Killerton had an absentee landlord until about 1770. The 7th Bart was an established landowner in Somerset as well as Devon and the whole of the hunting season was spent in Somerset at either Pixton or Holnicote. The house at Holnicote was destroyed by fire in 1779 but from the early 1770s Sir Thomas had taken a more active part in the life of Devon. Little is known of the day-to-day administration of the Killerton estates until then although Hodge's Rental at the back of his Atlas, made in 1756, was updated concerning the lives of the lessees of the tenements. Estate account books kept by Robert Batten detail expenditure on the estate from 1771 to 1788. Batten, sometimes referred to as 'Farmer Batten', signs the accounts on

145. D.R. Hainsworth, 'The Estate Steward' in Wilfred Prest, ed., *The Professions in Early Modern England* (London, New York, Sydney: 1987), 154–81.

146. Edward Hughes, 'The Eighteenth-Century Estate Agent' in H.A. Cronne,

T.W. Moody and D.B. Quinn, eds *Essays in British and Irish History* (London, 1949), 196.

147. CRO, PB/6/40, Letter 17 May 1818, AL to PB.

an annual basis and on occasions they are also signed by the 7th Bart. There is no evidence that Batten served as Agent on any other estate. According to the list of lives in being on Cross Tenement and Pims Cott in the Manor of Kildrington (Killerton) Francis in Hodge's Rental, Batten was 21 years of age in 1758. His father, also Robert, is described as 'gent.' in a lease of 1746, whereas son Robert is described as 'yeoman' in a lease of 1772.[148] However, in the 1770s the development and management of the Killerton estate required other skills than those of a local farmer and it was probably for this reason that in 1779 John Veitch was appointed Steward.

In the period following the death of the 7th Bart in 1785[149] the Agent played an increasingly important role. However, the expertise of an attorney did not always extend to the detailed knowledge required for planning, valuations and surveys, which were the special skills of the Stewards and Surveyors. Charles Vancouver, in his *General View of the Agriculture of the County of Devon* identified clearly the respective roles of lawyers and stewards when he stated '. . . in no part of England are the care and management of estates so generally deputed to the super-intendance of attornies and other unqualified persons as in the county of Devon: in what view their education, professional pursuits, and habits can be deemed qualifications for the important duties of land agent is not to be easily understood . . . Different, however, are the qualifications for a land steward, for

it is to him, and him only, that we must look for projecting, directing, and carrying into execution such works as the nature of the estate requires, and by the most economical and judicious means, effecting the permanent improvement of the employer's property'.[150]

Two men, John Weech and John Day, both of Milverton in Somerset, were the attorneys primarily responsible for the later administration of the Acland estates. John Weech served as Agent after Robert Batten until his death in 1815 when he was followed by John Day. The Account books in the Acland archive[151] provide much information about their duties even though they do not form a continuous record. After 1808 when Sir Thomas Dyke Acland, the 10th Bart, came of age the annual statements bear his signature, as well as that of either Weech or Day, reflecting his active involvement and supervision of the conduct of estate business. Of interest in the present context are the constant records of payments to John Veitch as Steward, sums paid to Alexander Law and Mr Hayward of Truro for mapping and details of the income generated by the Somerset, Cornwall and Devon estates which are itemised separately. The entry for 1815 is shown below as it appears in the account ledger together with the details of Weech's salary. The two lists demonstrate the relative importance of the various elements in the Acland land-holdings.

1815 Receipts	Somerset Estates	4357.0.4¾	
	Cornish "	428.19.4	
	Devon "	5331.12.3¾	
	Blackford & Newton Manors	13.11.6	10131.7.2½ (sic)
Weech's Salary	Devon Estates	150	
	Park "	30	
	Holnicote	100	
	Blackford	6.6	
	Newton	4.4	
	Cornish Estates	70	360.10

[148]. DRO, 1148M add/2/L15/322 and 1148M add/2/L15/33.

[149]. The 8th Bart, his grandson, died two months later. The 9th Bart (uncle of the 8th Bart) chose to live on his Somerset estates leaving John Veitch to look after Killerton. The 9th Bart died in 1794 and his son, Sir Thomas

Dyke Acland, 10th Bart, did not come of age until 1808.

[150]. Charles Vancouver, *General View of the Agriculture of the County of Devon* (London, 1808), 80–1.

[151]. DRO, 1148M General Accounts.

Occasionally other lawyers' names appear, usually in connection with a particular problem. Mr Cridland, another attorney from Milverton, seems to have been concerned with the settlement of the 7th Bart's estate. John Symes, who may have come from Bridport and Weymouth, is mentioned by Alexander Law in a letter which revealed the problems which could arise when more than one attorney was involved. When seeking particulars of Sir Thomas's estates he was told to apply to Mr Symes who told him to refer to Mr Weech: he suggested he should approach Mr Veitch who in turn passed him back to Mr Symes.[152] Another lawyer, Ralph Barnes, clerk to the Dean and Chapter, seems to have been concerned with Mr Weech with the sale of estates prior to 1808, a transaction which was not to Sir Thomas's advantage.[153] George Short, an Exeter attorney, was agent for the Oxenham estates which came into the possession of John (Palmer) Acland; the legal business associated with this property was also handled by Brutton and Ford, attorneys in Exeter. The name of Edward Collins, a lawyer from Exeter, did not appear until 1831 when he was concerned with the possible sale of the Manor of Goviley in Cornwall.[154]

The Surveyors

The surveyors, concerned with measuring land, calculating acreages and plotting the results on a map, were few in number in the seventeenth century. However, the demand for men qualified to produce maps and their accompanying surveys increased dramatically in the next hundred years. Skills, which were disseminated through the many books published on surveying techniques and plotting were acquired by local men. Some

worked with independent land stewards, others alone satisfying the demands of many employers.[155]

The names of some 21 surveyors appear on, or are associated with, the maps of Acland properties. Of these three are associated only with maps of Somerset and two with Cornish landholdings. Of the remaining 16 eight were concerned solely with Devon estates, five were active in both Devon and Somerset and three in Devon and Cornwall. Little can be added to what has already been published about some of these men[156] but surviving documents and letters recording the work of the others have given us a greater knowledge of their working methods, an insight into their characters and their relations with their employers and employees.

More than any other it is the name of Alexander Law which is the most important in any study of the Acland estate maps. The cartographic literature associates the name Law with Aberdeen.[157] An Alexander Law, son of Charles Law and Helen Tytler was baptised at Midmar, Aberdeen on 19 February 1755; there are considerable records of the Law family in that town and so identifying the West Country Alexander Law with Charles and Helen is unavoidably tentative.[158] What is certain is that he was not born in England[159] and in a letter to John Acland of 15 October 1812 Alexander Law revealed a little more of his early life. 'My Father was a Builder & Architec (sic) in an extensive Line with whom I lived till I was 18 years of Age and by which means I had an insight into that Business which few of my Profession ever had'.[160]

By 1772/3 he was assistant to William Hole of Barnstaple[161] and from that date on Law's experience as a practical surveyor and map-maker was extensive. Working independently from

152. SRO, DD/AH Box 24/FT9/1–2 Bundle 1, Letter 14 March 1808, AL to JPA.
153. SRO, DD/AH Box 24/FT9/1–2 Bundle 1, Letter 25 April 1809, AL to JPA.10.
154. DRO, 1148M add/36/434 and 441 Letters 20 Dec. 1830 and 21 Jan. 1831.
155. For example, Robert Ballment worked 'under the direction' of William Hole of Barnstaple and for most of his professional life Alexander Law was self-employed.
156. Mary R. Ravenhill and Margery M. Rowe, eds *Devon Maps and Map-*

Makers (DCRS, 2000, 2002).
157. A Sarah Bendall, *Dictionary of Land Surveyors and Local Map-Makers of Great Britain and Ireland 1530–1950* (London, 1997), 307; WCL, The Burnet Morris Index.
158. Aberdeen Record Office.
159. CRO, PB/6/20, Letter 15 September 1807, AL to PB, '. . . but not being myself born in England . . .'.
160. SRO, DD /AH/Box 24/FT9/1–2, Bundle 2, Letter 15 October 1812, AL to JPA.
161. *SM*, 11 August 1777.

Truro in 1778[162] and from Littleham, Exmouth about 1787 he produced many estate maps and atlases for the principal land-owners in Devon and Cornwall, amongst whom were the Earl of Devon, Lord Rolle, Lord de Dunstanville, the Rev. Charles Prideaux Brune and the Dean and Chapter of Exeter. The Act of Parliament of 1804 'disqualifying Agents not being Attorneys from drawing Deeds'[163] was the reason why Law sought admission to the Inns of Court. This he achieved in 1805[164] which made it possible for him to draw 'leases covenants and all instruments under seal'; this enabled Law to fulfill those duties required of an Agent and it was as an Agent that he acted for the Rev. Charles Prideaux Brune and John (Palmer) Acland as well as continuing to conduct Surveys and produce estate maps for them and other important landowners.

These, however, were not the only professional activities in which Alexander Law was involved. From his home and farm at Littleham, Exmouth, where he bred horses and produced cider of considerable quality, he travelled throughout Devon, Somerset, Dorset and Hampshire on business as Agent for Prideaux Brune and John Acland, writing regular reports on the conditions on the farms, their buildings and tenants. Included in these Reports were many comments on the state of agriculture and the problems caused by bad weather in the second decade of the nineteenth century. The surviving letters in the Record Offices of Cornwall and Somerset reveal the daily activities of a man conscientiously carrying out many and varied duties. It is unfortunate that this record is marred by what can only be described as an aggressive and disputatious attitude when dealing with other Agents and attorneys often over money matters. Alexander Law seems to have had an innate mistrust of lawyers which characterised his relations with them over many years and to have been convinced

that they felt a similar hostility towards him. He claimed they sought to cause trouble for him, that they regard him as 'one in their way' and that they would be glad to see matters go wrong.[165] In February 1818 he criticised one attorney as 'one of the meanest Scoundrels existing to act in such a manner . . . I have been nearly 40 Years in Business on my own Acct . . . In short I am surrounded with a set of Sharks . . .' and in July he said of Mr Barnes Clerk to the Dean and Chapter 'I wish I had never known him, he has been a great enemy to me. My Valuations of the Dean and Chapters property he hath put into the Hands of an Ironmonger in Exeter and made him their Surveyor in my place. In fact he is the only Man on Earth that I could not do Business with – with Pleasure.'[166] Some time later, in October 1818, Law was critical of Brutton and Ford (John Acland's lawyers) suggesting that they were deliberately obstructive and in the following month equally censorious about those serving Sir Thomas at Holnicote and the Earl of Carnarvon. 'I have had nothing but trouble from Agents ever since, and instead of following my advice; acted contrary to everything I recommended . . . At Holnicote Sir Thomas has a Footman for his Bailif(sic) and who is now the greatest Farmer in all that Country and possessed of Property above anything that I can boast of, and Mr Pearce who was a Country Carpenter, and Bailiff to the Earl of Carnarvon, keeps a better House than I could afford, yet these men are in full confidence, but if they had not been better paid than I have they would not have been in the affluence they are now'.[167]

It is hardly surprising that this hostility had unfortunate repercussions. When doubts were raised about Law's financial probity, relations with John Day, the Agent, and Sir Thomas Acland almost reached breaking point. Problems over payments to Summers and Shillibeer,[168] accusations of exorbitant fees being

---

162. *SM*, 9 November 1788.
163. CRO, PB/6/12, Letter 20 Jan. 1805, AL to PB.
164. CRO, PB/6/12, Letter 30 Sept. 1805, AL to PB expressing thanks for PB's assistance; EFP, 7 November 1805.
165. SRO, DD/AH/ Box 24/FT9/1–2, Bundle 1, Letter 5 April 1809, AL to JPA; CRO, PB/6/31, Letter 28 Aug. 1813, AL to PB.
166. SRO, DD/AH/ Box 24/FT9/1–2, Bundle 2, Letters 9 Feb. and 8 July

1812, AL to JPA.
167. SRO, DD/AH/ Box 11/15/1–4, Bundle 1, Letters 18 Oct. and 13 Nov, 1818, AL to JPA.
168. DRO, 1148M add/36/181, Letter 15 April 1813, William Summers to TDA; DRO,1148M add/36/241, Letter 10 Jan. 1817, William Summers to John Day.

charged for valuing timber[169] and claims for outstanding monies due to him led Law into several acrimonious exchanges with Sir Thomas and John Day. If Law found problems dealing with his employers, their lawyers and his own employees they also found him a difficult man to deal with. As early as 1813 John Weech, who preceded John Day as Agent to the Aclands, expressed his doubts about Law's openness and sincerity; 'Mr Law has a happy knack of shifting or rather endeavouring to shift every —— or blame in conduct from himself to another, and so long as he escapes he cares not who is the sufferer . . .'.[170] Charles Prideaux Brune felt much the same describing him in a letter to his solicitor in 1819 as having 'a perverse obstinacy of temper', and later stating that 'Mr Law has always unfortunately for his own Candour at least made his blunder concur with his own Interest'[171] and that he was 'not exempt from Cunning and Chicanery'.[172]

In his work for the Aclands Law relied on several assistants of whom Thomas Bradley, his nephew, was the most important. From 1802 on Bradley's name appears with his uncle's on 19 maps, 15 of which are of Acland land.[173] Other surveyors employed directly or indirectly were William Summers, William Shillibeer and Charles Chilcott and it must be said that Law does not seem always to have valued these associates or spared them from criticism. Bradley's relationship with his uncle was not without problems. In September 1803 Law writes that he 'withdrew from his protection, went to London on a frolic spent all his Money and wrote that he did not know where to find a Shilling'.[174] No doubt it was for this reason that in January 1804 Bradley became a 'Clerk to the Hazard Sloop of War' only to seek reinstatement in Exmouth in June of that year. It seems

that Alexander Law did restore him to his employment for his 'Nephew' is reported as making a survey in 1807. However, he did not seem wholly to have regained his uncle's confidence for in 1809 Law was writing that he 'appears sensible of his late imprudencies and if I can be the means of making him a useful Member of Society I shall think my trouble and expence well bestow'd'. A few years later Bradley is castigated 'few men are more capable but he certainly does not love work . . . more shew than substance'.[175] It seems probable that it was William Summers who replaced Bradley when he went off to sea. Law did not feel that it was an entirely satisfactory arrangement; 'the manner in which he does business is in general correct but not in that particular manner in which I have been accustomed to adopt'.[176] Even so, Summers was thought competent to undertake the out-door surveys at Holnicote and Killerton. It was correspondence from Summers which added the name of William Shillibeer as another of Alexander Law's assistants.[177]

Charles Chilcott's position in relation to Alexander Law is uncertain. He was responsible for an estate atlas of 20 maps dating from 1795 (of land belonging to John Acland) which pre-dates Law's involvement with John Acland. However there was contact between them in December 1819[178] over maps and plans of Acland's lands in North Petherton. This may refer to the 1795 work or to a later Survey but in any event in the following April Law was also critical of Chilcott, querying the accuracy of his map.[179] It is interesting to note that Law himself was not immune to criticism. A paper in Sir Thomas Acland's hand enclosed in Weech's Accounts of 1811 includes a note of £200 to be paid to Law to correct his value of Broadclyst[180] and a letter from J. Rendle in 1815 details a mistake he made in valuing

169. DRO, 1148M add/36/235, Letter 27 Dec. 1816, John Day to TDA – copy of letter sent to Alexander Law and 1148M add/36/243, Letter 18 Jan. 1817, John Day to TDA.
170. DRO, 1148M/Box 17/6, Letter 19 Nov. 1813, J. Weech to TDA.
171. CRO, PB/6/26, Letters 2 June and 5 Sept. 1819, PB to Edward Coode.
172. CRO, PB/6/51, Letter 18 Dec. 1819, Letter PB to Edward Coode.
173. DRO, 96M/Box 27/12. Lease dated 8 July 1806 to commence after the death of Alexander Law and his nephew Thomas Bradley signed in the presence of William Summers.
174. CRO, PB/6/7, Letter 11 Sept. 1803, AL to PB.

175. CRO, PB/6/23, Letter 3 Dec. 1809, AL to PB; CRO, PB/6/31, Letter 14 July 1813, AL to PB.
176. CRO, PB/6/8, Letter 30 June 1804, AL to PB.
177. DRO, 1148M add/36/241, Letter 10 Jan. 1817, William Summers to John Day.
178. SRO, DD/AH/ Box 11/15/1–4, Bundle 2, Letter 4 Dec. 1819, AL to JPA.
179. SRO, DD/AH/ Box 11/15/1–4, Bundle 3, Letter 19 April 1820, AL to JPA.
180. DRO, 1148M General Accounts to April 1813/Weech. The corrections were to be made 'to the date of the present map'.

timber on South Tawton estates where he charged 'Taw Green with the timber on Taw Ground when there was no timber there.'[181]

It is true that Alexander Law can be criticised for many shortcomings and that some of his problems were of his own making. In spite of this his professional life was one of consider-able achievement, one which to date has not been properly documented or recognised. In the present context it must be said that his maps and surveys of the various Acland properties have added immeasurably to our knowledge and understanding of these estates in the early nineteenth century.

5. The Documents

Provenance

The extensive estates of the Acland family are documented for the most part in two large collections of archives. The deposit in the Devon Record Office (1148M) of the papers of the main branch of the family was made over a period of 30 years, the bulk of the collection coming in 1962. It is listed quite fully in four binders in the Search Room except that 'out-county' deeds are simply 'bundle-listed'. It is from this 1148M collection that 22 of the maps and 20 of the surveys which are described in this present volume have been found. The other large deposit (some 66 boxes of material) relating to the Aclands is in the Somerset Record Office: the Acland Hood of Fairfield, Stogursey (DD/AH) collection relates chiefly but not exclusively to the Palmer Acland branch of the family. Of particular interest for the present study is the full listing of deeds of Devon properties which relate to the Aclands' Oxenham family inheritance. The list of the Acland Hood manuscripts is contained in five binders in the Record Office Search Room in Taunton. Five maps and one survey from this source are included in the text of the present volume. A smaller corpus of Acland material is located in a collection deposited in the Devon Record Office in 1970 by Anstey and Thompson, solicitors in 1970, which has the reference 1926B.

As might be expected, not all the maps of the Acland estates were found in their own family archives. Estates were sold and sometimes the map was passed on to the purchaser of the land. This occurred in the case of two of John Bowring's maps of 1757, one being given to the Fortescue family who bought land in East Buckland and one to South Molton Borough, which purchased properties in the town. The Newman family, who bought estates in Kenton which was formerly part of the Aclands' Oxenham inheritance, preserved a map of estates in the parish among their family archives and an atlas of the Aclands' Cornish estates made in 1828 is now in the possession of the present owner of property in Bude. A map of farms in Broadclyst is now in the Wyndham archives in the Somerset Record Office, possibly because Anne Oxenham married William Wyndham in 1743. Maps have always been of interest to archaeologists and two maps described in the present volume are taken from the Somerset Archaeological Society's collection in the Somerset Record Office. The 1762 map of 'Coomroy' in Broadclyst was found in a Plymouth solicitor's collection of documents in the Plymouth

---

[181] DRO, Z17/3/35, 30 July 1815 Letter J. Rendle to AL.

and West Devon Record Office. The building of roads and canals has always generated maps which were preserved in local government archives: hence a copy of the map of the new road at Killerton is in the Devon Quarter Sessions records and maps of the proposed Bude Canal are in Bude Museum and in the Cornwall Record Office amongst their Deposited Plans material.

The letters from Alexander Law, which are referred to in the main text and in Section III of this present volume, are to be found in the Devon, Somerset and Cornwall Record Offices. They not only chart the journeys made for various landowners, including the Aclands, but record the business he conducted on their behalf as agent, steward, surveyor and map-maker. In addition these letters provide an insight into the private life and interests of one of the most prolific independent professional men of the late-eighteenth and early-nineteenth centuries.

Listing

The maps and surveys are listed in date order within the three counties of Devon, Somerset and Cornwall. The aim is to provide sufficient detail for a student of cartography interested in the development of maps and for the social and landscape historian seeking information in the surveys on estate management and valuation. Twenty-four maps are illustrated in colour in the volume but unfortunately, others are either too large or faded to merit photography. However the modern grid reference is given on all the map descriptions to pinpoint the area covered. (In most cases this has been supplied from the 1" to the mile O.S. map with just a few taken from the 6" to the mile map). Any information supplied solely by the editors on the map and survey descriptions is placed between square brackets. Details of the scale of the maps are provided and these appear as on the document with no attempt made to convert them to metric measure, the representative fraction is given and the physical format and

the size of the map (in centimetres) are described. The orientation of the map, 'eastings' before 'northings', is supplied. Where the orientation is unclear, the horizontal measurement precedes the vertical. The 'content' describes the features which may be seen on the map and how these are shown. The natural features such as relief, rivers and ponds, precede fields, gardens, gates, roads and footpaths, buildings and contiguous parishes, estates and owners. The decoration (cartouche, compass rose, etc.) is also described and any other associated documents noted, as these often serve to place the map in context or to supply a date, a name of a surveyor or reason for making the map. Relevant letters from Alexander Law are included in this section. Finally, a reference is given if a map has been described or reproduced in any publication.

The surveys in the list vary greatly in size and information given. An attempt has been made to give details to conform to the map entries as far as possible, where the surveys exist as separate documents. Where both maps and surveys are present in atlases, details of the survey are given either in the general description or at the end of the map entry. Where there is a series of surveys covering several years, this is made clear although only one survey is listed in detail. Many surveys are unattributed, possibly because the steward would have been expected to compile them as part of his usual work in managing the estate, which was not always the case with the maps. Details on the listing of the abstracts of the three surveys and of the letters in Section III precede the relevant entries. In the abstracts of the three surveys place-names and surnames, upper and lower case letters and apostrophes in place-names appear as in the original: common Latin Christian names have been Anglicized. The names of manors are reproduced in their original spelling. A glossary is provided which lists the less familiar and local words which appear in the text.

Glossary

Advowson: the right to present an incumbent; used to include manorial rights and the jurisdiction of the church

Appurtenance: a minor property right or privilege that belongs to another as principal

Backside: yard containing a manure heap which was roofed over; back premises, also the privy

Ball: used as a place-name meaning round or smooth, probably referring to relief i.e. a small hill

Barton: usually courtyard farms with all the windows looking inwards, but came to mean the home farm

Burgage: urban plot consisting of the house, yard and garth, often with a narrow frontage and a long narrow strip of land behind

Capital messuage: dwelling house with its outbuildings and adjacent land occupied by the owner or lord of a property which contained a number of messuages

Cellar: storehouse or barn

Close: a small enclosed field or plot

Conventionary tenure: a seven-year lease at a free-market rent with negligible services and no renewal as of right; there were entry fines and relief or heriot at the death of a tenant

Copyhold: a form of tenure in which the title was substantiated by the tenant's ability to produce a copy of the entry in the court roll noting his acquisition of the property by inheritance or some other means

Courtlage: yards and buildings close to the dwelling house

Estover, common of: the right of taking sufficient wood from the demesne, lord's waste or woods for fuel, making implements etc

Fulling or tucking mill: a mill to scour or beat as a means of finishing or cleansing woollens

Furze: gorse

Germine wood: either young new woods or those regrowing after coppicing

Grist mill: corn mill

Ham: subdivided field usually near a river

Herbage: a payment for pasturing all sorts of animals other than swine on the demesne

Heriot: a payment made to the lord on the death of a tenant

High rent or chief rent: a lease for three lives and £25 down, paid until the death of the third life and then the property reverted to the lord

Horreum: storehouse for grain

Landscore: a bundle of strips, not all the same size, still surrounded by a grass balk and cultivated by tenants

Linhay: an open-fronted building with a loft above, standing in a farmyard or a field

Messuage: the portion of land occupied by the dwelling house and garden

Moiety: a half

Pound: a walled enclosure in which to keep beasts which had strayed on to the open fields

Quillet: a strip of land without any visible demarcation of ownership

Quine: a corner stone

Searwood: dried i.e. dead wood, thus dead wood taken from the coppice probably for fuel

Shambles: stalls erected by the town and let out to townsmen or strangers on market days for the sale of fish and meat

Shutthouse (shitthouse): a separate building housing the privy

Turbary: the right to pare off peat for use as fuel or to make charcoal

The information in this glossary has come principally from I.H. Adams, *Agrarian landscape terms: a glossary for historical geography* and the *OED*.

Section I

Abstracts of Surveys

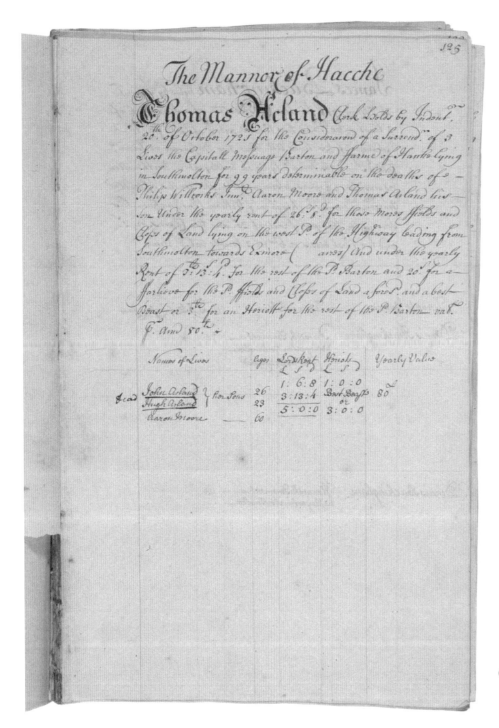

Page from the Survey of Devon
Estates, 1726
(DRO, 1148M add/6/11, by courtesy of
the National Trust and the Acland
Family)

Survey 1

Devon

This is a substantial volume of almost 400 pages, size 23.6cms x 37.5cms. It has a leather cover, tooled in gold, with a second outer loose leather cover which is rather worn. The binding of the volume has suffered, probably from damp.

The survey made in 1726 by Thomas Nott, Steward to Sir Hugh Acland, occupies the first 261 pages of the book: a survey made in 1765 of the same manors although the properties within the manors are not necessarily listed in the same order, accounts for the remaining pages (262–383). The 1765 survey has not been abstracted. There is an index to the manors which includes 'Kildrington alias Killerton Manor' and 'Kildrington alias Killerton Franceis'. No survey of these two manors appears in the volume in 1726 or 1765 but the index has a note 'vide Kill. Rent Book'.

In the 1726 survey the premises are described in a paragraph at the top of each page with details of the lease. Underneath, in columns, are details of tenants' names, tenements' names, acres, dates of leases and fines, names of lives and their ages, the lord's rent, heriots and yearly value. In the following abstract, only details of the premises, tenants and yearly value have been reproduced but some discussion of the other information given is to be found in the Introduction.

The Survey was made just a few years after the marriage of Sir Hugh Acland with Cecily Wroth in 1721. The lands listed represent the Acland family's estates in Devon in the 1720s which they had accrued in former centuries, many by advantageous marriages.

ABSTRACT OF SURVEY

[HEADING] A Survey of the Manors Farms Lands Tenem^{ts} Hereditaments lying in the County of Devon of Sr Hugh Acland Bar^t Taken from former Surveys Rent Rolls and Counterparts of Leases in the year of our Lord 1726 by Mr Thomas Nott Steward

LANDKEY PARISH

PREMISES: 'Farme of Akelane' [Acland Barton SS 595325]; LESSEES: Edward Ratclyffe and part let to Gregory Davy; TENANT: Samuel Wreford; ANNUAL VALUE: £79

'To this farm there belongs an Isle in the Parish Church of Lankey where many of the Ancestors Sr Hugh Acland ly Interred, this Isle is repaired by the Owner of the Farme. Notwithstanding it is Charged with Church Rates, which being thought unreasonable it was Contested at Law, but given for the Parish they proving the Ancient Usage of the same so that I suppose the Isle was Built by some of the Family for their own conveniency and the Rates still continued as before but whatever Seat there was before in the Church it is now lost.'

MANOR OF RIVERTON

[Riverton SS 638300]

SWIMBRIDGE PARISH

PREMISES: Riverton Northdown and Black alias Blackwood Meadow, part of Riverton barton; LESSEE: Margery Joce, widow; TENANT: John Cowell; ANNUAL VALUE: £10

PREMISES: Higher Eastdown, the Middle down and the lower Eastdowne, 25a., Riverton Moore, 26a., part of Riverton Barton; LESSEE: John Joce; TENANT: John Joce; ANNUAL VALUE: £10

PREMISES: Easterwell Brake [crossed through], Easterwell Park, the Bramblecombe alias Tong Close, Yelland Meadow, the Wester Well park, the Broadpark and Broompark, part of Riverton Barton, 28a.; LESSEE: John Saunders; TENANT: William Berry; ANNUAL VALUE: £17

PREMISES: the Town Place, 2a., the Town Place Meadow, 3a., the herbage and pasture only of Riverton Wood 'at such times and with such beasts only as the Germine and Coppice Woods may not be dampnified', 30a.; LESSEE: John Saunders; TENANT: William Berry; ANNUAL VALUE: £7

PREMISES: Riverton Close, 5a. and a quillet called the Hemphay; LESSEE: John Joce; TENANT: John Joce; ANNUAL VALUE: £2

PREMISES: Wester Stoodleigh parke, 5a., the Broomclose alias Easter Balesparke, 6a., Wester Bales parke, 8a., one meadow. 1¼a., part of Riverton Barton; LESSEE: William Mayne; TENANT: William Mayne; ANNUAL VALUE: £11

PREMISES: Easter Studley Park; LESSEE: William Mayne; TENANT: John Dalling; ANNUAL VALUE: £5

PREMISES: higher broomclose, 3a., the lower broomclose, 2½a., the higher hill, 2½a., the lower hill, 2a., the meadow, 2a.,

part of Riverton Barton; LESSEE: John Heddon; TENANT: Thomas Southwood; ANNUAL VALUE: £5

PREMISES: 2 water grist mills called Riverton mills and dwelling-houses, orchards, lands, meadows, leats and 'wares' belonging; LESSEE: John Williams; TENANT: Anthony Ball; ANNUAL VALUE: £10

PREMISES: cottage and garden; LESSEE: [not stated] Leworthy; TENANT: John Thorn; ANNUAL VALUE: £1

LANDKEY PARISH

PREMISES: messuage and tenement called Westcott [Westacott SS 585328]; LESSEE: Henry Cowell; TENANT: Henry Cowell; ANNUAL VALUE: £30

Hugh Acland de Acland in the County of Devon Esqre gave by his last Will &Testament dated xº Aprilis 1620 to the poor of Lankey to be bestowed in Bread weekly ... to be paid out of his lands in Westcott ...

PREMISES: the Lower tenements called Bathey or Boughtey, 4a.; LESSEE: Gregory Davey; TENANT: John Davey; ANNUAL VALUE: £5

PREMISES: messuage and garden in Wester=newland [Newland SS 597313]; LESSEE: Philip Westacot; TENANT: Eleanor Westacott; ANNUAL VALUE: £1

BISHOP'S TAWTON PARISH

PREMISES: tenement and close in Newport, 5a.; LESSEE: [not stated]; TENANT: George Prideaux; ANNUAL VALUE: 11s

PREMISES: close, 2a., in Newport; LESSEE: [not stated] Cooke; TENANT: James Kidwell; ANNUAL VALUE: £4

PREMISES: 2 closes, 3a., and a barn in Rompsham in Newport; LESSEE: the widow Rowley; TENANT: Nicholas Cooke; ANNUAL VALUE: £5

BARNSTAPLE PARISH

PREMISES: messuages in Lichton; LESSEE: Joan Mitchell; TENANT: Mary Horred; ANNUAL VALUE: £5

PREMISES: garden or shop or workhouse now new erected into a dwellinghouse and malthouse in Litchdon; LESSEE: Joan Mitchell; TENANT: George Webber; ANNUAL VALUE: £4

PREMISES: moiety of tenement in Holland Street; LESSEE: Susanna Badcock; TENANT: Martha Babb; ANNUAL VALUE: £3

PREMISES: the other moiety of the tenement in Holland Street; LESSEE: Martha Pope; TENANT: Martha Babb; ANNUAL VALUE: £3

PREMISES: messuages on the Key in or near Holland Street; LESSEE: Thomas Harris; TENANT: John Day; ANNUAL VALUE: £12

PREMISES: messuage and garden in Well Street; LESSEE: William Hills; TENANT: Henry Wilcocks; ANNUAL VALUE: £4

PREMISES: dwellinghouse and garden in Well Street; LESSEE: Joan Gagg; TENANT: Samuel Drake; ANNUAL VALUE: £4

PREMISES: dwellinghouse and garden in Well Street: LESSEE: Walter Tucker; TENANT: Henry Drake; ANNUAL VALUE: £4

BISHOP'S TAWTON PARISH

PREMISES: close called Goldspark, 2a.; LESSEE: George Moole; TENANT: John Gregory; ANNUAL VALUE: 50s

EAST DOWN PARISH

PREMISES: messuage called Booden alias Bowden; LESSEE: Mary Rogers; TENANT: Robert Ward; ANNUAL VALUE: £40

LANDKEY PARISH

PREMISES: messuage and tenement and 4 closes called Bathey, 5a.; LESSEE: George Prideaux; TENANT: George Webber; ANNUAL VALUE: £5

CHARLES PARISH

PREMISES: messuage late Fairchilds, herbage and coppice wood, 28a., and commons in Littlebray commons; LESSEE: John Scott; TENANT: [not stated]; ANNUAL VALUE: [not stated]

PREMISES: Littlebray; LESSEE: John Scott; TENANT: [not stated]; ANNUAL VALUE: [not stated]

PREMISES: messuage called Stocke; LESSEE: John Scott; TENANT: [not stated]; ANNUAL VALUE: [not stated]

PREMISES: dwellinghouse and 2 gardens adjoining Broomwell Gate and one little orchard and part of Littlebray; LESSEE: George Treble; TENANT: Thomas Kingdon; ANNUAL VALUE: £20

EAST DOWN PARISH

PREMISES: messuages called Indicott alias Endicott; LESSEE: Philip Lancey; TENANT: Thomas Harding; ANNUAL VALUE: [not stated]

BERRYNARBOR AND EAST DOWN PARISHES

PREMISES: messuage called Brimscott; LESSEE: Robert Harding; TENANT: Thomas Harding; ANNUAL VALUE: £45

High and Chief rent paid yearly to this Manor [specified] by the heirs or assigns of John Giffard of Brightley for lands in Chittlehampton, Marwood and East Down, total £28. 02. 10. Payments yearly out of this manor for Chief rent £7. 18. 04

THE MANOR OF HACKWORTHY

TEDBURN ST MARY PARISH

PREMISES: part of the barton or farm of Hackworthy; LESSEE: Henry Stone; TENANT: Jane Stone; ANNUAL VALUE: £40

PREMISES: part of the barton or farm of Hackworthy; LESSEE: Henry Stone; TENANT: Jane Stone; ANNUAL VALUE: £20

PREMISES: messuage called Lower Hackworthy; LESSEE: Alexander Nosworthy; TENANT: Charles Browning; ANNUAL VALUE: 18s

PREMISES: messuage called Pykes alias Peekes; LESSEE: Thomas Dyer; TENANT: Elizabeth Soper; ANNUAL VALUE: [blank]

PREMISES: messuage called Lakehead; LESSEE: Thomasin Belworthy; TENANT: Thomas Brimblecombe; ANNUAL VALUE [not stated]

PREMISES: close called Lakehead park, 16a., now divided into several closes and a house erected thereon; LESSEE: Richard Pond; TENANT: Thomas Brimblecombe; ANNUAL VALUE: £5

[The next entry is crossed through]

Chief rents paid yearly to this Manor total £14. 19. 07 and chief rents paid out of this Manor total £1. 05. 11

THE MANOR OF NIMET ST GEORGE

SOUTH MOLTON AND GEORGE NYMPTON PARISHES

PREMISES: capital messuage of great hele, 458a.; LESSEE: Gertrude Broad widow; TENANT: [not stated]; ANNUAL VALUE: [not stated]

SOUTH MOLTON PARISH

PREMISES: tenement in Combrewe [Comberew SS 653262] called Southcombes Tenement alias King's Tenement, 38a.; LESSEE: John Hele; TENANT: Richard Hele; ANNUAL VALUE: £20

PREMISES: tenement in Combrewe called Pearse's tenement being the Lower tenement and close called worthie, 37a.; LESSEE: John Hele; TENANT: Elizabeth Whitefield; ANNUAL VALUE: £20

PREMISES: tenement called Amerys or Symons in Combrew; LESSEE: John Hele; TENANT: Richard Hele; ANNUAL VALUE: £15

SOUTH MOLTON AND GEORGE NYMPTON PARISHES

PREMISES: tenements called Bury-Slade; LESSEE: William Kerslake; TENANT: William Kerslake; ANNUAL VALUE: £25

SOUTH MOLTON PARISH

PREMISES: messuage called Fore; LESSEE: Anne Nott and George Nott, her son; TENANT: Mary Badcock; ANNUAL VALUE: [not stated]

PREMISES: East Stone and Newnham park; LESSEE: Thomas Daw; TENANT: Richard Gay; ANNUAL VALUE: [not stated]

PREMISES: messuage called Weststone, 70a.; LESSEE: Thomas Daw; TENANT: Thomas Brooking; ANNUAL VALUE: [not stated]

GEORGE NYMPTON PARISH

PREMISES: messuage called Martens parkes or Stone; LESSEE: Joan Gread; TENANT: Mary Gread; ANNUAL VALUE: [not stated]

PREMISES: lands called Dowerland; LESSEE: Elizabeth Thorne; TENANT: John Snow; ANNUAL VALUE: £25

PREMISES: messuages called Little Hele alias Under Hele, 115a.; LESSEE: John Pawle; TENANT: Walter Broad; ANNUAL VALUE: £30

SOUTH MOLTON PARISH

PREMISES: fulling mill, millhouse and close called the Mill-ham; LESSEE: John Bawden; TENANT: Oliver Kingdon; ANNUAL VALUE: £6 or £7

PREMISES: fulling mill called Haynes Mill alias Middle Mill; LESSEE: John Bawden; TENANT: Oliver Kingdon; ANNUAL VALUE: £4

GEORGE NYMPTON PARISH

PREMISES: The Church House [George Nympton Church SS 700229]; LESSEE: Thomas Lake; TENANT: Thomas Lake; ANNUAL VALUE: £1

PREMISES: a new house, the Glebeland, and Greads Close, 1¼a.; LESSEES: Charles Veysey and Amory Chilcot; TENANT: Charles Veysey's widow; ANNUAL VALUE: £3. 10s

PREMISES: dwellinghouse and garden; LESSEE: Thomas Knott; TENANT: Philip Gread; ANNUAL VALUE: £1. 10s

PREMISES: house in George Nympton Green and a little garden; LESSEE: Thomasine Elworthy; TENANT: Robert Chappell; ANNUAL VALUE: 10s

PREMISES: another house and garden; LESSEE: Robert Chappell; TENANT: John Clarke alias Corney; ANNUAL VALUE: 10s.

PREMISES: house and garden; LESSEE: Henry Hampton; TENANT: [not stated]; ANNUAL VALUE: 10s

List of high and chief rents paid to the Manor Total 19s. 2¾d

The Advowson of the Church of Nymet St George belongs to the Lord of this Mannor Et valet per annum £100. 00. 00 Payments from the Manor 13s. 00d

THE MANOR OF SOUTHMOLTON

SOUTH MOLTON PARISH

PREMISES: messuage, tenement and garden and closes of land and meadow in Burseland, 10a.; LESSEE: John Anthony; TENANT: Mary Anthony; ANNUAL VALUE: £25 to £30

PREMISES: tenement and 4 closes of land in the town of South Molton, 17a.; LESSEE: James Broad; TENANT: Walter Broad; ANNUAL VALUE: £30 to £40

PREMISES: 2 closes called Spurwayes parks in Adderlane, 10a.; LESSEE: John Pawle; TENANT: James Langdon; ANNUAL VALUE: £10

PREMISES: 2 closes near the way leading to Southaller, 5a.; LESSEE: Richard Gay; TENANT: Richard Gay; ANNUAL VALUE: £8

PREMISES: messuages in South Molton, 2a. or 3a.; LESSEE: William Thorne; TENANT: John Howell; ANNUAL VALUE: £8

PREMISES: shamble lying in the norther row of the Shambles; LESSEE: George Badcock; TENANT: John Thorne; ANNUAL VALUE: £1

PREMISES: messuage, tenement, 2 gardens and backside; LESSEE: John Bawden; TENANT: Ann Bawden; ANNUAL VALUE: £12 or £16

PREMISES: fulling mill and 2 closes of land, formerly one close called Culvermead alias Blackpooll ham; LESSEE: John Bawden; TENANT: Ann Bawden; ANNUAL VALUE: £7 or £8 or £9

SOUTH MOLTON AND BISHOP'S NYMPTON PARISHES

PREMISES: moiety of messuages and 2 parcels of land near Mole water and moiety of 3 closes called Rackpark, Stilepark and Belly park, and the moiety of a messuage and close adjoining, 12a.; LESSEE: Richard Bawden; TENANT: Sarah Bawden; ANNUAL VALUE: £6

SOUTH MOLTON PARISH

PREMISES: meadow now divided into 2 closes, 7a., called Brookes Closes, and a barn; LESSEE: Richard Bawden; TENANT: Trustees for John Bawden an infant; ANNUAL VALUE: £10 or £12 or £14

PREMISES: messuage and meadow [name blank], 2a., in Borough of South Molton; LESSEE: Joshua Bawden; TENANT: Richard Bawden; ANNUAL VALUE: £9

PREMISES: close in Combe Down alias Winford lane now deep lane in Borough of South Molton; LESSEE: Joshua Bawden; TENANT: Sarah Bawden widow; ANNUAL VALUE: £4 or £5

PREMISES: dwellinghouse and garden in Parsonage Lane in South Molton; LESSEE: Joshua Bawden; TENANT: Joshua Bryan; ANNUAL VALUE: £1 or £2

PREMISES: messuage in South Molton; LESSEE: Elizabeth Shepheard; TENANT: Bartholomew Hele; ANNUAL VALUE: £4

PREMISES: 5 closes in the Borough of South Molton [boundaries given]; LESSEE: Christopher May; TENANT: Hannah Bennick; ANNUAL VALUE: £11 or £12

PREMISES: 2 closes, one in Adder lane one of which is 2a. at Preston well; LESSEE: Thomas Daw; TENANT: Samuel Thorn; ANNUAL VALUE: £11

PREMISES: messuage late the sign of the Bell; LESSEE: William Lamb; TENANT: George Anthony; ANNUAL VALUE: £16

PREMISES: part of the Gatehouse; LESSEE: John Osmond; TENANT: Matthew Hodge: ANNUAL VALUE: £2.10s

PREMISES: messuage and garden, part of the Gatehouse; LESSEE: Richard Hodge; TENANT: Lovell Hodge; ANNUAL VALUE: £1 or £2

PREMISES: Tinkers Close in Deep Lane; LESSEE: James Broad; TENANT: Walter Broad; ANNUAL VALUE: £8 or £2 [discrepant totals in 2 sections]

PREMISES: messuage, garden and backside in South Molton; LESSEE: John Hele; TENANT: Richard Hele; ANNUAL VALUE: £5 or £8

PREMISES: moiety of messuage at Colemans Corner and of Selley's Close in Adderlane; LESSEE: John Hele; TENANT: William Thorn; ANNUAL VALUE: £4 or £5

PREMISES: moiety of 2 closes called Howells Close in Neildstown Lane; LESSEE: John Gay; TENANT: George Gay; ANNUAL VALUE: 50s or £3

PREMISES: close in Mill Lane and close in Gullacombe Lane; LESSEE: John Gay; TENANT: George Gay; ANNUAL VALUE: £7

PREMISES: messuage in South Street and messuage adjoining called Buckinghams; LESSEE: Eleanor Sheere; TENANT: William Gould; ANNUAL VALUE: £9 or £12

Premises; 3 closes called Molfordhayes near Mill Lane, 8a.; LESSEE: Emanuel Tucker; TENANT: John Thorn; ANNUAL VALUE: £8

PREMISES: close in Adderlane called Chapples Field, 3a.; LESSEE: Emanuel Tucker; TENANT: John Widgery; ANNUAL VALUE: £3

PREMISES: moiety of close in Comb=Down Lane; LESSEE: Emanuel Tucker; TENANT: Thomas Amory; ANNUAL VALUE: £2

PREMISES: moiety of messuage, garden and backside, LESSEE: John Mildon; TENANT: John Mildon; ANNUAL VALUE: £3. 10s

PREMISES: 2 closes called Verdown, 7a.; LESSEE: William Harding; TENANT: Ann Handford; ANNUAL VALUE: £5

PREMISES: close in Mill Lane called Kents Close, 4a.; LESSEE: Thomas Nott; TENANT: Philip Tapp; ANNUAL VALUE: £5

PREMISES: messuage and garden; LESSEE: Hugh Landman; TENANT: Squire Hunt; ANNUAL VALUE: £3

PREMISES: close in Adderlane, ½a.; LESSEE: Elizabeth Underhill; TENANT: John Widgery; ANNUAL VALUE: £1. 10s

PREMISES: messuage, tenement and garden and 2 meadows called Hacche Meadows alias Gifford Meadows, 4a.; LESSEE: Arthur Sharland; TENANT: John Hole *clericus*; ANNUAL VALUE: £6 or £8

PREMISES: tenement called Nieldstown, 27a.; LESSEE: Thomas Harris; TENANT: James Langdon; ANNUAL VALUE: £16

SOUTH MOLTON AND GEORGE NYMPTON PARISHES

PREMISES: 3 closes called Holmesparks in South Molton and a barn in George Nympton; LESSEE: Richard Hodge; TENANT: Matthew Hodge; ANNUAL VALUE: £8 or £9

SOUTH MOLTON PARISH

PREMISES: the Town Hall and shops, cellars and chambers belonging; LESSEE: the Mayor and Burgesses; TENANT: the Mayor and Burgesses; ANNUAL VALUE: £8

PREMISES: moiety of close in Mill Lane called Perrymans, 2a.; LESSEE: executors of Richard Perryman; TENANT: Richard Gay; ANNUAL VALUE: 30s

PREMISES: Gullacombe Meadow in Gullacombe Lane, 5½a.; LESSEE: Widow Odam and William Badcock; TENANT: Philip Tapp; ANNUAL VALUE: £6

PREMISES: close called Broadmead, 4¼a.; LESSEE: Thomas Nott; TENANT: George Gay; ANNUAL VALUE: £6

PREMISES: moiety of barn and backside, ¾a.; LESSEE: Thomas Nott; TENANT: John Hole; ANNUAL VALUE: [not stated]

PREMISES: moiety of messuage, 2 gardens and close, ¾a.; LESSEE: William Tucker; TENANT: Oliver Kingdon; ANNUAL VALUE: £3

PREMISES: moiety of close near Mill Lane called Thorn Close; LESSEE: Thomas Nott; TENANT: John Hole *clericus*; ANNUAL VALUE: £1. 5s

PREMISES: messuage, tenement, garden and closes called Crossparks and burgage and field called Dominicks Close, 9 or 10a.; LESSEE: Richard Parkin; TENANT: John Rowcliffe; ANNUAL VALUE: £12 or £14

BISHOP'S NYMPTON PARISH

PREMISES: five closes near Mole Bridge, 10½a.; LESSEE: John Badcock; TENANTS: John and Thomas Badcock; ANNUAL VALUE: £13

SOUTH MOLTON PARISH

PREMISES: moiety of a messuage, tenement and backside and of 3 closes in Adderlane, 4a.; LESSEE: Thomas Mildon; TENANT: Thomas Mildon; ANNUAL VALUE: £5

PREMISES: moiety of closes called Rudges Close near Molebridge; LESSEE: John Badcock; TENANT: Joan Badcock; ANNUAL VALUE: £2

PREMISES: moiety of dwellinghouse, garden, backside and close of land; LESSEE: [blank] Chilcott; TENANT: [not stated] 'in hand'; ANNUAL VALUE: £3

PREMISES: messuage and garden; LESSEE: Thomas Lake; TENANT: Thomas Lake; ANNUAL VALUE: £4 or £5

PREMISES: barn and garden in Mill Lane; LESSEE: William Perkin; TENANT: Walter Broad; ANNUAL VALUE: 30s

PREMISES: 2 shambles; LESSEE: Hannibal Vawden; TENANT: Henry Almsworthy; ANNUAL VALUE: 30s

PREMISES: 2 shambles; LESSEES: Emanuel Tucker and John Rowcliffe; TENANT: Joshua Dunn; ANNUAL VALUE: 30s

PREMISES: shamble or a moiety of 1 large shamble; LESSEE: George Gay; TENANT: 'in hand'; ANNUAL VALUE: 10s

PREMISES: moiety of courtlage now a dwellinghouse; LESSEE: John Oliver; TENANT: Mary Oliver; ANNUAL VALUE: 4s

Conventionary rent yearly £44. 03s. 0d

Payments out yearly

To the Lords of the sd. Borough out of Spurways Parkes yearly 00. 05. 00 There is a chiefe Rent of 6s a yeare paid to Sr Arthur Chichester now Sr John Chichester Bart out of the Lands called Flemings in Southmolton or called by some other name or lying in some other place 00. 06. 00

THE MANOR OF HACCHE

SOUTH MOLTON PARISH

PREMISES: capital messuage, barton and farm of Hacche [Hacche Barton SS 714278], 363a.; LESSEE: Thomas Acland clerk; TENANT: Mrs Acland; ANNUAL VALUE: £80

NORTH MOLTON PARISH

PREMISES: Pincombs tenement in Withyeat [Withygate SS 707347], 70a.; LESSEE: James Buckingham; TENANT: Dennis Buckingham; ANNUAL VALUE: £35 or £40

PREMISES: Honacotts tenement in Witheyeat, 65a.; LESSEE: James Buckingham; TENANT: Dennis Buckingham; ANNUAL VALUE: £30

PREMISES: Moreman's tenement in Witheyeat, 50a.; LESSEE: James Buckingham; TENANT: Dennis Buckingham; ANNUAL VALUE: £28 or £30

PREMISES: Scotts tenement in Witheyeat, 40a.; LESSEE: Christopher Dennis; TENANT: Dennis Buckingham; ANNUAL VALUE: £20 or £24

SOUTH MOLTON PARISH

PREMISES: moiety of Hacche mills, 10a.; LESSEE: Thomas Nott; TENANT: John Hole *clericus*; ANNUAL VALUE: £6

NORTH MOLTON PARISH

PREMISES: tenement called Beare [Bere SS 706351], 76a.; LESSEE: William Baker; TENANT: William Baker; ANNUAL VALUE: £40

SOUTH MOLTON PARISH

PREMISES: moiety of Snurridge, 50a.; LESSEE: Elizabeth Fursen widow; TENANT: James Handford; ANNUAL VALUE: £20

EAST BUCKLAND PARISH

PREMISES: part of West Brayley; LESSEE: Henry Jenkins; TENANT: Elias Locke; ANNUAL VALUE: £30

PREMISES: another part of West Brayle[y], the whole 215a.; LESSEE: Henry Jenkins; TENANT: Elias Locke; ANNUAL VALUE: £70 both parts

SOUTH MOLTON PARISH

PREMISES: Southaller [South Aller SS 699274], 55a.; LESSEE: assigns of Lewis Southcombe; TENANT: Richard Bawden; ANNUAL VALUE: £24

High and Chief Rents paid yearly to the Manor Total £14. 11s. 04d

Payments yearly 4s

There are Salewoods called Hatch wood lying in South Molton and Beerwood lying in Northmolton belonging to this Manor

THE MANOR OF ROMANSLEIGH

ROMANSLEIGH PARISH

[Romansleigh Church SS 727206]

PREMISES: barton and farm of Romansleigh, 247a.; LESSEE: John Sanger; TENANT: Jonathan Sanger's executors; ANNUAL VALUE: £50 or £60

PREMISES: Horridge [Horridge SS 722195], cont. 156a.; LESSEE: Samuel Cheldon; TENANT: Samuel Childon (sic); ANNUAL VALUE: £20 or £25

PREMISES: Whitehouse, 48a.; LESSEE: Edward Radford; TENANT: Peter Allen; ANNUAL VALUE: £13

PREMISES: messuage called Droocombe, 58a.; LESSEE: Edward Radford; TENANT: Peter Allen; ANNUAL VALUE: £20 or £25

PREMISES: Duboundisland, 33a.; LESSEE: Edward Radford; TENANT: Thomas Holmes; ANNUAL VALUE: £10

PREMISES: close called Duxford, 3a.; LESSEE: Richard Webber; TENANT: Richard Webber; ANNUAL VALUE: £1

PREMISES: the Church House and wasteland; LESSEE: Edward Allen; TENANT: Robert Crocker; ANNUAL VALUE: 10s

PREMISES: cottage and garden; LESSEE: John Treble; TENANT: John Rumbelow; ANNUAL VALUE: 10s

PREMISES: messuage and closes called Oxenparks and Littleham, 2½a.; LESSEE: [not stated] Delve; TENANT: William Delve; ANNUAL VALUE: £2

CHULMLEIGH PARISH

PREMISES: Toblis=Coombe, Pitt and Beare, 160a.; LESSEE: Roger Cock; TENANT: Henry Venn; ANNUAL VALUE: £35 or £40

CHAWLEIGH PARISH

PREMISES: Dockworthy, 35a.; LESSEE: Samuel Partridge; TENANT: John Partridge; ANNUAL VALUE: £6 or £10

High Rents due yearly Total 6s. 10d

High Rents lost time out of mind 7s. 2d

THE MANOR OF WOOLLEIGH OMER AND HUNSHAW

[Woolleigh Barton SS 532168]

ST GILES IN THE WOOD PARISH

PREMISES: Lower Alscott; LESSEE: Jeremiah Hackwill; TENANT: Jeremiah Hackwill; ANNUAL VALUE: £6 or £7. 10s

BEAFORD PARISH

PREMISES: Wolleigh Mills; LESSEE: Francis Payne; TENANT: John Budd; ANNUAL VALUE: £10 or £12.10s

PREMISES: Wayhouse, 19a.; LESSEE: Joan Beare; TENANT: Joan Beare; ANNUAL VALUE: £6 or £10

ST GILES IN THE WOOD PARISH

PREMISES: tenement in Alscott, 15a.; LESSEE: Elizabeth Luxton; TENANT: Scipio Luxton; ANNUAL VALUE: £7 or £11

PREMISES: barn and closes called Higher Alscott, 79a.; LESSEE: Elizabeth Luxton; TENANT: Scipio Luxton; ANNUAL VALUE: £35

LITTLE TORRINGTON PARISH

PREMISES: East Hollam alias Lower Hollam in Taddyport and 5 closes, 56a.; LESSEE: Francis Elston; TENANT: James Bale; ANNUAL VALUE: £15

ST GILES IN THE WOOD PARISH

PREMISES: Kingscott, 30a.; LESSEE: Agnes Hackwill; TENANT: Jeremiah Hackwill; ANNUAL VALUE: £15, £16 or £20

BEAFORD PARISH

PREMISES: tenement and 12a. land in Blinsham; LESSEE: Lawrence Payne; TENANT: Agnes Chappleman; ANNUAL VALUE: £6, £7 or £8

PREMISES: Dillons or Hoopers and part of the barton of Blinsham, 55a.; LESSEE: Lawrence Payne; TENANT: Agnes Chappleman; ANNUAL VALUE: £25

PREMISES: 2 messuages and 10a. land near Woolleigh Mills; LESSEE: John Webber; TENANT: John Budd; ANNUAL VALUE: £4 or £6

PREMISES: cottage and garden; LESSEE: Arthur Chappelman; TENANT: Abraham Bright; ANNUAL VALUE: 15s or 20s

PREMISES: tenement and close called Southdown, 3 closes called Waresdown and a little plot of ground; LESSEE: Arthur Chappelman; TENANT: Agnes Chappelman; ANNUAL VALUE: £12

PREMISES: 2 tucking mills and close called Broomhill, 3a.; LESSEE: Christopher Lamb; TENANT: [not stated]; ANNUAL VALUE: £3

LITTLE TORRINGTON PARISH

PREMISES: tenement and garden in Taddyport and ¾a. of ground; LESSEE: [blank] Sweet; TENANT: Richard Moore; ANNUAL VALUE: £3. 10s

GREAT TORRINGTON PARISH

PREMISES: tenement, backside and garden in Chipping; LESSEE: William Davy; TENANT: [not stated]; ANNUAL VALUE: [not stated]

HUNTSHAW PARISH

PREMISES: barton of Hunshaw (sic); LESSEE: Richard Acland, Esq.; TENANT: John Acland, Esq.; ANNUAL VALUE: [not stated]

GREAT TORRINGTON PARISH

PREMISES: Hollaways Head, 4a.; LESSEE: Peter Glubb; TENANT: Thomas Langdon; ANNUAL VALUE: £5 or £6

PREMISES: 2 tenements, a garden and 3a. of land; LESSEE: Thomas Blackmore; TENANT: Bridget Esworthy; ANNUAL VALUE: £4

PREMISES: moiety of Doddacott and cottage (coppice excepted) divided, 36a.; LESSEE: John Cleverdon; TENANT: Elizabeth Vickary widow; ANNUAL VALUE: £8 or £10

PREMISES: moiety of tenement and ¼a.; LESSEE: William Aishton; TENANT: William Aishton; ANNUAL VALUE: £2 or £1 'real value £1. 10s. 00'

LITTLE TORRINGTON PARISH

PREMISES: moiety of messuage called East or Lower Hollam, 15+25a.; LESSEE: [not stated] Kingdon's trustees; TENANT: Samuel Burdon; ANNUAL VALUE: £6 or £9 'the whole'

PREMISES: moiety of messuage, 3 closes and 1 meadow, 12a.; LESSEE: [not stated] Kingdon's trustees; TENANT: Samuel Burdon; ANNUAL VALUE: £5 or £8 'the whole'

PREMISES: tenement called Omer and 3a. of coppice; LESSEE: Francis Elston; TENANT: Henry Elston; ANNUAL VALUE: £25

ST GILES IN THE WOOD PARISH

PREMISES: tenement called Somerwill, 18a.; LESSEE: Francis Payne; TENANT: Roger Blinsham; ANNUAL VALUE: £5 or £7

BEAFORD PARISH

PREMISES: closes called Skinners and Hanging Cleave alias tenement called Geatons or South Wooleigh; LESSEE: Thomas Geaton; TENANT: Grace Geaton; ANNUAL VALUE: £7

PREMISES: cottage and garden at Blinsham; LESSEE: Roger Howell; TENANT: Richard Taylor; ANNUAL VALUE: 10s

PREMISES: new erected cottage, garden and orchard; LESSEE: Peter Nanskevill; TENANT: Agnes Chappelman; ANNUAL VALUE: 25s or 30s

PREMISES: Quarry Close; LESSEE: John Webber; TENANT: John Budd; ANNUAL VALUE: 16s

In hand Blinsham Mills and pasture in the coppice
High and Chief rents paid yearly to this manor total 14s
Conventionary rent yearly totals £50. 02. 10
Payments out of the manor yearly £1. 17. 04

MANOR OF ESSEBEARE ALIAS AISHBEARE

WITHERIDGE PARISH

PREMISES: moiety of Barton of Essebeare alias Aishbeare, 200a.; LESSEE: John Thomas; TENANT: John Thomas's executors; ANNUAL VALUE: £45 or £50

PREMISES: $^1/_5$ part of the barton and farm of Bradford Tracy and all Taylors Meadow: LESSEE: Richard Shortridge; TENANT: Richard Shortrudge (sic); ANNUAL VALUE: £16 or £20

PREMISES: moiety of North Combe and Bynhay; LESSEE: Robert Tanner; TENANT: Robert Tanner; ANNUAL VALUE: £10

PREMISES: moiety of Down and all Rew Meadow; LESSEE: Mary Crooke; TENANT: Joan Fletcher widow; ANNUAL VALUE: £12

RACKENFORD PARISH

PREMISES: moiety of Lower Bulworthy, 60a., and common in Bulworthy Moor; LESSEE: Thomas Gun; TENANT: Thomas Gunn (sic); ANNUAL VALUE: £16

WITHERIDGE PARISH

PREMISES: Pile Moor and Pile Close; LESSEE: Hugh Greenslade; TENANT: Hugh Greenslade; ANNUAL VALUE: £9 or £10

PUDDINGTON PARISH

PREMISES; moiety of Bamsdon, 60.; LESSEE: Thomas Bodley; TENANT: Thomas Bodley; ANNUAL VALUE: £9 or £12

CREACOMBE PARISH

PREMISES: moiety of East Backworthy; lesssee: Mary Greenslade; TENANT: Thomas Veysey; ANNUAL VALUE: £12

PREMISES: moiety of West Backworthy; LESSEE: Jonathan Tanner; TENANT: John Tanner; ANNUAL VALUE: £15

ROSEASH PARISH

PREMISES: moiety of Franckhill, 70a.; LESSEE: Jonathan Tanner; TENANT: John Tanner; ANNUAL VALUE: £8. 15s

KNOWSTONE AND EAST ANSTEY PARISHES

PREMISES: moiety of Whitfield in Knowstone and moiety of Noddesdon in East Anstey; LESSEE: Thomas Hanford; TENANT: James Handford; ANNUAL VALUE: £16 or £20

KNOWSTONE PARISH

PREMISES: moiety of Bowbeare and Rochill, 20a.; LESSEE: Jonas Follet; TENANT: John Follett; ANNUAL VALUE: [£]5 or [£]6

WITHERIDGE PARISH

PREMISES: ¼ part of Westcott, 100a.; LESSEE: John Tolley; TENANT: James Cleeve of Crediton; ANNUAL VALUE: £10

EAST ANSTEY PARISH

PREMISES: moiety of Smallacombe Moor, 50a.; LESSEE: William Barne; TENANT: William Barnes (sic); ANNUAL VALUE: £4

PUDDINGTON PARISH

PREMISES: moiety of Combehayes, 34a.; LESSEE: John Melhuish; TENANT: George Brooke; ANNUAL VALUE: £10

CREACOMBE PARISH

PREMISES: moiety of Crowdall, 40a.; LESSEE: John Tanner; TENANT: John Tanner; ANNUAL VALUE: £6

STOODLEIGH PARISH

PREMISES: moiety of Blackworthy, 50a.; LESSEE: Thomas Tolley; TENANT: Thomas Tolley; ANNUAL VALUE: £10

EAST WORLINGTON PARISH

PREMISES: 1a. called Halshanger near Hartford; LESSEE: Thomas Nott; TENANT: 'in hand'; ANNUAL VALUE: 10s or 20s

ROSEASH PARISH

PREMISES: moiety of Willhayes, 30a.; lessee; John Gallen; TENANT: John Gallen; ANNUAL VALUE: £5

EAST ANSTEY PARISH

PREMISES: moiety of 6a. called The Tongue; LESSEE: Philip Hill; TENANT: James Handford; ANNUAL VALUE: [not stated]

RACKENFORD PARISH

PREMISES: the Landscore in West Bapton and Bapton Moor; LESSEE: William Colman; TENANT: Mr Lyddon; ANNUAL VALUE: none – held for 1000 years absolute

High and Chief rents total £11. 04. 10
Payments out yearly total £01. 01. 01

THE MANOR OF LEIGH

LOXBEARE PARISH

PREMISES: Churchill [Churchill SS 904165], 90a.; LESSEE: Hugh Ven or John Payne; TENANT: John Payne; ANNUAL VALUE: £40
PREMISES: Leigh Barton; LESSEE: John Quick; TENANT: 'in hand'; ANNUAL VALUE: [£]85

TIVERTON PARISH

PREMISES: Lurely [Lurley SS 924148], 80a.; LESSEE: Richard Densham; TENANT: Richard Densham; ANNUAL VALUE: £55 or £60

LOXBEARE PARISH

PREMISES: Sedborough [SS 901150] and Fordland; LESSEE: Elizabeth Sharland; TENANT: 'in hand'; ANNUAL VALUE: [not stated]

RACKENFORD PARISH

PREMISES: Laneland [SS 851184], 30a.; LESSEE: Richard Thomas; TENANT: Richard Thomas; ANNUAL VALUE: £7 or £8
PREMISES: Backstone [SS 835191], 70a.; LESSEE: [blank] Ayre; TENANT: Richard Ayre; ANNUAL VALUE: £20 or £25 or £30
PREMISES: Canworthy, 100a., besides commons; LESSEE: Mary Gammon; TENANT: Mary Gammon; ANNUAL VALUE: £20

TIVERTON PARISH

PREMISES: cottage and garden; LESSEE: William Clapp; TENANT: Alexander Maunder; ANNUAL VALUE: £1.10s

LOXBEARE PARISH

PREMISES: Leigh Mill [SS 907149], Millham, 4½a., and Hollow Cleave, 6a.; LESSEE: Edward Delve; TENANT: Richard Yea; ANNUAL VALUE: £10
PREMISES: Venhay, 22a.; LESSEE: Richard Melhuish; TENANT: William Snell; ANNUAL VALUE: £14 or £18
PREMISES: Ham Tenement; LESSEE: Barnard Voysey; TENANT: George Portbury *clericus*; ANNUAL VALUE: [£]5
PREMISES: messuage and 6a. land in Leigh Town [SS 914149]; LESSEE: Caleb Burridge; TENANT: Henry Bidgood; ANNUAL VALUE: [£]4 or [£]5
PREMISES: tenement in Leigh Town, 18a.; LESSEE: Elizabeth Sharland; TENANT: Mr Troyte's executors; ANNUAL VALUE: [£]15 or [£]16
PREMISES: Chapland, Dipland and tithing meadow in Leigh Town,

20a.; LESSEE: Richard Yea; TENANT: Richard Yea; ANNUAL VALUE: £20

PREMISES: tenement and 16a. land in Leigh Town; LESSEE: Humphry Daw and John Daw; TENANT: John Bidgood; ANNUAL VALUE: £10 or £12

PREMISES: cottage and garden, part of Leigh Barton [SS 909148]; LESSEE: Stephen Tolley; TENANT: Hugh Tolley; ANNUAL VALUE: 40s

Paid yearly out of the manor £13. 08. 08

MANOR OF LOXBEARE

LOXBEARE PARISH

PREMISES: Loxbeare Barton [SS 913159]; LESSEE: Thomas Duckham; TENANT: 'in hand'; ANNUAL VALUE: [£]88

TIVERTON PARISH

PREMISES: Ford [SS 900146]; LESSEE: William Crooke; TENANT: 'in hand'; ANNUAL VALUE: [not stated]

LOXBEARE PARISH

PREMISES: Gills Tenement: LESSEE: John Gill; TENANT: James Marsh; ANNUAL VALUE: £12

PREMISES: Churchill Park; LESSEE: Joan Saunders; TENANT: 'in hand'; ANNUAL VALUE: [not stated]

PREMISES: tenement called Wood, 15a.; LESSEE: Thomas Duckham; TENANT: William Duckham; ANNUAL VALUE: £13 or £15 or £18

WASHFIELD AND LOXBEARE PARISHES

PREMISES: cottage, garden and 2 closes of land in Loxbeare and Buttermores [SS 917161] in Washfield; LESSEE: Thomas Troyte clerk in trust for Mary the wife of Thomas Duckham late called

Mary Bidgood; TENANT: Thomas Duckham; ANNUAL VALUE: £3. 10 for the cottage and 2 closes and £6 for Buttermores

LOXBEARE PARISH

PREMISES: cottage, garden and orchard, 16 yards; LESSEE: Mark Daw; TENANT: Mark Daw; ANNUAL VALUE: £2. 10s

PREMISES: Hiram Arters cottage and 4a. land; LESSEE: John Greenslade; TENANT: Richard Yea; ANNUAL VALUE: £5

PREMISES: close, 2a., being part of Pantacrudge [Pantacridge SS 905158]; LESSEE: John Greenslade; TENANT: Richard Yea; ANNUAL VALUE: £1

PREMISES: cottage and orchard called Beere, 1a.; LESSEE: Alexander Maunder; TENANT: Alexander Maunder; ANNUAL VALUE: £3

PREMISES: cottage, garden and orchard; LESSEE: Andrew Can; TENANT: William Duckham; ANNUAL VALUE: £2

PREMISES: Beards Cottage; LESSEE: Hannah Beard; TENANT: Hiram Arter; ANNUAL VALUE: £2

PREMISES: cottage and small orchard and garden; LESSEE: John Edney; TENANT: Robert Marshall; ANNUAL VALUE: £1. 10s

WASHFIELD PARISH

PREMISES: Wester Winbow [Wester Winbow SS 919166], 6a.; LESSEE: Alexander Maunder; TENANT: Richard Yea; ANNUAL VALUE: [not stated]

LOXBEARE PARISH

PREMISES: cottage, orchard and garden, 12 yards, and plot of ground, ¾a. [described as 2 separate tenements]; LESSEE: Samuel Thorn; TENANT: John Copp; ANNUAL VALUE: £2. 10s

WASHFIELD PARISH

PREMISES: Little Winbow; LESSEE: Henry Copp; TENANT: Abraham Arter; ANNUAL VALUE: £8 or £10

PREMISES: Way's Tenement; LESSEE: Henry Copp; TENANT: Alexander Maunder; ANNUAL VALUE: £5 or £6

PREMISES: Great Winbow; LESSEE: Isaac Clark; TENANT: Isaac Clark; ANNUAL VALUE: £20 or £24

High and chief rents paid yearly to the manor 1s. 6d.

THE MANOR OF COLLOM:JOHN

[Columbjohn SX 960997]

BROADCLYST AND REWE PARISHES

PREMISES: Week's Tenement, fields called Fetherstones Marsh, the Horne and the 2 Beeres in Rewe and Bernard Johns Tenement in Broadclyst; LESSEE: Philip Wilcocks; TENANT: Philip Wilcocks; ANNUAL VALUE: £40 or £45

REWE PARISH

PREMISES: Guns Marsh otherwise the Higher Marsh; LESSEE: Philip Wilcocks; TENANT: Philip Wilcocks; ANNUAL VALUE: £6 or £7

PREMISES: 2 closes called Walthams Marshes and the Higher Marsh alias the Little Marsh and Dennis's Ragg; LESSEE: Philip Wilcocks; TENANT: Philip Wilcocks; ANNUAL VALUE: [not stated]

BROADCLYST PARISH

PREMISES: tenement called Slaughter house, 14a.; LESSEE: John Taswell; TENANT: Robert Taswell; ANNUAL VALUE: £14

PREMISES: the Two Marshes and a close, part of the Bottom Closes, 10a.; LESSEE: John Taswell; TENANT: Robert Taswell; ANNUAL VALUE: £10

PREMISES: cottage called Rookhouse and 2 closes; LESSEE: Christian Wilson; TENANT: John Cox; ANNUAL VALUE: [not stated]

PREMISES: Fetherstones Tenement; LESSEE: John Cox; TENANT: John Cox; ANNUAL VALUE: £14 or £16

REWE PARISH

PREMISES: tenements, gardens, orchard and closes, 5½a.; LESSEE:

George Dennis; TENANT: Nicholas Melhuish; ANNUAL VALUE: £4 or £5

HUXHAM PARISH

PREMISES: Southpark Tenement; LESSEE: Gilbert Coombe alias Ratcliffe; TENANT: John Perry; ANNUAL VALUE: £6

BICKLEIGH PARISH

PREMISES: 3 closes called Rashlake, 8a. and 9a.; LESSEE: Joan Drake; TENANT: Robert Comings; ANNUAL VALUE: £10

BROADCLYST PARISH

PREMISES: tenement, orchard and meadow called Penroses; LESSEE: Edward Bishop; TENANT: 'in hand'; ANNUAL VALUE: [not stated]

PREMISES: house, garden and orchard; LESSEE: John Dunsford; TENANT: Edward Southwood; ANNUAL VALUE: [not stated]

SILVERTON PARISH

PREMISES: close called Coles Platt, 2a.; LESSEE: Henry Osmond; TENANT: John Hayward; ANNUAL VALUE: £2

BROADCLYST PARISH

PREMISES: house, orchard and 3 parcels of land, 2a.; LESSEE: John Ramsey; TENANT: John Cox; ANNUAL VALUE: £3. 10s

SILVERTON PARISH

PREMISES: closes of land, ¾a., belonging to Etherleigh's Marshes; LESSEE: Eleanor Rix; TENANT: Edward Southwood; ANNUAL VALUE: £1

PREMISES: Elworthy Marshes; LESSEE: Richard Shepheard; TENANT: [not stated], ANNUAL VALUE: £50

BROADCLYST PARISH

PREMISES: Fursepark, part of Newhall; LESSEE: Christopher

Hawkins; TENANT: Christopher Hawkins; ANNUAL VALUE: [not stated]

PREMISES: cottage and tenement, part of Newhall; LESSEE: George Palmer; TENANT: David Loyde; ANNUAL VALUE: [not stated]

Rent payable to the manor total £7. 06. 06

Note of purchase of part of Gunns Tenement by Sir Hugh Acland from Mary Gunn, value £8.10s per annum and another part of Gunns Tenement purchased of Sarah Vinnicombe

Survey 2

Somerset

SURVEY	
1746–7 and later additions	DRO, 1148M add/6/20

A volume, size 23cms x c.35cms, with limp parchment covers (which formed part of a deed) entitled 'Holnycote Surveys 1747 Avill Bossington Holnycote West Luckham Exbridge Ryphay'. The actual surveys are preceded by rentals for one year to Lady Day 1746 for the Manors of Avil, Bossington, West Luckham, Holnicote and Exbridge Riphay. These rentals have columns for dates of leases (all blank), the apportioned number in the survey, premises and rents but details of these have not been reproduced in the Abstract of the survey printed below. The surveys proper have columns for a number within the manor (each manor is listed separately), dates of original leases and who granted them, lessees and fines, premises, lives and ages, present tenants, the lord's rent, heriots, yearly value and notes and miscellaneous

remarks. Only the premises, tenants and yearly value have been abstracted below but there is a discussion of some of the information given in the Survey in the Introduction.

Much of the property listed came to the Acland family on the marriage of Sir Thomas Acland with Elizabeth Dyke in 1745 and this would seem to be the reason for making the survey.

ABSTRACT OF SURVEY

MANOR OF AVIL

A Survey of the Manor of Avil near Dunster & Lying in the severall Parishes of Bicknaller Crocombe Carhampton Cutcombe Old Cleeve Dunster St Decumans & Timberscombe

BICKNOLLER PARISH

1. PREMISES: messuage and tenement called Culverhays; LESSEE: John Lethbridge; TENANT: William Lane; ANNUAL VALUE: £15
2. [This entry is crossed through]

CROWCOMBE PARISH

3. PREMISES: messuage and tenement called Water; LESSEE: William Gore; TENANT: John Gore; ANNUAL VALUE: £21

ST DECUMANS PARISH

4. PREMISES: messuage and garden called Pinck's cottage in the north-east corner of a close called Harridge, part of Kentsford demesnes [Kentsford ST 058426]; LESSEE: William Bartlet of St Decumans, weaver; TENANT: Robert Bartlet; ANNUAL VALUE: [not stated]

DUNSTER PARISH

5. PREMISES: barn near Frackford, the close behind it and 2 meadows between Frackford House and Frackford Bridge; LESSEES: Edward Dyke, Walter Coffin and Barbara Blackwell, widow; TENANT: Thomas Blackwell; ANNUAL VALUE: £10
6. PREMISES: messuage, burgage and tenement in a street leading to the Church; LESSEE: Thomas Griffin; TENANT: Elizabeth Bastone, widow and William Elsworthy (1782); ANNUAL VALUE: [not stated]
7. PREMISES: messuage, garden and close of arable or pasture adjoining on the south called Long Close, with stones from Kitswall Common for building and repairing and water from Avil ground 'in a friendly manner'; LESSEE: Baldwin Knight of Dunster, clothier; TENANT: Abraham Blackmore in right of Rebecca, his second wife; ANNUAL VALUE: [not stated]

DUNSTER AND CARHAMPTON PARISHES

8. PREMISES: messuage, burgage and tenement in Gallox Street, viz. a convenient dwellinghouse and outhouses, garden, orchard and meadow near Gallox Cross, wood, close near Holly hill and 3 yards in Skilacre; LESSEES: William Hurford of Dunster, clothier, James Wilkings, mercer and William Warman, millwright; TENANT: Thomas Hanniford of Gallox Street, husbandman by right of Anne, his wife; ANNUAL VALUE: [not stated]

TIMBERSCOMBE PARISH

9. PREMISES: dwellinghouse, garden under the hill called Black Ball, a little outlet or a place for a garden on the north side of the house and the liberty to erect a 'Shutthouse'; LESSEE: John Cole of Timberscombe, husbandman [agric]; TENANT: John Cole, Parish Clerk of Timberscombe; ANNUAL VALUE: [not stated]

DUNSTER PARISH

10. PREMISES: messuage and garden on the Ball, formerly Crosses; LESSEE: John Collimore of Dunster, labourer; TENANT: Edith Collimore, widow; ANNUAL VALUE: [not stated]
11. PREMISES: reversion of the above premises; same lessee and tenant; ANNUAL VALUE: [not stated]
12. PREMISES: dwellinghouse, orchard, garden and little parcel of land containing ½ yard; LESSEE: William Chilcot; TENANT: [not stated]; ANNUAL VALUE: [not stated]
13. PREMISES: reversion of the above premises; lessee; John Slocombe of Clatworthy, yeoman; TENANT: [not stated]; ANNUAL VALUE: [not stated]
14. PREMISES: messuage and tenement near March [Marsh SS 994444], being a convenient dwellinghouse, barn, garden and and about 3a. of arable land, late in the possession of George Close and then of Henry Thomas, labourer; LESSEE: Joan Slocombe of Dunster, widow; TENANT: William Chilcot by right of Frances (formerly Frances Escot, widow, who bought it); ANNUAL VALUE: [not stated]
15. PREMISES: messuage and tenement called Overborough and 50a. belonging to it in Avil; LESSEE: John Blake of Dunster, yeoman; TENANT: Benjamin Escot during John Blake's life; ANNUAL VALUE: [not stated]
16. PREMISES: reversion of same premises; LESSEE: Benjamin

Escott of Dunster, yeoman; TENANT: Benjamin Escott; ANNUAL VALUE: [not stated]

DUNSTER AND CARHAMPTON PARISHES

17. PREMISES: messuage and tenement called Kitswall in the possession of Frances Blake for her widowhood only [marked 'mort']; LESSEES: Thomas Hill and Robert Taylor; TENANT: Benjamin Escott; ANNUAL VALUE: [not stated]
18. PREMISES: reversion of above premises; TENANT: Benjamin Escott: ANNUAL VALUE: [not stated]

TIMBERSCOMBE PARISH

19. PREMISES: messuage consisting of 2 chambers late in the possession of Andrew Long and the garden and the coppice near and belonging to the messuage; LESSEE: John Hobbs of Timberscombe, husbandman; TENANT: Joan Hobbs, widow; ANNUAL VALUE: [not stated]
20. PREMISES: reversion of above premises; LESSEE: Anthony Hobbs of Timberscombe, carpenter; TENANT: [not stated]; ANNUAL VALUE: [not stated]
21. PREMISES: messuage and tenement consisting of 2 ground rooms late in the possession of John Kerridge deceased and 1 little chamber in the possession of Andrew Long, a hanging or wood house in the possession of Andrew Long and 2 little gardens lying before the windows of the ground room; LESSEE: Joan Portman of Timberscombe, widow; TENANT: [not stated]; ANNUAL VALUE: [not stated]

DUNSTER PARISH

22. PREMISES: 2 messuages and tenements called the Two Upper or Higher Tenements and Illicombe [Ellicombe SS 983444]; LESSEE: Joan Barrow of Minehead, widow; TENANT: 'Bonnemer's'; ANNUAL VALUE: [not stated]
23. PREMISES: messuage and tenement called Row; LESSEE: William Barrow of Minehead, merchant; TENANT: David Price; ANNUAL VALUE: [not stated]

WITHYCOMBE PARISH

24. PREMISES: mesuage and 5a. land; LESSEE: John Question junior; TENANT: John Question: ANNUAL VALUE: [not stated]

DUNSTER PARISH

25. PREMISES: piece or parcel of land cont. 2[a.], and 3a. called Common Aller; LESSEE: William Moore of Dunster, husbandman; TENANT: 'Mary Smith lives in it'; ANNUAL VALUE: [not stated]
26. PREMISES: 2 meadows called Danters and a piece of ground called Coxmoore; LESSEE: Mary Smith of Dunster, widow; TENANT: Mary Smith [marked 'dead']; ANNUAL VALUE: [not stated]
27. PREMISES: messuage and burgage and tenement in Marsh; LESSEE: Henry Proole, clothier; TENANT: John Shenton by purchase; ANNUAL VALUE: [not stated]

TIMBERSCOMBE PARISH

28. PREMISES: messuage and tenement late in the possession of John Leigh deceased viz. a convenient dwellinghouse, several outhouses and 2a. land adjacent in orchards and gardens, 1 mead[ow] at the Townsend cont. 2½a. and close called Wood Close; LESSEE: John Spurrier of Timberscombe, feltmaker; TENANT: 'Mary Spurrier holds for Joan Bell's life'; ANNUAL VALUE: [not stated]
29. PREMISES: barn near his [i.e. John Leigh's] dwellinghouse and garden there in his possession; LESSEE: George Hammet of Timberscombe, tailor; TENANT: [not stated]; ANNUAL VALUE: [not stated] 'This is a Reversion. Joan Bell still living'
30. PREMISES: orchard and garden in St George Street and piece of ground called Grabust Close cont. 2a.; LESSEE: Thomas Stadden of Dunster; TENANT: Thomas Stadden; ANNUAL VALUE: [not stated]
31. PREMISES: cottage and garden near Duddings Farm at Stentwells and also sufficient turbary heath and furse to be taken yearly on Avill Common; LESSEE: John Snow senior 'dead'; TENANT: [not stated]; ANNUAL VALUE: [not stated]
32. PREMISES: reversion of the same premises; LESSEE: Charles

Strong of Carhampton, yeoman; TENANT: [not stated]; ANNUAL VALUE: [not stated]

ST DECUMANS PARISH

33. PREMISES: moiety of dwellinghouse on the north side in which Richard Chedzoy then lived near the highway from a village called Stream to Watchet and a piece of hedge; LESSEE: Robert Slocombe of Clatworthy; TENANT: Robert Slocombe; ANNUAL VALUE: [not stated]

DUNSTER PARISH

34. PREMISES: messuages and tenements in Illicombe late in the possession of Robert Giles, junior, deceased; LESSEES: Mary Withycombe of Carhampton, widow and John, son of John Smith, of Stogumber, yeoman; TENANT: John Smith, clerk; ANNUAL VALUE: [not stated]

ST DECUMANS PARISH

35. PREMISES: 6a. land called Goat hanger; LESSEES: [crossed through]; TENANT: Thomas Towell; ANNUAL VALUE: [not stated]

TIMBERSCOMBE PARISH

36. PREMISES: messuage and tenement called Cuffs alias Lower or Little Kitswall and 2 closes near adjoining called Puddymoore Close and Puddymoore meadow; LESSEE: Richard Snow of Selworthy, yeoman; TENANT: 'Lewis Taylor owns this'; ANNUAL VALUE: [not stated]
37. PREMISES: reversion of the same premises; LESSEE: Lewis Taylor of Carhampton, yeoman; TENANT: Lewis Taylor; ANNUAL VALUE: [not stated]

DUNSTER PARISH

38. PREMISES: messuage, burgage and tenement in West Street; LESSEE: Lewis Taylor of Carhampton, yeoman; TENANT: [not stated]; ANNUAL VALUE: [not stated]

OLD CLEEVE PARISH

39. PREMISES: messuage and tenement on Cleeve Hill in Old Cleeve [Old Cleeve Church ST 041419] called the Warren cont. 60a.; LESSEE: John Smith of Old Cleeve, limeburner, 'mort'; TENANT: William Weller by right of his wife, formerly Ann Smith; ANNUAL VALUE: £17

CUTCOMBE AND TIMBERSCOMBE PARISHES

40. PREMISES: capital messuage and tenement called Oak Trow [SS 942404]; LESSEE: Joseph Webb of Cutcombe, yeoman; TENANT: Joseph Webb; ANNUAL VALUE: [not stated]

DUNSTER PARISH

41. PREMISES: messuage, burgage and garden in New Street called Whites House; LESSEE: William Estcott of Dunster, carpenter; TENANT: Margaret Estcott, widow; ANNUAL VALUE: [not stated]

LUCCOMBE PARISH

42. PREMISES: copyhold messuage and tenement cont. 26a. called Holtball near the Church; LESSEE: Joan Blackford, widow; TENANT: Joan Blackford; ANNUAL VALUE: [not stated]

TIMBERSCOMBE PARISH

43. PREMISES: messuage and garden and 2 little meadows adjacent cont. 2a. late in the possession of Thomazin Hawkwell deceased; LESSEE: John Evans of Timberscombe, tailor; TENANT: John Evans; ANNUAL VALUE: [not stated]

DUNSTER PARISH

44. PREMISES: the reversion of no. 25, premises sometime since called Common Allers on part of which a dwellinghouse called Bondington House was built; LESSEE: Robert Smith of Dunster, yeoman; TENANT: [not stated]; ANNUAL VALUE: [not stated]
45. PREMISES: messuage, burgage or dwellinghouse and premises late in the possession of Thomas Warren in West Street; LESSEE:

Mary Baker of Dunster, spinster; TENANT: Mary Baker; ANNUAL VALUE: [not stated]

46. PREMISES: messuage or dwellinghouse late in the possession of John Baker in West Street which lies on the left hand side of the same street leading from Dunster Church to Avill; LESSEE: Susanna Baker of Dunster, spinster; TENANT: Susanna Baker; ANNUAL VALUE: [not stated]

47. PREMISES: reversion of no. 38; LESSEE: Thomas Staddon in trust for Lucas's; TENANT: [not stated]; ANNUAL VALUE: [not stated]

48. PREMISES: messuage and garden on the Ball called Morckhams Tenement with a barn and stable and also Burges Barn adjacent to the dwellinghouse of Edith Cullimore, widow; LESSEE: Samuel Hancock of Dunster, husbandman; TENANT: [not stated]; ANNUAL VALUE: [not stated]

49. PREMISES: reversion of no. 9, except 'the little outlett for a garden in order to erect a Shutthouse'; LESSEE: Sarah Cole of Timberscombe, spinster; TENANT: [not stated]; ANNUAL VALUE: [not stated]

50. PREMISES: messuage in West Street late in the possession of Grace Wilkins deceased; LESSEE: Thomas Mortifie of Dunster, husbandman; TENANT: [not stated]; ANNUAL VALUE: [not stated]

51. PREMISES: messuage in West Street consisting of 2 dwellings, one of which is late in the possession of 'Jos' [possibly Joseph] Bond and the other is now in the possession of John Wilkins; LESSEE: John Napcott of Dunster; TENANT: [not stated]; ANNUAL VALUE: [not stated]

52. PREMISES: messuage in George Street in the possession of John Nicolls, father of Thomas Nicolls; LESSEE: Thomas Nicolls TENANT: [not stated]; ANNUAL VALUE: [not stated]

53. PREMISES: messuage, curtilage, orchard and garden lying on the west side of Gallox Street late in the possession of Benjamin Copp deceased and now of Anstice Williams; LESSEE: Hugh Poole junior; TENANT: [not stated]; ANNUAL VALUE: [not stated]

54. PREMISES: messuage or dwellinghouse, garden, curtilage amd one close of meadow cont. 1a. on the west side of Gallox Street late in the possession of Mary Watts, widow; LESSEE: Henry Leigh of Dunster, clothier; TENANT: [not stated]; ANNUAL VALUE: [not stated]

55. PREMISES: the reversion of no. 5; LESSEE: Thomas Blackwell of Carhampton, yeoman; TENANT: [not stated]; ANNUAL VALUE: [not stated]

DUNSTER AND ST DECUMANS PARISHES

56. PREMISES: the reversions of nos. 13 and 33; LESSEE: John Slocombe of Clatworthy, yeoman; TENANT: [not stated]; ANNUAL VALUE: [not stated]

MANOR OF BOSSINGTON

Survey of the Manor of Bossington lying in the several Parishes of Porlock, Selworthy, Minehead, Timberscombe and Luckham

[Bossington SS 897479] [Porlock Church SS 886466]

PORLOCK PARISH

1. PREMISES: messuage and tenement; LESSEE: William Creech, junior, of Porlock, yeoman; TENANT: [not stated]; ANNUAL VALUE: £6

2. PREMISES: messuage and tenement in the village and Manor of Bossington called Rawls Tenement cont. about 13a.; LESSEE: Grace Beague of Selworthy, spinster; TENANT: William Clarke; ANNUAL VALUE: £15

3. PREMISES: customary messuage and tenement in the possession of Mary Hensleigh 'dead' [entry crossed through]; LESSEE: George Hensleigh of Porlock, yeoman; TENANT: Mr Wiseman Sydenham; ANNUAL VALUE: £15. 15s

4. PREMISES: several parcels of land, meadow and pasture, viz. the Cleale, Marland and Maire, the 'heal' and little mead and ½ part of all the ground in the Wester haven formerly parcel of a messuage held in common between WB and L Spark; LESSEE: Andrew Kitner of Porlock, yeoman; TENANT: Nicholas Harding; ANNUAL VALUE: £6

SELWORTHY PARISH

5. PREMISES: messuage and tenement near West Linch [Lynch SS 902476]; LESSEE: Mary Hensleigh of West Linch in Selworthy, widow; TENANT: Isaac Clarck [John Hensleigh crossed through]; ANNUAL VALUE: £20

PORLOCK PARISH

6. PREMISES: tenement in Bossington in reversion of Andrew Kitner 'dead', 'reversionary Lease granted by Sr Thos Acland to Dr Hall vide 28'; LESSEE: John Kitner; TENANT: Emma Kitner 'dyed abt Febry 1749 when No. 28 commenced'; ANNUAL VALUE: £20

LUCCOMBE PARISH

7. PREMISES: messuage and tenement called Higher Tenement late in the possession of John Rositer, afterwards of Robert Quircke; LESSEE: John Kent of Luckham, yeoman; TENANT: Agnes Crocombe; ANNUAL VALUE: £8

8. PREMISES: messuage and tenement called Lower Tenement held as in no. 7, 'A Barn on it but no dwelling house'; LESSEE: John Kent of Luckham, yeoman; TENANT: Agnes Crocombe; ANNUAL VALUE: £8

PORLOCK PARISH

9. PREMISES: 2 pieces of meadow, arable ground and land in the possession of Mary Loram, widow by right of widowhood as widow of William Loram; LESSEE: John Kent of Porlock, yeoman; TENANT: Mary Loram 'dead'; ANNUAL VALUE: £5

LUCCOMBE PARISH

10. PREMISES: an overland in and near Haldridge Wood cont. 5a. of arable and pasture and 2a. of coppice wood; LESSEE: William Poole alias Hayward of Meere in Minehead, yeoman; TENANT: William Poole; ANNUAL VALUE: £5

PORLOCK PARISH

11. PREMISES: messuage and tenement in Bossington; LESSEE: William Clare of Oare, clerk; TENANT: Andrew Rawle who bought it of Mr Clare; ANNUAL VALUE: £6 [crossed through and £8 substituted]

12. PREMISES: 1a. of ground in the Manor of Bossington lately inclosed from the waste and 1 plot of ground to the east of Bossington pound 56ft broad and 110ft long adjacent to William Creech's orchard in Bossington Green; LESSEE: Andrew Rawle of Porlock, carpenter; TENANT: Andrew Rawle; ANNUAL VALUE: £1

13. PREMISES: reversion of 1 tenement in Bossington called Higher Tenement cont. 5a.; LESSEE: John Stephens; TENANT: John Stephens; ANNUAL VALUE: £6

LUCCOMBE PARISH

14. PREMISES: messuage and tenement in Dovehay; LESSEES: Thomas Kent and Abraham Phelps; TENANT: Elizabeth Sparke; ANNUAL VALUE: £20

15. PREMISES: as in 14 and 2a. coppice wood more or less now in the possession of Elizabeth Sparke, widow, being part of Haldridge Wood; LESSEE: Richard Snow of Luckham, gent.; TENANT: Richard Snow; ANNUAL VALUE: [not stated]

LUCCOMBE PARISH

16. PREMISES: messuage and tenement called the Lower Tenement; LESSEE: Philip Spurrier, junior, of Oare, yeoman; TENANT: John Spurrier of Oare; ANNUAL VALUE: £16

PORLOCK PARISH

17. PREMISES: messuage and tenement in Bossington; LESSEE: Joan Snow of Bossington, spinster; TENANT: Joan, May and Elizabeth Snow; ANNUAL VALUE: £20

18. PREMISES: messuage and tenement in Bossington; LESSEE: Richard Tirrell of Porlock, yeoman; TENANT: Richard Tirrell the son; ANNUAL VALUE: £7

19. PREMISES: messuage and tenement in the village and manor of Bossington; LESSEE: Cecill Beague of Selworthy, spinster; TENANT: Cecil Taylor, widow; ANNUAL VALUE: £13

20. PREMISES: messuage and tenement in and near Porlock; LESSEE: Henry Webber of Porlock, mercer; TENANT: Henry Webber; ANNUAL VALUE: £15

21. PREMISES: messuage and tenement in Bossington late in the possession of William Joole and a moiety of a lime kiln erected on Bossington beach occupied by Robert Griffith and John Phelps and the liberty to lay stones and culme on Bossington beach whilst the kiln is in use without obstructing the passage there; LESSEE: Robert Griffith of Porlock, yeoman; TENANT: Robert Griffith; ANNUAL VALUE: £23

22. PREMISES: messuage and tenement in the village and manor of Bossington, formerly John Snow's; LESSEE: George Hensleigh of Porlock, yeoman; TENANT: George Hensleigh; ANNUAL VALUE: £11

23. PREMISES: reversion of premises in no. 22; LESSEE: George Hensleigh of Porlock, gent.; TENANT: [not stated]; ANNUAL VALUE: [not stated]

24. PREMISES: messuage and tenement cont. about 9a. in Bossington; LESSEE: George Hensleigh; TENANT: George Hensleigh; ANNUAL VALUE: £12

25. PREMISES: messuage and tenement in Bossington called Robsingsons Tenement formerly William Stoat's; LESSEE: Grace Stoate of Bossington, widow; TENANT: Grace Stoate; ANNUAL VALUE: £28

26. PREMISES: messuage and tenement in Bossington late in the possession of John Phelps, deceased, and licence to lay stones and culme on Bossington beach near to the lessee's lime- kiln there without obstructing the passage there; LESSEE: John Oland of Bossington, yeoman; TENANT: John Oland; ANNUAL VALUE: £24

27. PREMISES: water grist mill and millhouse called Bossington Mill; LESSEE: John Williams of Bossington, miller; TENANT: John Williams; ANNUAL VALUE: £3

28. PREMISES: messuage and tenement in Bossington late in the possession of John Kitner, deceased, in reversion of Emma Kitner's widowhood ('dead'); LESSEE: Peter Hall of Porlock, yeoman; TENANT: Peter Hall; ANNUAL VALUE: £20

29. PREMISES: 2 copyhold tenements in Bossington now in the possession of Robert Griffith; LESSEE: Cecilia Taylor of Selworthy, widow; TENANT: [not stated]; ANNUAL VALUE: [not stated]

30. PREMISES: customary messuage and tenement with appurtenances; LESSEE: Wiseman Sydenham of Bossington, tanner; TENANT: [not stated]; ANNUAL VALUE: £15. 15s

SELWORTHY PARISH

31. PREMISES: tenement with appurtenances cont. 8a. 3 rodds at East Lynch [SS 927462]; LESSEE: Alice Siderfin of Perriton [in Minehead], widow; TENANT: Mrs Siderfin; ANNUAL VALUE: £6

PORLOCK PARISH

32. PREMISES: reversion of premises in no. 11; LESSEE: Andrew Rawle, yeoman; TENANT: [not stated]; ANNUAL VALUE: [not stated]

33. PREMISES: reversion of premises in no. 9; LESSEE: George Crocombe of Brindon [? Brendon], yeoman; TENANT: [not stated]; ANNUAL VALUE: £7. 10s

MANOR OF WILMERSHAM AND WEST LUCKHAM

A Survey of the Manor of Wilmersham and West Luckham Lying in the several Parishes of Luckham Stoke Pero Exford and Selworthy

STOKE PERO PARISH

1. PREMISES: ¹/₃ part of a messuage, garden and tenement in Stock Pero in reversion of Lucy Arnold's widowhood ('dead') 'its

called Wilmersham'; LESSEE: Andrew Arnold of Stoke Pero, yeoman; TENANT: Christian Arnold; ANNUAL VALUE: [not stated]

2. PREMISES: ⁵/₁₂ parts of above premises; LESSEE: Andrew Arnold; TENANT: Andrew Arnold; ANNUAL VALUE: £18. 10s

3. PREMISES: ³/₁₂ parts of above premises. Note that Mrs Blackford was entitled to part of the tenement; LESSEE: Andrew Vauter of Stoke Pero, yeoman; TENANT: Robert Chaplin by right of his wife, late Mary Reed; ANNUAL VALUE: [not stated]

4. PREMISES: ⁵/₁₂ parts of a messuage with the appurtenances parcel of the said manor called Tarball [Tarr Ball Hill SS 865440]; LESSEE: Richard Ridler; TENANT: Mary, widow of Richard the son for her widowhood; ANNUAL VALUE: [not stated]

5. PREMISES: the late part, purparty and undivided portion of Andrew Snow in a messuage and tenement called Bucket Hole; LESSEE: Andrew Snow of Stoke Pero, yeoman; TENANT: Andrew Snow; ANNUAL VALUE: [not stated]

6. PREMISES: ⁵/₁₂ parts of a tenement called Bucket Hole [SS 872453] and 2a. of underwood at Horner gate between the wood of Richard Blackford and Henry Phelps; LESSEE: Richard Snow; TENANT: [not stated]; ANNUAL VALUE: [not stated]

7. PREMISES: ⁴/₁₂ part of a messuage and tenement called Tarr Ball; LESSEE: Thomas Paramore of Luckham, yeoman; TENANT: Thomas Paramore; ANNUAL VALUE: £2. 10s

MANOR OF WEST LUCKHAM

LUCCOMBE PARISH

1. PREMISES: part of Cloudisham Farm [Cloutsham SS 882432] late in the possession of Wilmot Rublin; LESSEE: Andrew Arnold of Stoke Pero, yeoman; TENANT: Andrew Arnold; ANNUAL VALUE: [not stated]

STOKE PERO PARISH

[Stoke Pero Church SS 878434]

2. PREMISES: ⁵/₁₂ parts of a tenement within the Parish and manor with the appurtenances called Feiris' Tenement in Wilmers-

ham; LESSEE: John Ferris; TENANT: Andrew Ferris; ANNUAL VALUE: £17. 10s

LUCCOMBE PARISH

3. PREMISES: water grist mill and millhouse or millroom called Horner Mill [Horner (at river) SS 897454] late in the possession of Robert Chaplin and part of a dwellinghouse and garden late in the possession of the said Robert Chaplin situated near Horner Mill and a little dwellinghouse with appurtenances situate near the other dwellinghouse late in the possession of William Tuck, and parcels of coppice wood; LESSEE: Jonas Fish of Luckham, carpenter; TENANT: Jonas Fish; ANNUAL VALUE: [not stated]

4. PREMISES: little dwellinghouse, garden and orchard late in the possession of Agnes Rendall deceased and a certain waste plot or parcel of ground lying between the said house, garden and orchard and Horner river, and 1a. of coppice on Horner wood late in the possession of Robert Cor deceased; LESSEE: Richard Cridland, gent. in trust for Mary Hole; TENANT: Mary Hole; ANNUAL VALUE: [not stated]

5. PREMISES: reversion of messuage, garden and acre of coppice wood late in the possession of Margaret Aubert, widow, after the deaths of Joan and Susan, daughters of the lessee ('both dead'); LESSEE: Joan Ellis of Luckham, widow; TENANT: Francis Tame by right of Ann his wife; ANNUAL VALUE: [not stated]

6. PREMISES: part of a messuage and a certain parcel of coppice wood cont. 2a. in Horner and the woods thereunto belonging late in the possession of Henry Hooper and ⁸/₁₂ parts of a close near Horner Wood called Rack Close; LESSEE: Peter Rawle of Horner, clothier; TENANT: John Goss by right of his wife, formerly Anne Rawle; ANNUAL VALUE: [not stated]

7. PREMISES: 3 plots of ground in Horner Coombe; LESSEE: John Goss; TENANT: [not stated]; ANNUAL VALUE: [not stated]

8. PREMISES: ground inclosed in Horner Coombe late Goss's vineyard and High Park and an orchard; LESSEE: [not stated]; TENANT: [not stated]; annual value; £3

9. PREMISES: messuage, water grist mill and tenement in the Manor of West Luckham [Luccombe SS 899462] late in the

possession of Thomas Taylor, clothier and 7a. coppice in Horner wood; LESSEE: John Harding of Porlock, yeoman; TENANT: Nicholas Harding; ANNUAL VALUE: £17

10. PREMISES: messuage and tenement called Cloutisham alias Huishe, part of Cloutsham Farm, late in the possession of William Baker and all that coppice wood or woodland ground lying in Horner Woods between the woods of Edward Kitner and John Blewett, cont. 8a.; LESSEE: Thomas Rublin of Luckham, yeoman; TENANT: John Hole, given to him by Thomas Rublin's will; ANNUAL VALUE: 'Tenant says it is £10 per annum'

11. PREMISES: messuage, fulling mill and premises with the use of the furnace and other materials thereon; LESSEE: John Hill of Luckham, fuller; TENANT: John Hill; ANNUAL VALUE: [not stated]

12. PREMISES: part of a dwellinghouse and garden of late years occupied by the said John Hill near to Horner tucking mill; LESSEE: John Hill of Horner, fuller; TENANT: John Hill; ANNUAL VALUE: [not stated]

13. PREMISES: messuage and tenement in Luckham and 7a. of coppice wood in Horner Wood; LESSEE: [not stated]; TENANT: Peter Hall; ANNUAL VALUE: £6. 10s

14. PREMISES: part and parcel of Cloudisham Farm late called Warrs in the possession of Emmet Rublin, widow of Richard Rublin for her widowhood; LESSEE: John Gardiner in trust for Wilmott Rublin; TENANT: John Cole; ANNUAL VALUE: [not stated]

15. PREMISES: messuage and tenement called Easter Tenement; LESSEE: John Kent of Porlock, yeoman; TENANT: Thomas Kent; ANNUAL VALUE: £12. 12s

16. PREMISES: messuage and tenement with appurtenances in the village and manor of West Luckham late in the possession of Joan Cole, widow; LESSEE: John Kent of Porlock, yeoman; TENANT: Thomas Kent; ANNUAL VALUE: [not stated]

17. PREMISES: messuage and tenement called Blewits Wester Tenement; LESSEE: Thomas Kent of Luckham, yeoman; TENANT: Thomas Kent; ANNUAL VALUE: £13

18. PREMISES: $5/12$ parts of Easter Tenement; LESSEE: [not stated]; TENANT: [not stated]; ANNUAL VALUE: £13. 10s [entry crossed through]

19. PREMISES: piece and parcel of meadow ground near the gate leading from Allerford towards West Luckham Green late in the possession of David Knight called Holesmead or the Broom Close; LESSEE: Edward Kitner of Luckham, yeoman; TENANT: Nathaniel Langhwell [possibly Laughwell]; ANNUAL VALUE: 'about 50s per annum'

20. PREMISES: dwellinghouse, garden and orchard in Horner Green, 1a. in Horner Wood near Recombfoot and 1 day's cut of turf on West Luckham Hill; LESSEE: Christopher Neale; TENANT: 'now Henry Webbers'; ANNUAL VALUE: £4. 5s

21. PREMISES: messuage and tenement near the village of West Luckham consisting of a convenient dwellinghouse, barn, outhouses, garden and orchard and 3a. ground called the Burrow, higher and lower Crater [Crawter Hill SS 892458], late in the possession of William Westcott; LESSEE: William Hayward alias Poole of Minehead, yeoman; TENANT: William Poole alias Hayward; ANNUAL VALUE: [not stated]

22. PREMISES: 'Mr B. granted 7 pts in 12 of 2 orchards near Hakety Bridge late Thos Taylors and late W Westcotts Orchard adj. to Christopher Neal's orchard near Horner Green and also late Ellis's potatoe garden in Horner Green near the gate leading in[to] the meadow belonging to Horner Farm and the potatoe garden in Halescombe now inclosed by George Phelps. Mr Wood granted the other 5 parts'; LESSEE: George Phelps of Luckham, yeoman; TENANT: William Poole alias Hayward by marrying Mary, widow of George Phelps; ANNUAL VALUE: £4

23. PREMISES: 4th part of a messuage and tenement and of 7a. wood in Horner Wood; LESSEE: David Ridler of Luckham, yeoman; TENANT: David Ridler; ANNUAL VALUE: [not stated]

24. PREMISES: $1/4$ part of a messuage and tenement, parcel of the manor; LESSEE: David Ridler of Porlock, tanner; TENANT: Walter Ridler; ANNUAL VALUE: [not stated]

25. PREMISES: $1/4$ part of messuage and tenement sometime heretofore Phelps and $7/12$ parts of 6a. coppice wood in Horner Wood between the woods of Simon Warr and Mary Phelps, $7/12$ of another acre there between the woods of John Blewit and John Hensley; LESSEE: Mary Ridler of Porlock, widow; TENANT: Thomas Browne by right of his wife; ANNUAL VALUE: [not stated]

26. PREMISES: $^4/_{12}$ part of a messuage and tenement in Luckham [Luccombe Church SS 911445] and parcel of Luckham Manor with $^4/_{12}$ part of 6a. coppice wood in Horner wood between the woods of William Thomas and his fellows and the woods of George Hole and his fellows and 1a. coppice wood in Horner wood between the wood of Thomas Taylor and George Hole; LESSEE: Edward Kitner; TENANT: David Ridler; ANNUAL VALUE: [not stated]

27. PREMISES: $^3/_{12}$ of a messuage and tenement in Luckham and $^3/_{12}$ of 6a. coppice woods in Horner woods between the woods of William Sparke and Joan Foy, widow and $^3/_{12}$ of 1a. wood in the same wood between the wood of Sarah Cole and Joan Foy and for depasturing 100 sheep, 15 bullocks and 2 horse beasts upon the hills of West Luckham; LESSEE: David Ridler of Porlock, tanner; TENANT: Christopher Ridler; ANNUAL VALUE: [not stated]

28. PREMISES: messuage and tenement in the village of West Luckham late in the possession of John Hensley and since of Lawrence Yorke and 6a. of coppice wood; LESSEE: Abraham Phelps of Porlock; TENANT: Richard Snow; ANNUAL VALUE: £14

29. PREMISES: messuage and tenement in Luckham heretofore in the possession of Henry Langworthy and 7a. wood in Horner wood; LESSEE: Elizabeth Sparke, widow; TENANT: Richard Snow; ANNUAL VALUE: £12

30. PREMISES: messuage and tenement in the Manor of West Luckham called Burrow Hayes in the possession of Roger Henson, 6a. coppice wood in Horner wood adjoining to that of Thomazin Taylor, widow, 1a. coppice wood in the same wood, common for 200 sheep, 40 bullocks and 5 horse beasts; LESSEE: Mary Stephens of Porlock, spinster; TENANT: John Bales 'now Mr Henry Webbers'; ANNUAL VALUE: [not stated]

31. PREMISES: an old tallet near the decayed house in Horner in Luckham and 3 fields in Horner called the Dovehouse mead and the Down Close in the possession of Thomas Dollen; LESSEE: Philip Spurrier of Oare, gent.; TENANT: John Spurrier; ANNUAL VALUE: [not stated]

32. PREMISES: reversion of 2 messuages and tenements called Woodcocksleigh [Woodcocks Ley SS 881450] and a coppice wood thereunto belonging called Woodcocksleigh wood in

Luckham in the possession of Agnes Snow, widow, except 4a. of coppice wood at the lower side of the wood adjoining to John Ridlers; LESSEE: Nicholas Snow of Luckham, yeoman; TENANT: Nicholas Snow; ANNUAL VALUE: £50

33. PREMISES: barn, court and several closes in Luckham then in the possession of John Hall, butcher, called The Hams; LESSEE: Nicholas Snow of Luckham, yeoman; TENANT: Nicholas Snow; ANNUAL VALUE: [not stated]

34. PREMISES: premises as in no. 33 in reversion; LESSEE: Nicholas Snow, junior, of Luckham; TENANT: the said Nicholas Snow; ANNUAL VALUE: [not stated]

35. PREMISES: messuage, barn and tenement and closes of land belonging called Burnols Tenement near Horner in Luckham late in the possession of Ethelred Ellis; LESSEE: John Stoate of Selworthy, yeoman; TENANT: John Stoate; ANNUAL VALUE: [not stated]

STOKE PERO PARISH

36. PREMISES: part of a messuage and tenement called Ley Poole [Pool Farm SS 873443] in Stoke Pero late in the possession of Nicholas Paramore, deceased; LESSEE: John Paramore of Stock Pero, yeoman; TENANT: John Paramore; ANNUAL VALUE: [not stated]

LUCCOMBE PARISH

37. PREMISES: plot of ground lying between the Horner river and the mill leat below the edge mill of Walter Spurryes towards Horner and one other little plot of land being between the mill leat and river abutting upon the west end of a close called Rack Close; LESSEE: John Goss of Luckham, dyer; TENANT: William Tuck by right of his wife, formerly Ann Goss; ANNUAL VALUE: [not stated]

38. PREMISES: $^3/_{12}$ part of a messuage in West Luckham sometime Reeds Tenement and $^3/_{12}$ of 6a. coppice wood in Horner Wood between Edward Kitner and William Thomas and $^3/_{12}$ part of 1a. wood there between George Hole and Joan Foy, widow, and common of pasture for 100 sheep, 15 bullocks and 2 horse

beasts on Manor downs and common of turbary; LESSEE: Philip Jones of Luckham, husbandman; TENANT: William Tucker by right of his wife formerly Ann Phelps; ANNUAL VALUE: [not stated]

39. PREMISES: one messuage or tenement with appurtenances in Wilmersham [SS 874437]; LESSEE: Andrew Vauter; TENANT: [not stated]; ANNUAL VALUE: £17

40. PREMISES: [not stated]; LESSEE: [not stated]; TENANT: Robert Way; ANNUAL VALUE: £12

41. PREMISES: reversion of premises in no. 30; LESSEE: Abraham Phelps of Porlock; TENANT: Mr Henry Webber; ANNUAL VALUE: [not stated]

42. PREMISES: messuage and tenement in West Luckham with appurtenances, i.e. a dwellinghouse, garden, backside and 1 close of arable called Valebridge cont. 2a. and 1 yard adjacent to a close called Four acres, 1 close called Barrow cont. 3 yards lying near the same leading to the Hill from West Luckham and closes called the Crators cont. 1a., and ⁵/₁₂ parts of '/a. wood in Horner Wood between Nicholas Snow of Wood Cocksleigh and William [? Wilii] Quartly; LESSEE: Henry Webber of Porlock, merchant; TENANT: Henry Webber; ANNUAL VALUE: [not stated]

43. PREMISES: ¹/₃ part and ³/₄ part of a messuage and tenement, viz. 3 parts of all that messuage or dwellinghouse, court, courtilage, outhouses, 2 orchards, a garden cont. 1a., 1 closes of ground called Laze head adj. to the hill called Crator towards the south cont. 3a. and 1 close called the Woolland cont. 3a. and 1 close called Little Crator cont. ½a. and 2 closes called Langlands cont. 4a., and 6a. wood in Horner Wood between Thomas Rublins and near a place called Norborow; LESSEE: William Ridler of Porlock, yeoman; TENANT: John Rawle; ANNUAL VALUE: [not stated]

STOKE PERO PARISH

44. PREMISES: 3 part [?¹/₃] of a messuage and tenement called Tarr ball [Tarr Ball Hill SS 866440] at Stock Pero [entry crossed through]; LESSEE: Thomas Paramore; TENANT: Thomas Paramore; ANNUAL VALUE: [not stated]

LUCCOMBE PARISH

45. PREMISES: ⁵/₁₂ part of a messuage and tenement with appurtenances in Luckham and ⁵/₁₂ part of 6a. of coppice wood in Horner woods between the woods now of Thomas Kent and Peter Hall, and ⁵/₁₂ part of 1a. wood there between the woods now or late of Sarah Hole and Joan Foye, widow, with common of pasture at all times for depasture [of] 100 sheep, 15 bullocks and 2 horse beasts upon the hills of West Luckham; LESSEE: Christopher Ridler of Luckham, yeoman; TENANT: Christopher Ridler; ANNUAL VALUE: [not stated]

46. PREMISES: ⁵/₁₂ part of a messuage in West Luckham adjoining West Luckham Green and a small piece of garden ground adjoining and of 1a. wood lying in Horner Wood; LESSEE: David Ridler of Luckham, husbandman; TENANT: David Ridler; ANNUAL VALUE: [not stated]

47. PREMISES: the reversion of premises in no. 29; LESSEE: Richard Snow of Luckham, yeoman; TENANT: [not stated]; ANNUAL VALUE: [not stated]

48. PREMISES: the reversion of premises in no. 32; LESSEE: Nicholas Snow, junior; TENANT: [not stated]; ANNUAL VALUE: [not stated]

MANOR OF HOLNICOTE

A Survey of the Manor of Holnicote Lying in the several Parishes of Selworthy, Luckham, Minehead, Porlock, Dulverton, Brompton Regis and Exford [Note: no property in Brompton Regis is specified in this Section.]

SELWORTHY PARISH

[Selworthy Church SS 920468]

1. PREMISES: messuage and tenement late Elizabeth Blakes with other lands; LESSEE: Robert Beague; TENANT: Robert Beague, son of lessee; ANNUAL VALUE: [not stated]

2. PREMISES: reversion of above premises, viz. messuage and

tenement heretofore of Elizabeth Blake and close called Charlands and another close called Willclose; LESSEE: Robert Beague of Selworthy, yeoman; TENANT: [not stated]; ANNUAL VALUE: [not stated]

3. PREMISES: shop and chamber within the shop, the east part of the entry and part of the orchard downward from the Quine of the wall without the back door right over to the East hedge in Allerford [SS 904470]; LESSEE: James Beague; TENANT: John Beague, tanner; ANNUAL VALUE: [not stated]

4. PREMISES: cott or dwellinghouse and garden and orchard adj. called Pitt at Buddlehill, one parcel of land formerly converted into a garden, 1 close called Little Stretford cont. 1½a., 2 closes called Little Buddles cont. 1½a. and 1 closes called Barn Oak cont. 1½a.; LESSEE: John Beague of Selworthy, tanner; TENANT: John Beague; ANNUAL VALUE: [not stated]

5. PREMISES: late copyhold tenement with appurtenances and 4a. heretofore in the possession of John Rawle deceased and several pieces of arable and pasture called Farthing and Holtridges cont. 6a.; LESSEE: John Beague of Skilgate, gent.; TENANT: [not stated]; ANNUAL VALUE: [not stated]

6. PREMISES: tenement at West Linch [Lynch SS 901477] with appurtenances, one orchard cont. ½a., close called Broom Close cont. 2½a.; LESSEE: John Bryant of Selworthy; TENANT: Robert Bryant 'the only life'; ANNUAL VALUE: [not stated]

7. PREMISES: cott and garden in Holnicote in the possession of Susan Shepherd and all sear wood from time to time in coppice wood happening or falling out; LESSEE: W. Martin Charity (lease made to Walter Coffin and James Blackford in trust for W. Martin being a minor); TENANT: John Budd by purchase or otherwise for Wm Martin's life; ANNUAL VALUE: [not stated]

PORLOCK AND SELWORTHY PARISHES

8. PREMISES: messuage, dwellinghouse and tenement called West Lynch in Selworthy, 1 piece of wood cont. 2a. in Porlock Meadow in Porlock and common of pasture for cattle upon certain waste grounds called Lynch otherwise West Lynch common and 1 small parcel of coppice wood or woodland ground adj. to the upper end of Henbeer; LESSEE: John Beague of West Lynch, yeoman; TENANT: William Clark by right of his wife; ANNUAL VALUE: £16

SELWORTHY PARISH

9. PREMISES: piece of pasture or arable near Down Lane on the north side of Holnicote village with the orchard at the lower end thereof cont. 3a., a piece or parcel of land between Holnicote village and New Cross cont. ¾a., a parcel of land beyond Hounsham cont. more than an acre and a piece of meadow ground lying west of the last cont. 1½a; LESSEE: William Taylor; TENANT: [not stated]; ANNUAL VALUE: £6

10. PREMISES: messuage and tenement with appurtenances cont. 13a. of land, meadow or pasture and common of pasture and common of tillage in Holnicote Coombe; LESSEE: William Taylor; TENANT: [not stated]; ANNUAL VALUE: £13

11. PREMISES: part of Strongs messuage and tenement 'made' to William Taylor by Henry Strong; LESSEES: John Beague and Philip Taylor; TENANT: [not stated]; ANNUAL VALUE: £6

12. PREMISES: reversion of the above premises; LESSEE: Cecilia Taylor in pursuance of a contract the 'testator' made with William Taylor, her husband; TENANT: Cecilia Taylor, widow; ANNUAL VALUE: [not stated]

[unnumbered entry for Mitchells tenement crossed through]

13. PREMISES: part of Mitchells tenement, viz. all those 2 closes of arable land, one of them cont. about 2a. and the other 3 yards adj. to John Giles's house, one piece of meadow opposite Holnicote mills [SS 911462] called Martins Mead cont. 1a.; LESSEE: Cecilia Taylor, widow; TENANT: [not stated]; ANNUAL VALUE: [not stated]

14. PREMISES: dwellinghouse, garden and backside called Slutfolds, Slutfolds barn adj. to the dwellinghouse and 4 closes of overland called Green Close above Long Shell Burrow and Foot Land situated in Allerford; LESSEE: Benjamin Coffin of Allerford, tanner; TENANT: Benjamin Coffin; ANNUAL VALUE: £5

15. PREMISES: dwellinghouse and garden or backside in Allerford; LESSEE: William Cooksley of Selworthy, husbandman; TENANT: [not stated]; ANNUAL VALUE: £1

16. PREMISES: messuage and tenement with appurtenances and 2 pieces of ground called the little Daglages cont 1½a.; LESSEE: Joan Doble of Selworthy, spinster; TENANT: Ethelred Ellis in the right of the said Joan, his wife; ANNUAL VALUE: £5

17. PREMISES: tenement with appurtenances heretofore in the possession of Mary Falvey, widow, in Holnicote; LESSEE: Luke Falvey of Holnicote, yeoman; TENANT: Luke Falvey; ANNUAL VALUE: £6

18. PREMISES: cottage, house and garden in Holnicote; LESSEE: David Gyles, junior; TENANT: Joan Giles, widow; ANNUAL VALUE: £1. 10s

EXFORD PARISH

19. PREMISES: moor called Hole Moor [Hoar Moor SS 863405] cont. 178a.; LESSEE: Arthur Hooper of Exford; TENANT: Arthur Hooper; ANNUAL VALUE: £7

LUCCOMBE AND SELWORTHY PARISHES

20. PREMISES: messuage in Holnicote village called Newhouse with the barn, stable, garden and orchard adj. with common as hath been used in and upon Holnicote Coombe and all other waste commonable places belonging to Holnicote manor, one day's cut of turf and one day's pulling of heath on Cloutisham Common with heath and turfs on Easthill or the Down Common lying east and west between St Anthony's Chapel [SS 906449] and Horner village, also 2a. coppice woods in Horner woods between Abraham Blackmors and Jan Woolcotts near Yeatcombes foot, 1a. more of coppice wood between the 2 ways in Yelscombe Plain and one other acre of coppice wood in Horner Hill adj. to the Parson of Luckham's wood in Selworthy, in Luckham and parcels of Holnicote and West Luckham manors; LESSEE: Wilmott Rublin of Selworthy, widow; TENANT: William Horne in the right of Wilmott, his wife; ANNUAL VALUE: £8

SELWORTHY PARISH

21. PREMISES: messuage and tenement with appurtenances

sometime in the possession of Peter Hensley deceased and a close or parcel of land called the half acre alias the Grove formerly in the possession of George Taylor otherwise Mitchael deceased and lately taken into the wester side of a close called New Cross, parcel of the said tenement and 2 charlands, Wet-close and one orchard in the possession of Robert Beague and John Strong excepted; LESSEE: Thomas Paramore of Selworthy, yeoman; TENANT: William Horne by purchase; ANNUAL VALUE: £7

22. PREMISES: reversion of the above premises; LESSEE: William Horne of Selworthy, yeoman; TENANT: [not stated]; ANNUAL VALUE: [not stated]

23. PREMISES: piece or parcel of meadow called Hanger Mead cont. 1a. [boundaries specified]; LESSEE: William Tirrel the elder in trust for George Hensley his grandson, an infant; TENANT: George Hensley; ANNUAL VALUE: [not stated]

DULVERTON PARISH

24. PREMISES: messuage called East Browford alias Brufford [Broford; farmstead, now only agricultural buildings. SS 921313. We are indebted to Dr Robert Dunning for this reference] [entry crossed through]; LESSEE: John Lyddon of Dulverton, yeoman; TENANT: John Lyddon 'dead'; ANNUAL VALUE: £50

25. PREMISES: messuage called West Browford [entry crossed through]; LESSEE: John Lyddon; TENANT: John Lyddon; ANNUAL VALUE: £60

26. PREMISES: coppice wood called Sale wood on the south side of Wester Broford House cont. 12a. with timber and the right to fell and carry away the same; LESSEE: Nicholas Lyddon of Dulverton, yeoman; TENANT: John Lyddon 'dead'; ANNUAL VALUE: £10

SELWORTHY PARISH

27. PREMISES: messuage in the possession of Frances Taylor in the village and manor of Holnicote; LESSEES: John Lee of Selworthy, husbandman and Frances Taylor, widow; TENANT: John Lee; ANNUAL VALUE: £4

28. PREMISES: messuage, tenement and 2 closes with appurtenances called Farthings cont. 17a.; LESSEE: John Hayward of Porlock, yeoman; TENANT: John Poole alias Hayward; ANNUAL VALUE: £12

29. PREMISES: dwellinghouse, cottage and garden with appurtenances heretofore in the possession of Ann Strong; LESSEE: John Phelps of Selworthy, husbandman; TENANT: Simon Mockridge [possibly Meckridge] by right of his wife, Mary Phelps; ANNUAL VALUE: £1. 10s

30. PREMISES: copyhold cottage with an orchard called Blacklake with appurtenances, parcel of the Manor of Holnicote; LESSEE: John Creech of Luckham, husbandman; TENANT: John Creech, junior; ANNUAL VALUE: £1

31. PREMISES: messuage and tenement; LESSEE: Alexander Stephens of Selworthy, cordwainer; TENANT: John Stephens, son of the said Alexander; ANNUAL VALUE: £6

32. PREMISES: orchard called Bove Town orchard with appurtenances cont. ¾a. in Holnicote; LESSEE: Alexander Stephens of Porlock, cordwainer; TENANT: John Stephens; ANNUAL VALUE: £1. 5s

LUCCOMBE PARISH

[Luccombe Church SS 911445]

33. PREMISES: 3 closes called Huish Balls and about 9a. land; LESSEE: Nicholas Snow of Luckham; TENANT: Nicholas Snow; ANNUAL VALUE: £10

34. PREMISES: 3 closes of land, meadow and pasture called Church fields, viz. closes called Middle church field, wester church field and easter church field or chapple close, Church field meadow, the whole containing 32a. and common of pasture, tillage and estovers on Easthill common in Luckham; LESSEE: Betty Stoate of Selworthy, widow; TENANT: Betty Stoate; ANNUAL VALUE: £22

SELWORTHY PARISH

35. PREMISES: dwellinghouse and orchard and one close of 'G:' [?garden] near the Down Gate; LESSEE: Edward Stoate; TENANT: Lewis Viccary, by right of his wife; ANNUAL VALUE: £1. 10s

36. PREMISES: reversion of the above premises; LESSEE: Lewis Viccary of Selworthy, carpenter; TENANT: [not stated]; ANNUAL VALUE: [not stated]

37. PREMISES: messuage, garden and orchard, 4a. land, meadow and pasture being a meadow adj. to the wester side of the said orchard, a piece called Ridge, a close called Long Close, a close called Broom Close and ½a. in a field called Somerway; LESSEE: John Stoate of Selworthy, yeoman; TENANT: Betty Stoate; ANNUAL VALUE: £5

WINSFORD PARISH

38. PREMISES: messuage and tenement with the coppice called Oldrey [SS 902378]; LESSEE: Richard Court of Winsford, yeoman; TENANT: Christian Skinner, widow, formerly Christian Thorn; ANNUAL VALUE: £45

SELWORTHY PARISH

39. PREMISES: dwellinghouse and garden with the hedge and ditch enclosing the same garden at the wester end of the village called Towshead in Holnicote; LESSEE: Richard Warr, husbandman; TENANT: Robert Sully of Holnicote, blacksmith, by purchase; ANNUAL VALUE: £1

40. PREMISES: reversion of the above premises; LESSEE: Robert Sully of Selworthy; TENANT: Robert Sully; ANNUAL VALUE: [not stated]

EXFORD PARISH

41. PREMISES: moiety of tenement called Over Priscott [Prescott SS 860392] and a moiety of the common belonging upon Priscott Down; LESSEE: Alexander Tudball of Exford; TENANT: Walter Tedball (sic); ANNUAL VALUE: £10

42. PREMISES: his part of a messuage and tenement called Priscott, 'formerly his fathers'; LESSEE: Alexander Tedball; TENANT: Walter Tedball; ANNUAL VALUE: £30

SELWORTHY PARISH

43. PREMISES: dwellinghouse and garden now in the possession of Susan Osmond with the barn and one other garden or orchard belonging called Chibbles; LESSEE: John Cheek of Selworthy, cordwainer; TENANT: the said John Chek (sic); ANNUAL VALUE: £2

44. PREMISES: tenement and several closes, pieces of land, meadow and pasture called Henry Horners Tenement with appurtenances and one close of arable ground called Kents Close cont. 2a.; LESSEE: William Horne of Selworthy, yeoman; TENANT: William Horne; ANNUAL VALUE: £6

45. PREMISES: dwellinghouse, outhouses, garden, backside and orchard belonging commonly called Flattholms at Allerford; LESSEE: Thomas Darch of Selworthy, carpenter; TENANT: Thomas Darch; ANNUAL VALUE: £1. 4s.

LUCCOMBE PARISH

46. PREMISES: messuage, dwellinghouse with garden and little orchard belonging and 4 closes of arable, meadow and pasture ground cont. 6a. near Luckham Church; LESSEE: James Darch of Luckham, carpenter; TENANT: James Darch; ANNUAL VALUE: £7. 12s.

SELWORTHY PARISH

47. PREMISES: messuage and tenement with appurtenances late in the possession of Katherine Eames, widow; LESSEE: William Falvey of Holnicote, butcher; TENANT: William Falvey; ANNUAL VALUE: [not stated]

48. PREMISES: dwellinghouse, outhouses, court and courtlage garden and orchard; LESSEE: John Giles of Selworthy, tailor; TENANT: [not stated]; ANNUAL VALUE: [not stated]

DULVERTON PARISH

49. PREMISES: 2 messuages called North Coombe [SS 917291] and 6a. coppice wood or woodland ground in North Marshwood [Marsh wood centred on SS 900294]; LESSEE: Robert Heard of Dulverton, gent., a gift of Sir Thomas Dyke Acland; TENANT: [not stated]; ANNUAL VALUE: [not stated]

SELWORTHY PARISH

50. PREMISES: messuage and tenement with appurtenances called Gilhams in Branding Street [Brandish Street approx. SS 911467] in Selworthy, a little meadow near Pyles Mill, one day's cut of turf for one man on Horner Common and one day's pull of heath by one man and pasture for 50 sheep on the said common, ¾a. in Sumerway late John Bryants and 1a. in the same field late Betty Stoates; LESSEE: Edward May of Holnicote, miller; TENANT: [not stated]; ANNUAL VALUE: [not stated]

MANOR OF EXBRIDGE RYPHAY

A Survey of the Manor of Exbridge Ryphay lying in the several Parishes of Brushford, Dulverton, Winsford, Hawkridge and Bampton [Note: no property in Dulverton specified in this section.]

BRUSHFORD PARISH

[Brushford Church SS 919257]

1. PREMISES: messuage and garden in Brushford called Seamans House with appurtenances; LESSEE: Hugh Addicot of Brushford, tailor; TENANT: [not stated]; ANNUAL VALUE: £1. 10s

2. PREMISES: ruinous messuage or dwellinghouse, garden and orchard near the Green late in the possession of Thomas Hawksland; LESSEE: William Budd of Brushford, husbandman; TENANT: [not stated]; ANNUAL VALUE: £1. 10s

3. PREMISES: the millhouse, water grist mill and malt mill, the little plot of ground adj. on the SE side of the mill leat and 2 closes of land near Blackwell and mill close cont. about 4a.; LESSEE: John Cox of Exebridge, merchant; TENANT: John Cox; ANNUAL VALUE: £11

4. PREMISES: 2 dwellinghouses or cottages with garden adj. called Ile land houses, both under one roof and near Exbridge [SS 930244]; LESSEE: Samuel Escott of Brushford, yeoman; TENANT: [not stated]; ANNUAL VALUE: £1

5. PREMISES: 3 messuage and gardens with appurtenances [crossed

through]; LESSEE: Joan Bowden of Brushford, widow; TENANT: [not stated]; ANNUAL VALUE: £2. 10s

6. PREMISES: messuage or tenement with appurtenances called Nighcott (sic) in the village of Nightcott [Nightcott SS894258]; LESSEE: Elie Hill of Brushford, widow; TENANT: 'Richard Stone says this estate is held by him and Martin Langdon of Spiring'; ANNUAL VALUE: £20

7. PREMISES: messuage and dwellinghouse converted into 3 dwellings with the gardens or garden plots of ground now of late years used with the same in the possession severally of Henry Herniman, Joan Cridge and Zachariah Parsons called New Rock [?Rocks SS 919246]; LESSEE: Henry Herniaman (sic) of Exbridge, thatcher; TENANT: the said Henry; ANNUAL VALUE: £4. 8s

BAMPTON PARISH (Devon)

8. PREMISES: messuage and tenement with appurtenances called Higher Lodfen alias Lodven [Lodfin Dairy SS 954237]; LESSEE: John Lewis of Dulverton, yeoman; TENANT: [not stated]; ANNUAL VALUE: £24

WINSFORD PARISH

9. PREMISES: messuage and tenement in the possession of Nicholas Lyddon called Nether Week [Week SS 914334]; LESSEE: Nicholas Lyddon of Winsford, yeoman; TENANT: [not stated]; ANNUAL VALUE: £28

BRUSHFORD PARISH

10. PREMISES: dwellinghouse, garden and plot of ground with appurtenances and all that barn sometime since converted into a small shop or forge and liney (sic), houses against the same with the courtlage and garden [belonging] to the last mentioned premises; LESSEE: Diana Melton of Brushford, widow; TENANT: [not stated]; ANNUAL VALUE: £2

BAMPTON PARISH (Devon)

11. PREMISES: messuage and tenement with appurtenances late

in the possession of John Edberry; LESSEE: John Oxenham of Bampton, yeoman; TENANT: [not stated]; ANNUAL VALUE: £5

BRUSHFORD PARISH

12. PREMISES: messuage called New Rock Kitchen with the garden thereunto belonging; LESSEE: Dorothy Collard of Brushford, widow; TENANT: [not stated]; ANNUAL VALUE: [not stated]

HAWKRIDGE PARISH

13. PREMISES: messuage and tenement called Cloggs alias Foxcombe [Cloggs Farm SS 839311] with appurtenances [entry crossed through]; LESSEE: George Langdon of Exton; TENANT: [not stated]; ANNUAL VALUE: £20

BRUSHFORD PARISH

14. PREMISES: messuage or tenement called Haynes Hill or Haynes Wood; LESSEE: Margaret Gorton of Tetton, spinster 'in consideration of her faithfull service done and performed for Lady Acland'; TENANT: [not stated]; ANNUAL VALUE: £11

15. PREMISES: reversion of premises in no. 2; LESSEE: Ann Budd of Brushford, widow; TENANT: [not stated]; ANNUAL VALUE: £1. 10s.

WINSFORD PARISH

[Winsford Church SS 904356]

16. PREMISES: reversion of premises in no. 9; LESSEE: Nicholas Lyddon of Winsford, yeoman; TENANT: [not stated]; ANNUAL VALUE: [not stated]

BRUSHFORD PARISH

17. PREMISES: messuages and gardens heretofore in the possessions of Mark Seaman, William Herniman and Thomas Broadmead; LESSEE: Nicholas Fisher of Brushford, husbandman; TENANT: [not stated]; ANNUAL VALUE: [not stated]

Survey 3

Cornwall, Devon and Somerset

	SURVEY
c.1802	DRO, 1110M add/6/13

This is a small volume of 72 pages, size 19.2cms x 23.6cms, with soft leather covers. Like many other surveys in the Acland collection it has been affected by damp. The information for eight Cornish manors, the Manor of East Luckham in Somerset and the Manor of Stockleigh Luckham in Devon is given in columns with headings for the names of the tenements, the lives in being and their ages, lives added, conventionary rent, capons, due days, the kind of heriots, the sum in lieu thereof and 'Observations'. A column showing acreages of the tenements in some of the manors and the name of the present tenant in all manors has been added in a later hand, as have details of leases granted by Mrs Kaye up to April 1802, the latter appearing in an 'Observations' column. In the following abstract, only details of the tenements (and acreages where given), the tenants and the conventionary rents have been reproduced but details of the other information given is to be found in the Introduction. Parishes and the grid reference, where found, have been supplied in the Abstract.

The original survey appears to date from c.1800. Mrs Augusta Kaye, who obtained the properties in 1799 after the death of Earl Strafford, is described as being 60 years of age in some of the leases. The later information in the Survey most probably dates from 1802 when Sir Thomas Dyke Acland, the 10th Bart, inherited the properties as the devisee of the last Lord Arundell.

ABSTRACT OF SURVEY

Cornwall

MANOR OF TRERISE

NEWLYN EAST PARISH

PREMISES: Trendrean House [Trendrean SW 833573], 29a.1r.10p.; LESSEE: John Thomas, esq.; RENT: £1.0s.6d

PREMISES: Trendrean late Bartlets, 39a. 1r. 11p.; LESSEE: Richard Andrews; RENT: £1. 6s. 8d

PREMISES: Trendrean late Kestles, 25a. 1r. 36p.; LESSEE: William James; RENT: £1

PREMISES: Trendrean Moor, 3r. 32p.; LESSEE: Thomas Cook; RENT: 2s. 6d.

PREMISES: Trendrean, 1r. 6p.; LESSEE: Samuel Symons; RENT: 6s. 8d.

ST COLUMB MINOR PARISH

PREMISES: Trethiggey [SW 846596], 62a. 1r. 20p.; LESSEE: John Cardell; RENT: £1. 6s. 8d.

PREMISES: Trevilley alias Ladys Close, 26a. 3r. 38p.; LESSEE: William Martyn; RENT: £1. 6s. 8d.

PREMISES: Trevilley Field, 23a. 0r. 2p.; LESSEE: William Martyn; RENT: £1

MAWGAN-IN-PYDAR PARISH

PREMISES: Trenance Maugan [SW 852681], 43a. 3r. 23p.; LESSEE: Mary Merifield; RENT: 16s.4d.

PREMISES: Trenance, 22a. 2r. 17p.; LESSEE: William Bonython; RENT: 8s. 4d.

PREMISES: Trenance late Hobbs, 19a. 1r. 3p.; LESSEE: Philip Gilbert; RENT: 8s. 4d.

PREMISES: Trenance late Blakes, 40a. 0r. 22p.; LESSEE: Philip Gilbert; RENT: 18s.

PREMISES: Trenance late Nicholls and Smiths, 39a. 1r. 39p.; LESSEE: Philip Gilbert; RENT: 16s. 8d.

ST ERVAN PARISH

PREMISES: Penrose 'in St Evell' (sic) [Penrose SW 876708], 2r. 1p.; LESSEE: Robert Hawke; RENT: 1s.

ST MERRYN PARISH

PREMISES: Tregannon 'in St Merryn', 21a. 2r. 7p.; LESSEE: John Bennet; RENT: £1

NEWLYN EAST PARISH

PREMISES: Trerise Mill, 6a. 1r. 35p.; LESSEE: John Varco; RENT: £2

PREMISES: a little orchard near Castle Mill, 2r. 23p.; LESSEE: John Benny now Samuel Symons; RENT: 1s

[Williams Moor 'lost many years' – entry crossed through]

PREMISES: Knights Moor, 5a. 2r. 28p.; LESSEE: Samuel Symons; RENT: 1s

Cornwall

MANOR OF TRESILLIAN

[Tresillion House SW 855584 in Parish of Newlyn East]

ST ENODER PARISH

PREMISES: Retyn [Retyn Farm SW 885587], 132a. 1r. 1p.; LESSEE: Ann Williams; RENT: £3

PREMISES: Retyn, 29a. 2r. 4p.; LESSEE: Richard Jenkin; RENT: 10s.

NEWLYN EAST PARISH

PREMISES: Trevighan [possibly Trevean SW 862588], 74a. 1r. 33p.; LESSEE: Samuel Symons; RENT: £3. 8s.

PREMISES: Carbus, 56a. 0r. 6p; LESSEE: Daniel Cook (alias Cock); RENT: £2

ST COLUMB MINOR PARISH

PREMISES: Manuells [Manuels SW 830600], 67a. 1r. 34p.; LESSEE: John Cardell; RENT: £2. 13s. 4d.

ST COLUMB MAJOR PARISH

PREMISES: Trencreek [SW 828608], 53a. 2r. 13p.; LESSEE: Silas Edward Martyn; RENT: £1. 15s. 4d.

PREMISES: Bonithons Trencreek, 8a. 2r. 36p.; LESSEE: John Bonython; RENT: 6s. 8d.

PREMISES: Trencreek, 7a. 1r. 7p.; LESSEE: William James; RENT: 6s. 8d.

ST COLUMB MINOR PARISH

PREMISES: Trethiggey [SW 846596], 22a. 3r. 4p.; LESSEE: John Cardell; RENT: 9s.

PREMISES: Hodges Tenement, 12a. 1r. 13p.; LESSEE: Rev. John Bennett; RENT: 10s.

PREMISES: Trethiggey, 27a. 2r. 10p.; LESSEE: John Cardell; RENT: 9s.

NEWLYN EAST PARISH

PREMISES: Tregonning [SW 866586], ['Great' added in a later hand], 278a. 0r. 24p; LESSEE: Rev. John Bennett; RENT: £4. 10s.

PREMISES: Tregonning, 9a. 1r. 9p.; LESSEE: Rev. John Bennett; RENT: £1

PREMISES: Tregonning, 17a. 1r. 9p.; LESSEE: John Oxnam; RENT: 10s.

PREMISES: Trewerry Field, 35a. 3r. 2p.; LESSEE: Zacheus Prater; RENT: £2

PREMISES: Trewerry Mill [SW 838581], 3a. 2r. 37p.; LESSEE: William James; RENT: £2

PREMISES: Pool Tenement or Trewerry Field and Moor, 4a. 1r. 35p.; LESSEE: John Oxnam; RENT: 15s. 10d.

PREMISES: Trewerry Moor [acreage not given]; LESSEE: Edward Church; RENT: 5s. 8d.

Cornwall

MANOR OF CRAGANTALLAN

NEWLYN EAST PARISH

PREMISES: Benney alias Trenance Wallas [Benney SW 840574], 23a. 3r. 24p.; LESSEE: Zacheus Prater; RENT: £1

PREMISES: Benney alias Trenance Wallas and mills, 34a. 2r. 23p.; LESSEE: Zacheus Prater; RENT: £2.

PREMISES: Trenance Martha [Trenance SW 815610], 50a. 2r. 5p.; LESSEE: Simon Lawer; RENT: £1. 6s. 8d.

PREMISES: Higher Trenance Treglidrick, 26a. 3r. 11p.; LESSEE: Simon Lawer; RENT: 13s. 4d.

CUBERT PARISH

PREMISES: Melingey [?Molingey SW 009502], 24a. 0r. 29p.; LESSEE: Samuel Symons; RENT: £1. 6s. 8d.

NEWLYN EAST PARISH

PREMISES: Trenance late Hedges, 50a. 0r. 3p.; LESSEE: Simon Lawer; RENT: £1. 12s.

ST COLUMB MINOR PARISH

PREMISES: Legonna [SW 833594], 38a. 0r. 6p.; LESSEE: Samuel Symons; RENT: £2. 6s. 8d.

PREMISES: Guills [SW 831592], 5a. 0r. 4p.; LESSEE: Grace Libbey; RENT: £1.

PREMISES: Trevilly late Turnivince [Trevilley SW 833598], 10a. 0r. 17p.; LESSEE: William Martyn; RENT:10s.

PREMISES: Trevilly Close, 4a. 1r. 3p.; LESSEE: Thomas Nicholls; RENT: 6s.

PREMISES: Trevilly late Sleemans and late Mays, 6a. 2r. 32p.; LESSEE: Joseph Row; RENT: 10s. 8d.

PREMISES: Trevilly late Sleeps, 22a. 2r. 21p.; LESSEE: William Salmon; RENT: £1. 6s. 8d.

NEWLYN EAST PARISH

PREMISES: Trevilson [SW 847557], 24a. 2r. 6p.; LESSEE: John Oxnam; RENT: 10s.

Cornwall

MANOR OF DEGEMBRIS

NEWLYN EAST PARISH

PREMISES: Degembris [SW 852568], 49a. 0r. 2p.; LESSEE: John Oxnam; RENT: £2. 10s.

PREMISES: Degembris Minor, 50a. 2r. 37p.; LESSEE: John Oxnam; RENT: £2. 10s.

PREMISES: Degembris Major, 133a. 1r. 8p.; LESSEE: William Roberts; RENT: £5.

PREMISES: Pallamounter [SW 850564], 130a. 1r. 6p.; LESSEE: Willliam Roberts; RENT: £2.

PREMISES: Nansmeer late Thomsons [Nansmear SW 856558], 47a. 0r. 21p; LESSEE: John Trevenon; RENT: £1. 6s. 8d.

PREMISES: Church Field and Wallence Trevel, Church Field and Wallence, 52a. 1r. 30p.; LESSEE: Zaccheus Prater; RENT: £2. 10s. 10d.

PREMISES: Delbridges Tenement in Trendean [SW 833573] 19a. 0r. 11p.; LESSEE: Agnes Prater; RENT: 13s. 4d.

ST COLUMB MAJOR PARISH

PREMISES: Vincents Tenement in Trevole [Trevole SW 836580], 23a. 2r. 22p.; LESSEE: John Row; RENT: £1. 6s. 8d.

PREMISES: Slade Tenement in Trevole, 4a. 1r. 15p.; LESSEE: Robert Varco; RENT: 4s.

NEWLYN EAST PARISH

PREMISES: Trevole, 36a. 2r. 32p.; LESSEE: Mr [Samuel] Symons; RENT: £1. 12s.

CUBERT PARISH

PREMISES: Colgreeze and Santer, 59a. 0r. 33p.; LESSEE: John Christian; RENT: £2. 6s.

ST COLUMB MAJOR PARISH

PREMISES: Trevol Field and Shop, or Wattys Tenement, acreage not given; LESSEE: John Row; RENT: 5s.

NEWLYN EAST PARISH

PREMISES: Nancemear, 47a. 0r. 21p.; LESSEE: John Treve[n]on esq.; RENT: £2.

PREMISES: Nancemear, 15a. 2r. 11p.; LESSEE: William Parks; RENT: £1. 6s.

ST COLUMB MAJOR PARISH

PREMISES: Trevole, acreage not given; LESSEE: Samuel May; RENT: 5s.

NEWLYN EAST PARISH

PREMISES: Tenhale alias Hailmern, 6a. 3r. 34p.; LESSEE: William Mitchell; RENT: 10s.

ST COLUMB MAJOR PARISH

PREMISES: Trevole, acreage not given; LESSEE: Andrew Dennis; RENT: 6s.

PREMISES: Trevole, acreage not given; LESSEE: Daniel Cornish; RENT: 4s. 6d.

PREMISES: Trevole, acreage not given; LESSEE: Andrew Dennis; RENT: 2s.

PREMISES: Trevole, acreage not given; LESSEE: John Merrifield; RENT: 10s.

PREMISES: Trevole House and garden, acreage not given; LESSEE: John Row; RENT: 6s. 8d.

PREMISES: Trevole Field, acreage not given; LESSEE: John Row; RENT: 10s.

PREMISES: cottage and garden at Trendrean [Trendrean SW 833573], acreage not given; LESSEE: Agnes Prater; RENT: 2s.

Cornwall

MANOR OF GOVILEY

No acreages given for properties in this manor

CUBY PARISH

PREMISES: Goviley Major [SW 945440]; LESSEE: Mr [Robert] Gummoe; RENT: £1. 13s. 4d.

PREMISES: Goviley Minor; LESSEE: Mr [Robert] Gummoe; RENT: £1. 2s. 4d.

PREMISES: Goviley Lower; LESSEE: Lieut. Plunket; RENT: £1.

PREMISES: Pencoose [SW 943446]; LESSEE: Mr Carlyon; RENT: £2.

LADOCK PARISH

PREMISES: Respaworth [?Resparveth in Ladock at SX 908500]; LESSEE: Mr Carlyon; RENT: £1. 6s. 8d

CUBY PARISH

PREMISES: Polglaze [SW 964498]; LESSEE: Mr Gummoe; RENT: £1. 6s. 8d

CUBY PARISH

PREMISES: Treluckey Mill [Treluckey SW 948431]; LESSEE: Peter Roberts; RENT: 13s. 4d.

PREMISES: Treluckey Major; LESSEE: Mr Gummoe; RENT: £2. 3s. 4d.

PREMISES: Treluckey Minor; LESSEE: Mrs Hearle; RENT: 16s. 8d.

PREMISES: Rose Vallin [Rosevallon SW 940437]; LESSEE: William Pearce; RENT: 11s.

VERYAN PARISH

PREMISES: Camels Major [Camels SW 928393]; LESSEE: Reverend Jeremiah Trist; RENT: £1. 6s. 8d.

PREMISES: Camels Minor; LESSEE: Reverend Jeremiah Trist; RENT: 13s. 4d

GERRANS PARISH

PREMISES: Crugurrel Field alias Way Close [Cargurrel SW 884375]; LESSEE: John Martyn; RENT: 4s. 8d.

ST COLUMB MAJOR

PREMISES: Trencreek the Higher alias Wallas [Trencreek SW 828608]; LESSEE: Reverend Richard Hannah; RENT: £1. 13s. 4d.

PREMISES: Trencreek the Lower alias Wallas; LESSEE: John Collier; RENT: £2. 6s. 8d.

VERYAN PARISH

PREMISES: Crugsillack [Crugsillick SW 903394]; LESSEE: John Kempe esq.; RENT: £5. 6s. 8d

GERRANS PARISH

PREMISES: Crugurrel; LESSEE: John Martyn; RENT: 8s.

VERYAN PARISH

PREMISES: Camels Cellar; LESSEE: John Luke esq.; RENT: 10s.

GERRANS PARISH

PREMISES: Parken Crowse in Trelingan [possibly now Park-an-Crows in Treluggan]; LESSEE: Richard Johns; RENT: 4s.

PREMISES: cottage, in hand only a smith's shop and not used; RENT: 6s. 8d.

PREMISES: cottage; LESSEES: Peter Roberts and Amos Weeks, the existing lives; RENT: 1s.

Cornwall

MANOR OF PENSTRASE MOOR

[Penstrace Moor in Kenwyn Parish SW 754459]

Acreages not given for holdings in this manor

KENWYN PARISH

PREMISES: the half of Ventonsith Moor [Ventongimps SW 793502]; LESSEE: Charles Williams (senior life); RENT: 7s. 6d.

PREMISES: the half of Ventonsith Moor; LESSEE: Solomon Williams (senior life); RENT: 10s.

PREMISES: Green Bottom [SW 769451]; LESSEES: Michael Grose and George Hicks; RENT: 6s.

PREMISES: Late Reynolds; LESSEE: James Hicks; RENT: 5s.

PREMISES: Late Harris; LESSEE: James Hicks; RENT: 4s.

PREMISES: House, etc.; LESSEE: Jacob Manuel; RENT: 4s.

PREMISES: Late Jane Gilberts; LESSEE: Thomas Cocking; RENT: 4s.

PREMISES: Late Gilberts; LESSEE: Charles Williams; RENT: £1.

PREMISES: Late Eslicks; LESSEE: Thomas Wilford (senior life); RENT: 4s.

PREMISES: Late Goodmans; LESSEE: Uddy Bray; RENT: 10s.

PREMISES: Stairs Moors; LESSEE: Edward James; RENT: 5s.

PREMISES: Late Edwards'; LESSEE: Thomas Trethouan (senior life); rent; 8s.

PREMISES: Late Honeys: LESSEE: Samuel Vials; RENT: 7s.6d

PREMISES: Cottage and an acre of land; LESSEE: John Williams; RENT: 5s.

PREMISES: Late Samsons; LESSEE: John Wall; RENT: 6s.

PREMISES: [blank]; LESSEE: Samuel Hoare; RENT: 4s. 6d.

PREMISES: Late Hix's; LESSEE: Thomas Whitford; RENT: 5s. 6d.

PREMISES: [blank]; LESSEE: Matthew Manuell; RENT: 9s.

PREMISES: [blank]; LESSEE: William Trerise; RENT: 7s. 6d.

PREMISES: Two cottage tenements; LESSEE: Jane Clima; RENT: 5s.

PREMISES: [blank]; LESSEE: Edward Merryfield; RENT: 7s. 6d.

PREMISES: [blank]; LESSEE: Thomas Tippet; RENT: 5s.

PREMISES: [blank]; LESSEE: Charles Williams; RENT: 5s.

PREMISES: Carbus's; LESSEE: Edward James; RENT: 5s.

PREMISES: [blank]; LESSEE: Ralph and Daniel Mackenne; RENT: 5s.

PREMISES: Part of Green Bottom; lessee; Margaret Rule, senior life; RENT: 6s.

PREMISES: [blank]; LESSEE: Sampson Deeble, senior; RENT: 3s.

PREMISES: Late Stephen Eslicks; LESSEE: William Hoar, senior life; RENT: 5s.

THE BARTON OF GARROWS

[Garras SW 819488]

PREMISES: small house, barn, etc and about 30 acres of uncultivated land; LESSEE: Thomas Powell; RENT: 6s. 8d.

PREMISES: [blank]; LESSEE: Elizabeth Francis; RENT: 6s. 8d.

PREMISES: [blank]; John Francis; RENT: 6s. 8d.

Cornwall

MANOR OF THURLIBEER

LAUNCELLS PARISH

PREMISES: Thurlibeer [SS 252048], 65a. 1r. 35p.; LESSEE: Thomas Row; RENT: £4. 12s.

PREMISES: Lower Shirnick [Shernick SS 274048], 112a. 0r. 23p.; LESSEE: Trustees of William Mill; RENT: £2.

PREMISES: Higher Shirnick; LESSEE: Sir William Pratt Call; RENT: £1.

PREMISES: Suddons, acreage with Higher Shirnick above, 138a. 2r. 18p; LESSEE: Sir William Pratt Call; RENT: £1. 6s. 8d.

PREMISES: Barley Mead Park and Rows Cottage 'see the end of this survey', 44a. 1r. 36p.; LESSEE: Wrey Ians, esq.; RENT: £3.

PREMISES: Saunders Pitton, 36a. 3r. 39p.; LESSEE: Sir William Pratt Call; RENT: 16s. 8d.

PREMISES: Harbour Moor or Heards Pitton, 58a. 3r. 31p.; LESSEE: Sir William Pratt Call; RENT: £1. 3s. 4d.

PREMISES: Pitton, 73a. 1r. 3p.; LESSEE: Sir William Pratt Call; RENT: £1. 3s. 4d.

PREMISES: Scoreham and Woodhouse [Scorsham SS 256053], 63a. 2r. 27p.; LESSEE: Thomas Bunbury; RENT: £1. 13s.

PREMISES: North Harbour [no acreage given]; LESSEE: Wrey Ians, esq.; RENT: £1. 13s. 4d.

PREMISES: Underwood Lower [SS 248056], 12a. 1r. 22p.; LESSEE: Dr John King; RENT: 12s.

PREMISES: Hobbacott alias Burrow [Hobbacott SS 244041], 81a. 1r. 14p.; LESSEE: Ann Bray, widow; RENT: £1. 10s.

PREMISES: Hobbicott Down, 89a.0r..29p.; LESSEE: Ann Bray , widow; RENT: £4. 5s.

PREMISES: Thorn [SS 261046], 94a. 0r. 13p.; LESSEE: Richard Hayman; RENT: £1. 17s. 4d.

PREMISES: Harbour, 37a. 0r. 37p.; LESSEE: Wrey Ians, esq.; RENT: £1. 13s. 4d.

PREMISES: Darts Butsper alias Butterbury [Butsper Close SS 265042], 39a. 0r. 19p.; LESSEE: John May; RENT: 17s. 4d.

PREMISES: Browns Butsper, 26a. 0r. 36p.; LESSEE: Samuel Row; RENT: 17s. 8d.

PREMISES: Norcotts or Barrotts Butsper, 31a. 3r. 7p.; LESSEE: John Ham; RENT: 16s. 4d.

PREMISES: Mabyns Butsper, 25a. 0r. 38p.; LESSEE: John Ham; RENT: 13s. 6d.

PREMISES: Bunbury's Butsper, 16a. 3r. 39p.; LESSEE: Thomas Bunbury; RENT: 11s. 2d.

PREMISES: Higher Underwood, 8a. 1r. 25p.; LESSEE: William Vogwell; RENT: £1.

PREMISES: Cob Thorns, 84a. 1r. 1p.; LESSEE: Nicholas Symons; RENT: £2.

PREMISES: Grove [SS 267036]; LESSEES: Richard Hayman and Thomas Bray, joint tenants; RENT: £1

PREMISES: Grove, 76a. 1r. 7p. for this and the last mentioned premises; LESSEES: Richard Hayman and Thomas Bray, joint tenants; RENT: £1.

PREMISES: Easter Mills's or Easter Windmill Parks, 45a. 1r. 23p.; LESSEE: Thomas Bunbury; RENT: £1. 13s. 4d.

PREMISES: Church Park, 12a. 0r. 32p.; LESSEE: Wrey Ians, esq.; RENT: 16s. 8d.

BRIDGERULE PARISH

PREMISES: Little Bridge or Bridge Rule, 14a. 3r. 26p.; LESSEE: John Wills; RENT: 12s.

LAUNCELLS PARISH

PREMISES: Windmill Parks, 40a. 0r. 12p.; LESSEE: John King, surgeon; RENT: £3. 1s. 8d.

PREMISES: A cottage late Row, 'this is included in the Lease of Barley Mead Parks', 0a. 0r. 27p.; LESSEE: Wrey Ians, esq.; RENT: 5s

PREMISES: A cottage [no acreage given]; LESSEE: Elizabeth Cornish; RENT: [crossed through]

PREMISES: A cottage, 0a. 0r. 0p.; lessee; John Chapman; RENT: 5s [in a later hand]

Cornwall

MANOR OF EBBINGFORD ALIAS EFFORD

STRATTON PARISH

PREMISES: Stratton or late Mary Davisons with Binamy [Stratton Church SS 231065], 9a. 2r. 37p. and 1a. 0r. 40p.; LESSEE: Wrey Ians, esq.; RENT: 18s.

PREMISES: Stratton three closes, 6a. 2r. 20p.; LESSEE: John Bryant; RENT: 9s.

PREMISES: Stratton dwellinghouse and plot, 0a. 2r. 34p.; LESSEE: James Tuke, surgeon; RENT: 8s. 6d.

PREMISES: Dodges Arnolds Fields, 0a. 2r. 24p; LESSEE: Reverend Richard Martyn; RENT: 4s.

PREMISES: Saunders's Brodinghams, 3a. 3r. 35p.; LESSEE: Roger Carwithen; RENT: 10s.

PREMISES: Gennys Lane, 6a. 1r. 7p.; LESSEE: Richard Burden Bray; RENT: 6s. 8d.

PREMISES: Groves, 19a. 1r. 27p.; LESSEE: Richard Symons; RENT: £1. 5s.

JACOBSTOW PARISH

PREMISES: Heale [Hele Barton SX 216978], 54a. 3r. 16p.; LESSEE: John Congdon; RENT: 13s. 6d.

WEST DOWN PARISH

PREMISES: Westdown, 24a. 1r. 3p.; LESSEE: Richard Mullins; RENT: 8s.

POUNDSTOCK PARISH

PREMISES: Penleen Webbs [Penlean SX 202901], 15a. 1r. 20p.; LESSEE: Richard Webb; RENT: 16s.

PREMISES: Penleen Bettisons, 12a. 2r. 8p.; LESSEE: Elias Bettinson; RENT: 10s.

STRATTON PARISH

PREMISES: Jewels Place on the Strand, 3a. 1r. 24p.; LESSEE: William Welsh; RENT: 10s.

PREMISES: Wheat Park at Efford, 15a. 3r. 15p.; LESSEE: Wrey Ians, esq.; RENT: £1. 5s.

PREMISES: Oston Park at Efford, 33a. 0r. 18p.; LESSEE: George Boughton Kingdon, esq.; RENT: £1. 5s.

PREMISES: Efford North Down [SS 202059], 76a. 3r. 8p.; LESSEE: William Welsh; RENT: £1. 5s.

PREMISES: Cleeve, 64a. 3r. 16p.; LESSEE: Richard Burden Bray; RENT: £1. 6s. 8d.

PREMISES: Upton late Hallets; LESSEE: Richard B. Bray; RENT: 9s.

PREMISES: Upton late Hallets Honeys, 12a. 3r. 4p. which includes the last mentioned tenement; LESSEE: Richard B. Bray; RENT: 9s.

1. Acland coat of arms from an estate atlas of 1828
(in private hands, reproduced by kind permission of the owner)

2. Map of the Manor of Killerton & CulmJohn, 1756, described on page 84.
(DRO, 1148M add23/E1, by courtesy of the National Trust and the Acland Family)

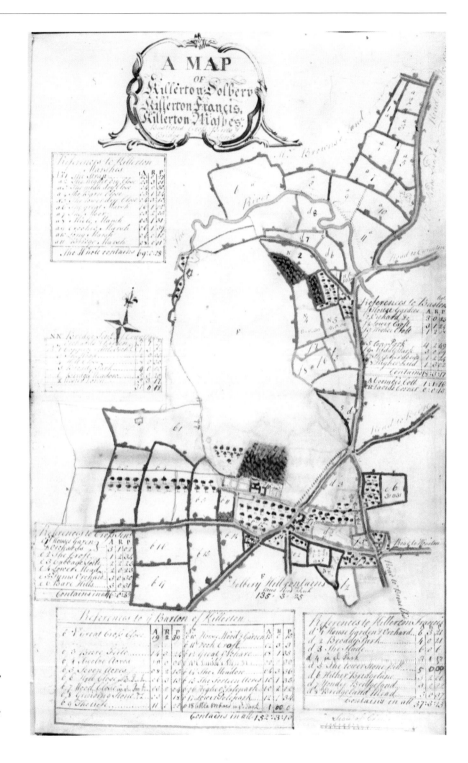

3. Map of Killerton, Dolberry, Killerton Francis, Killerton Ma[r]shes, Bastions, Cross, and Pimms Bridge Tenements, 1756, described on page 84.
(DRO, 1148M add23/E1, by courtesy of the National Trust and the Acland Family)

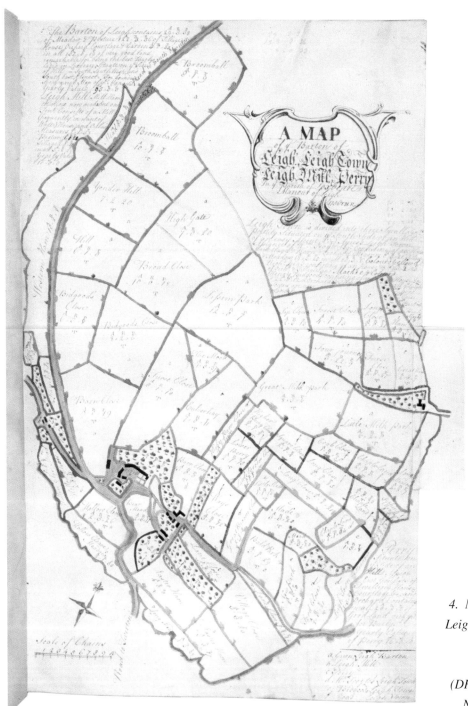

4. Map of the Barton of Leigh, Leigh Town,
Leigh Mill & Perry in the Parish of Loxbeare
& Manor of Leigh 'T H Fecit', 1756,
described on page 84.
(DRO, 1148M add23/E1, by courtesy of the
National Trust and the Acland Family)

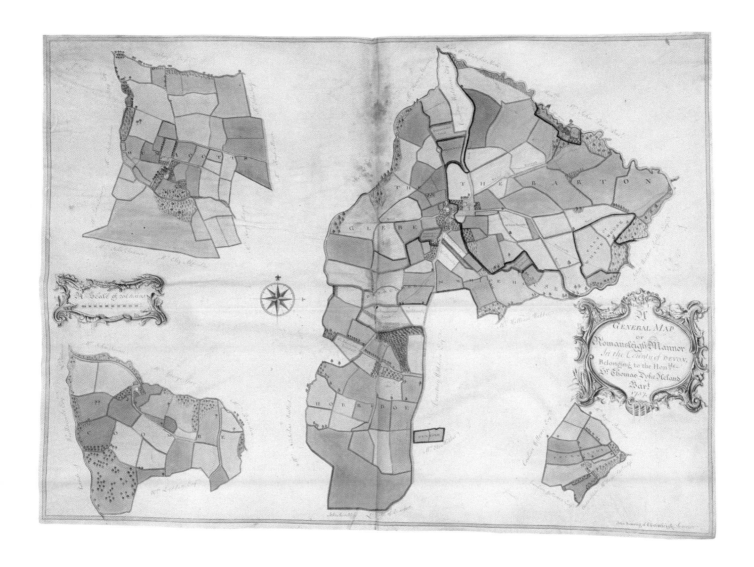

5. *A General Map of Romansleigh Manor in the County of Devon Belonging to the Honble*
Thomas Dyke Acland, Bart, 1757, described on pages 85–6.
(DRO, 1148M add/6/11, by courtesy of the National Trust and the Acland Family)

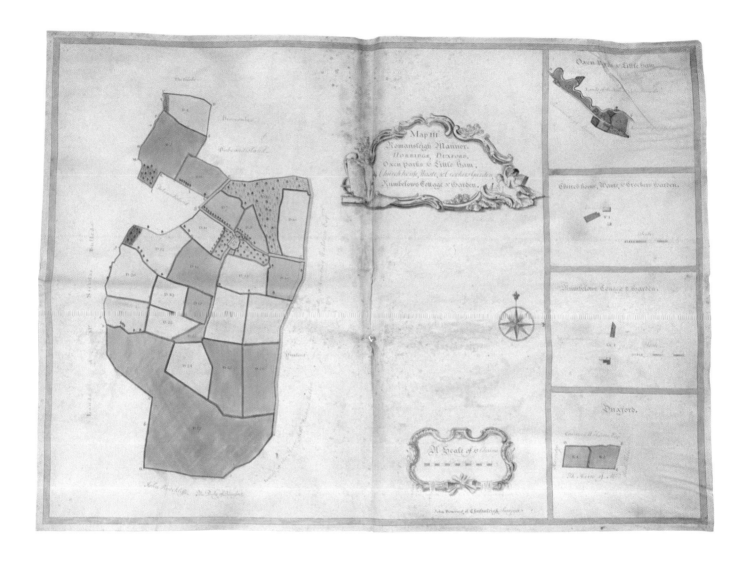

6. *Map of Romansleigh Mannor. Horridge, Duxford, Oxen parks & Littleham, Churchouse, Waste, & Crokers Garden,*
Rumbelows Cottage & Garden, described on page 86.
(DRO, 1148M add/6/11, by courtesy of the National Trust and the Acland Family.

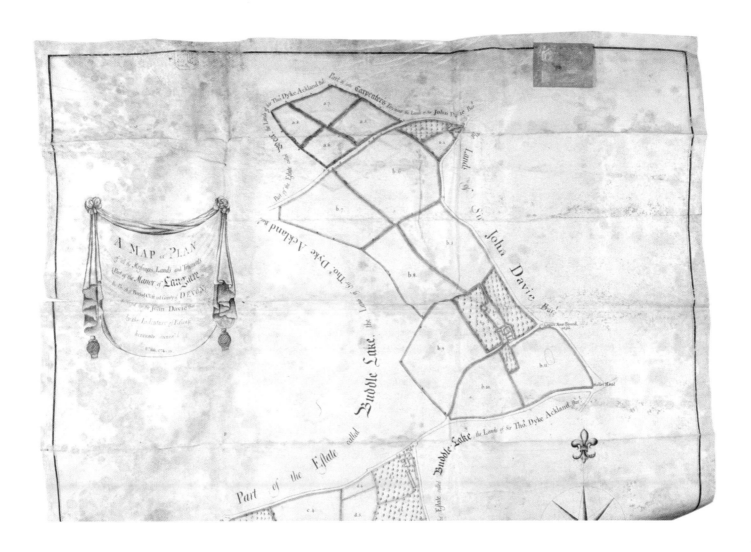

7. A Map or Plan of all the Messuages, Lands and Tenements (part of the Manor of
Langacre in the Parish of Broadclyst), 1774, described on pages 89–90.
(DRO, 1148M add/1/T8/168, by courtesy of the National Trust and the Acland Family)

8. *Map from* A Survey and Valuation of the Long Estate, *1805, described on page 96.*
(SRO, DD/AH/Box 14.5, by courtesy of Lady Gass)

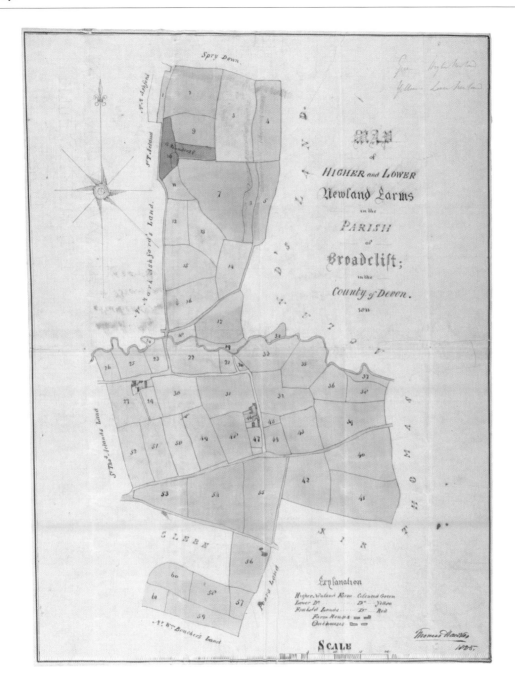

9. *Map of Higher and Lower Newland Farms in the Parish of Broadclyst, [1811–25], described on page 98.*
(SRO, DD/WY/Box 121, by courtesy of the Wyndham Estates)

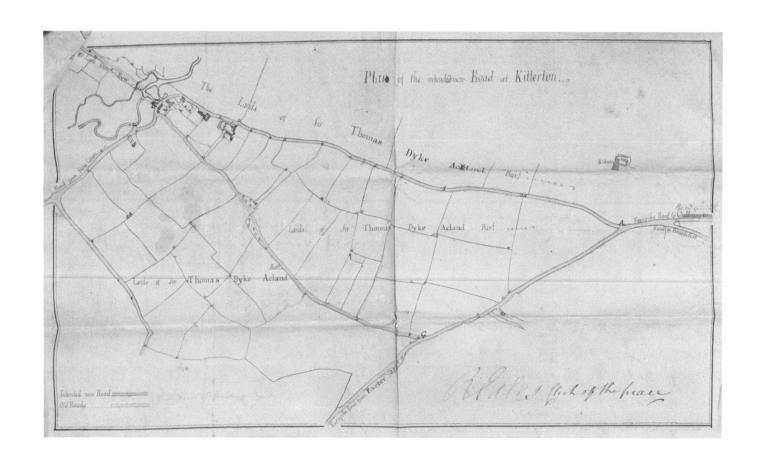

10. *Plan of the intended new road at Killerton, 1812, described on pages 98–9.*
(DRO, DQS 113A/34/1, by courtesy of Devon County Council)

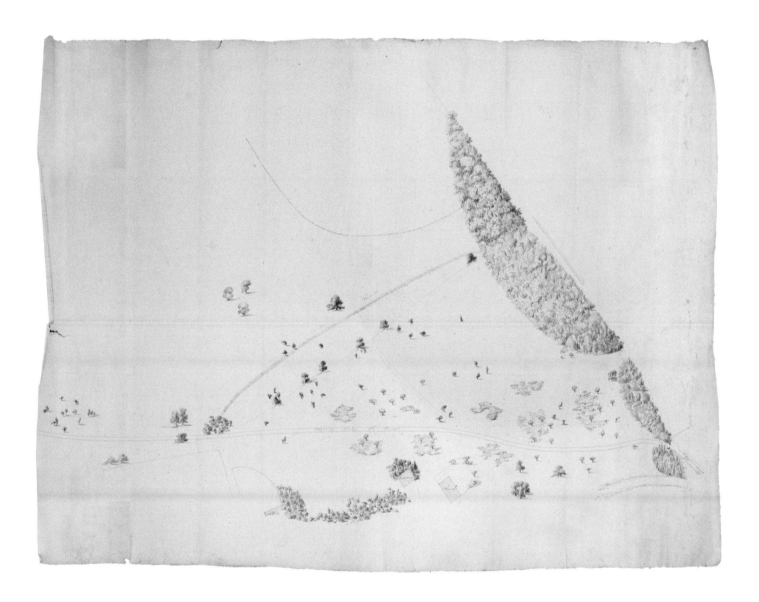

11. Early nineteenth-century plan of Killerton Park, (part), described on pages 100–1.
(DRO, 1148M add/10/5/15, by courtesy of the National Trust and the Acland Family)

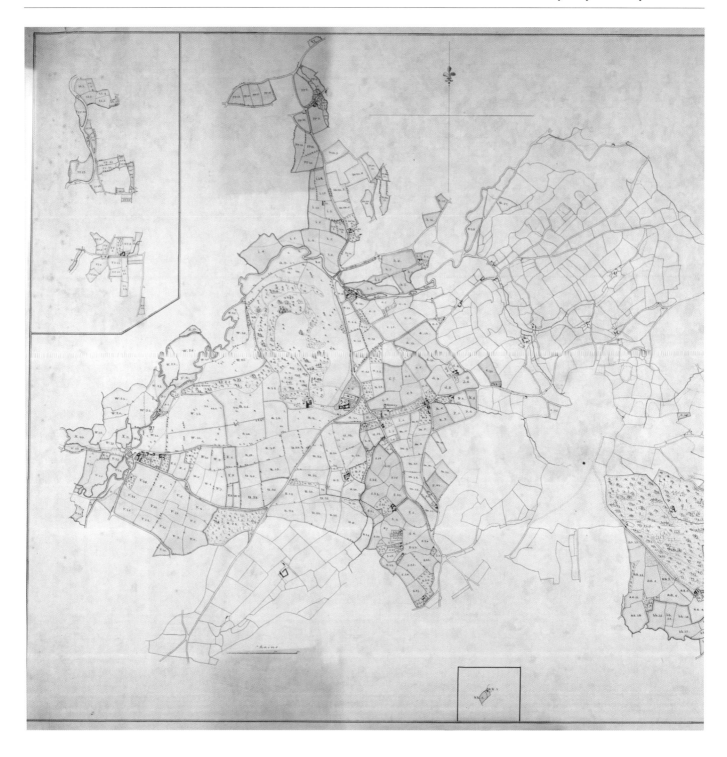

*12–13. Map of the Manors of Killerton and Aishclyst, early
nineteenth-century, described on page 99.
(SRO, DD/SAS c1540/12/1, by courtesy of Somerset Record Office)*

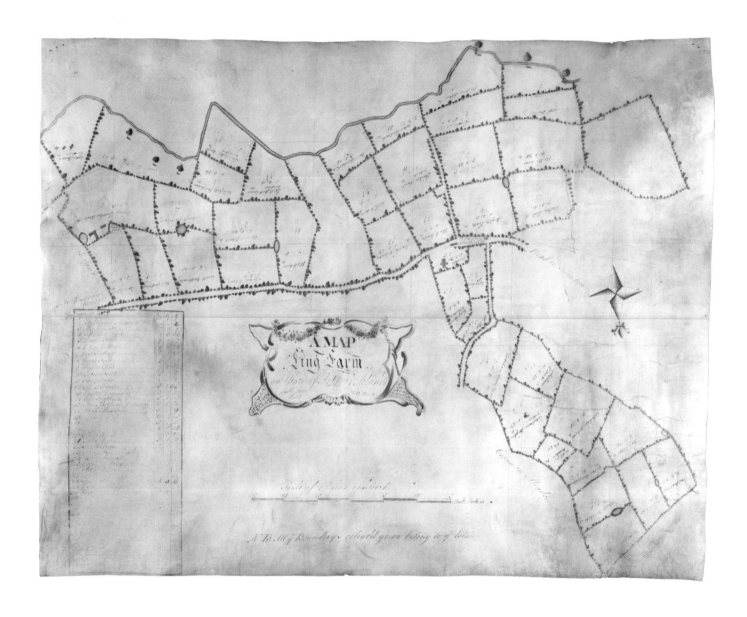

14. *A Map of Lyng Farm and Estate of Arthur Acland Esq.,' T.H. Fecit', c.1760, described on pages 104–5.*
(SRO, DD/AH 65/13c/2252, by courtesy of Lady Gass)

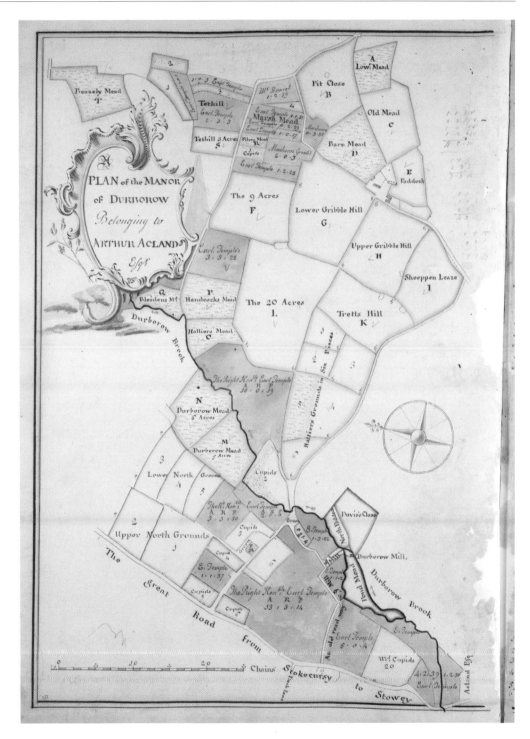

15. Map from an atlas entitled *A Plan of the Manor of Fairfield, the Seat of Arthur Acland Esq.ʳ, 1767,* described on page 106. (SRO, DD/AH/66/11, by courtesy of Lady Gass)

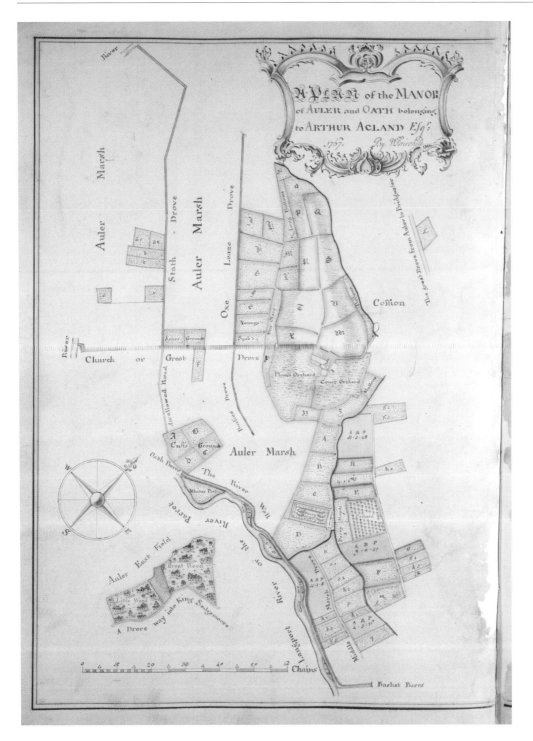

16. Map from an atlas entitled
A Plan of the Manor of
Fairfield, the Seat of Arthur
Acland Esqr, 1767, described
on page 106.
(SRO, DD/AH/66/11, by
courtesy of Lady Gass)

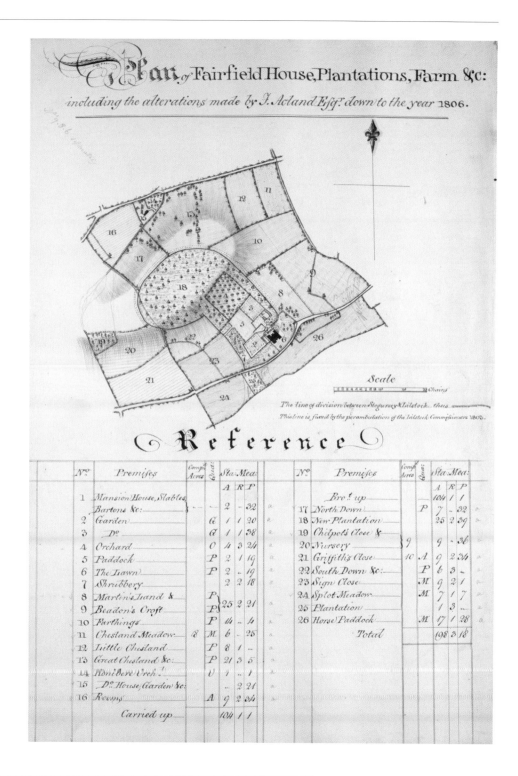

17. Plan of Fairfield House, Plantations, Farm &c from an Atlas entitled A Survey of the Manors of Fairfield and Durborow, 1795–1806, described on pages 107–8. (SRO, DD/AH/65/12, by courtesy of Lady Gass)

*18. Map of Petherton Park and Manor and Tithes of Newton=Roth & Regis
showing North Petherton only, 1809, described on page 109.
(DRO, 1148M add/10/23a, by courtesy of the National Trust and the Acland Family)*

*19. (opposite) Part of the Manor of Holnicote, general map, 1809–12, described on pages 110–11.
(DRO, 1148M add9/6/24, by courtesy of the National Trust and the Acland Family)*

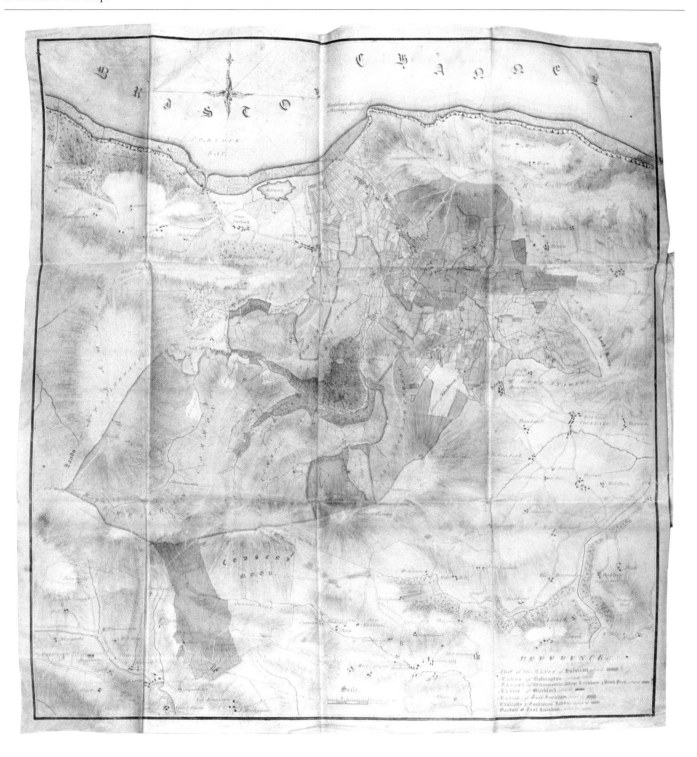

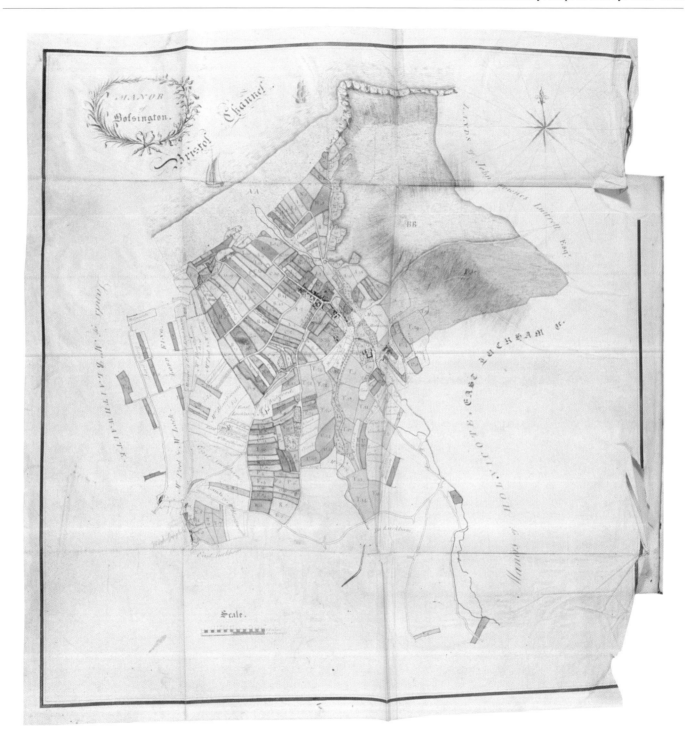

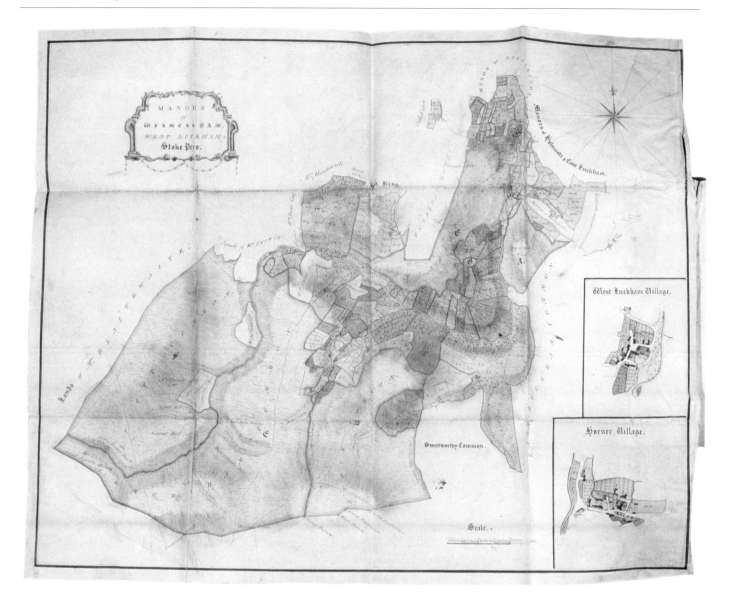

21. *Map of the Manors of Wilmersham West Luckham & Stock Pero, 1809–12, described on pages 111–12.*
(DRO, 1148M add9/6/24, by courtesy of the National Trust and the Acland Family)

20. *(opposite) Map of the Manor of Bossington, 1809–12, described on pages 111–12.*
(DRO, 1148M add9/6/24, by courtesy of the National Trust and the Acland Family)

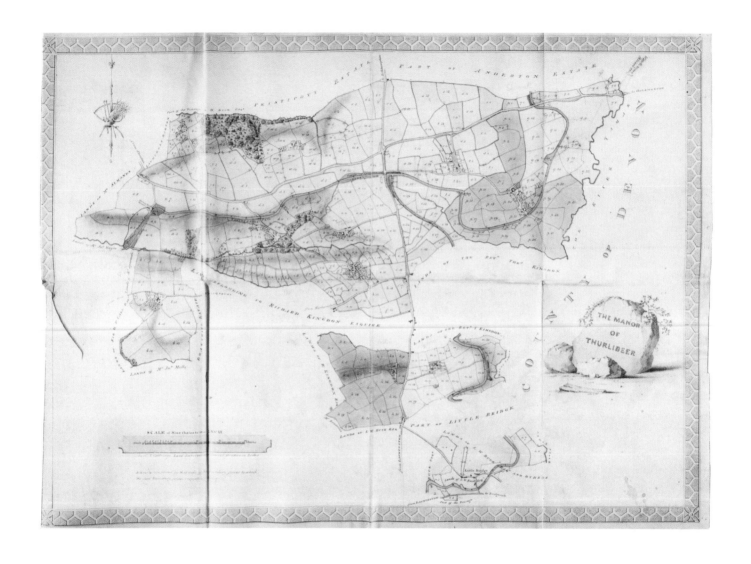

22. *Map of the Manor of Thurlibeer, 1828, described on page 119.*
(in private hands, reproduced by courtesy of the owner)

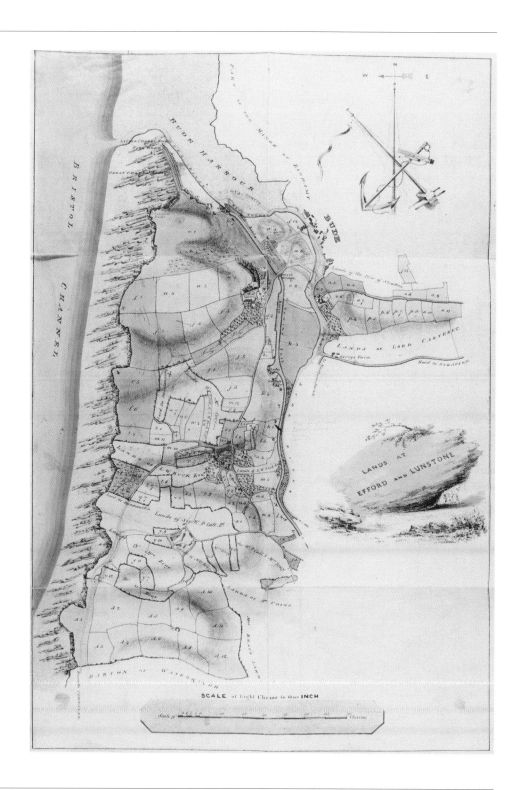

23. Map of Lands at Efford and Lunstone, 1828, described on page 119. (in private hands, reproduced by courtesy of the owner)

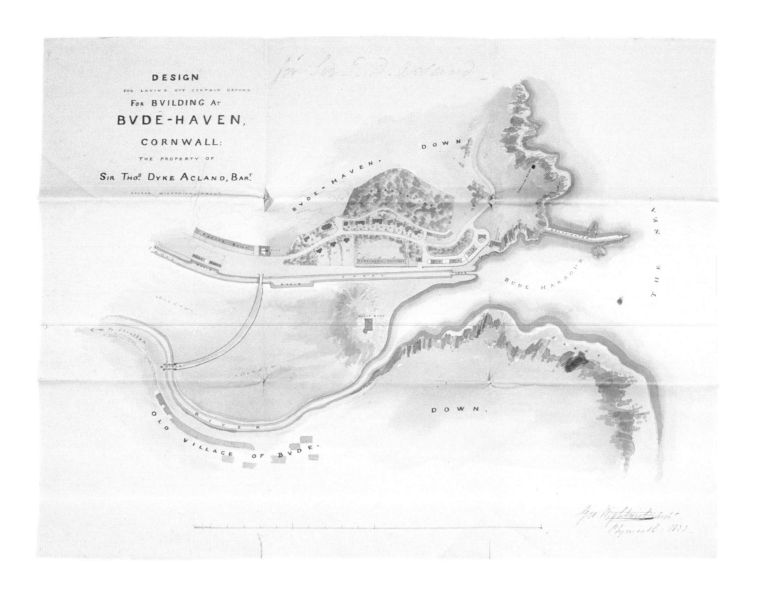

24. Design for laying out certain ground for Building at Bude-Haven, Cornwall, 1833, described on pages 121–22. (DRO, 1148M/Box 20/7, by courtesy of the National Trust and the Acland Family)

PREMISES: Moors Plot, 3a. 2r. 23p.; LESSEE: John Williams; RENT: 6s.

PREMISES: Lunestone [Lynstone SS 206052], [acreage not given]; LESSEE: Reverend Robert Martyn; RENT: 13s.

PREMISES: Lunestone late Phelps's, [acreage not given]; LESSEE: John Balhatchet; RENT: 13s.

Premises; Lunestone late Marshals, 13a. 2r. 19p.; LESSEE: Reverend Robert Martyn; RENT: 13s. 4d.

PREMISES: Lunestone late Richard Wallis's, 13a. 3r. 17p.; LESSEE: Reverend Robert Martyn; RENT: £1. 5s.

PREMISES: Efford House [Efford SS 205057], 58a. 0r. 14p.; LESSEE: William Welsh; RENT: £1. 5s.

PREMISES: Lunestone late Congdons, 3a. 3r. 21p.; LESSEE: Reverend Robert Martyn; RENT: 4s.

('with Saunders's Down included', 7a. 1r. 7p.; LESSEE: as above; RENT: 3s.)

PREMISES: Cooks Lunestone late Burdens, 14a. 2r. 31p.; LESSEE: Reverend Mr Martyn; RENT: 18s. 4d.

PREMISES: Bridge Park and Rodds Garden, 2a. 2r. 0p.; LESSEE: Wrey Ians, esq.; RENT: 4s.

PREMISES: Lunestone late Couths, 7a. 2r. 8p.; LESSEE: William Brown; RENT: 8s. 8d.

PREMISES: Efford Lower Cellar, [acreage not given]; RENT: 6s.

PREMISES: Efford Cellar, Mill and Blacksmith Shop, [acreage not given]; LESSEE: W. Ians, esq.; RENT: 2s. 6d.

PREMISES: Strand late Calls, 10a. 2r. 11p.; LESSEE: Mary Couch, senior life; RENT: £1.

PREMISES: Strand late Mills, 15a. 0r. 33p.; LESSEE: William Couch; RENT: 11s.

PREMISES: Bowden late Brown's, 0a. 3r. 34p.; LESSEE: William Horsewell; RENT: 2s.

PREMISES: Bowden late Cooks or Lobbs, 0a. 0r. 16p.; LESSEE: William Horsewell; RENT: 1s. 8d.

PREMISES: Trimbles or Bowden in Small Ridge Lane, 1a. 1r. 34p.; LESSEE: Reverend R. Martyn; RENT: 1s. 4d.

PREMISES: Bowdon late Calls, 3a. 3r. 26p.; LESSEE: Susanna Saunders; RENT: 4s.

PREMISES: Bowden late Miltons, 0a. 1r. 37p.; LESSEE: John Rowland; RENT: 6s.

PREMISES: Bowden late Williams's Copledicks, 0a. 0r. 34p.; LESSEE: Reverend R[ichar]d Martyn; RENT: 6s.

PREMISES: Bowden late Baileys, 7a. 2r. 37p.; LESSEE: Richard Burden Bray; RENT: 9s.

PREMISES: Tower Hill, 15a. 1r. 7p.; LESSEE: John and Walter Spry; RENT: 2s.

PREMISES: Bowden late Hutchins, 0a. 0r. 19p.; LESSEE: Richard Woodley; RENT: 1s.

PREMISES: Bowden late Trelevans, 1a. 2r. 15p.; LESSEE: James Heddon; RENT: 1s. 6d.

PREMISES: Bowden, [acreage not given]; LESSEE: Thomas King; RENT: 2s.

PREMISES: Cross Park, 1a. 1r. 33p.; LESSEE: Richard Heale; RENT: 4s.

PREMISES: Stratton Baytree late Warmingtons, 0a. 0r. 25p.; LESSEE: Reverend Richard Martyn; RENT: 13s. 4d.

PREMISES: Stratton Baytree late Calls, [acreage not given]; LESSEE: James Heydon; RENT: 14s. 2d.

PREMISES: Pound Field, 2a. 0r. 14p.; LESSEE: Joseph Honey; RENT: 10s.

PREMISES: Stratton Down, 1a. 1r. 35p.; LESSEE: Richard Heale; RENT: 1s. 6d.

PREMISES: Great Close alias Benamey and a field at Morris's Lane late Luggons, 4a. 3r. 30p.; LESSEE: Joseph Honey; RENT: 6s.

PREMISES: Strattons late Heddens, [acreage not given]; LESSEE: Thomas Ching; RENT: 2s.

PREMISES: Strattons late Woods, 8a .0r. 19p.; LESSEE: Elizabeth Woodley, widow; RENT: 14s. 4d.

PREMISES: Stratton Broda Parks, 2a. 2r. 19p.; LESSEE: James Tuke, surgeon; RENT: 5s.

PREMISES: Stratton late Bonds, 7a. 3r. 34p.; LESSEE: Richard Fanson; RENT: 13s. 4d.

PREMISES: Efford Cellar paid for by Mrs Welsh; RENT: 2s. 'NB This is on the Rolls but no Survey & not to be found'

Somerset

MANOR OF EAST LUCKHAM

Acreages of tenements not given for this manor

LUCCOMBE PARISH

PREMISES: Doverhay [SS 890465]; LESSEE: John Kent; RENT: £1. 2s. 6d.

PREMISES: Late Phelps's; LESSEE: Philip Taylor; RENT: 9s. 8d.

PREMISES: Hosgoods Tenement; LESSEE: Philip Taylor; RENT: 12s. 8d

PREMISES: Duderidges in Doverhay; LESSEE: William Oland; RENT: 13s. 4d.

PREMISES: Late Snows; LESSEE: John Kent; RENT: 18s. 8d.

PREMISES: Late Slowleys; LESSEE: John Kent; RENT: 11s. 8d.

PREMISES: Late Stoates; LESSEE: William Elsworthy; RENT: 9s. 4d.

PREMISES: Late Staddons; LESSEE: William Stoate; RENT: 10s. 4d

PREMISES: Part of late Stratons in Newbridge; LESSEE: John Beague; RENT: £1. 4s.

PREMISES: Late Hensleys called the Hanger Cleeve, the Parslers and the Harridge; LESSEE: William Baker, miller; RENT: 3s. 6d.

PREMISES: Coo Grass; LESSEE: William Baker; RENT: 3s. 4d

PREMISES: Brandy Street; LESSEE: William Stote of Brandy Street; RENT: 18s. 8d.

PREMISES: Part of late Staddens; LESSEE: William Stote of Brandy Street; RENT: 10s. 2d.

PREMISES: Piles Mill at Allerford [mill SS 911462; Allerford SS 905470]; LESSEE: Giles Randall; RENT: £2. 6s. 2d.

PREMISES: Rudgeway Fleet; LESSEE: John Gale; RENT: 3s. 8d.

PREMISES: House by Allerford Bridge; LESSEE: John Kent; RENT: 3s. 8d.

PREMISES: Late Piles's; LESSEE: Philip Taylor; RENT: 15s.

PREMISES: Late Phelps's formerly Piles; LESSEE: Philip Taylor; RENT: 7s. 1d.

PREMISES: Late David Kents; LESSEE: Philip Taylor; RENT: 7s. 1d

PREMISES: Late Andrew Kents; LESSEE: Robert Griffith; RENT: 12s. 5d.

PREMISES: Late White with Linch Field and orchard; LESSEE: Philip Taylor; RENT: 12s. 5d.

PREMISES: Late Eastcotts; LESSEE: John Giles; RENT: 17s. 11d.

PREMISES: Late Horns; LESSEE: Reverend Samuel Willis; RENT: 16s. 9d.

PREMISES: Late Bryants; LESSEE: Philip Taylor; RENT: 12s. 6d.

PREMISES: Higher and Lower Coo Cross late Henslays; LESSEE: Philip Taylor; RENT: 9s. 6d.

PREMISES: Zeals; LESSEE: John Snow; RENT: 11s. 6d.

PREMISES: Higher and Lower Cockerhills, Cross acre and Little Fields; LESSEE: John Snow; RENT: 5s. 4d.

PREMISES: Higher Linch [Lynch SS 903476; East Lynch SS 927462]; LESSEE: Sir Thomas Ackland; RENT: 5s.

PREMISES: Late Wythycombe; LESSEE: William Ellis, senior; RENT: 8s.

PREMISES: Late Hix's; LESSEE: James Darch; RENT: 7s. 4d

PREMISES: Churchhouse Croft; LESSEE: John Bustin; RENT: 2s

PREMISES: Late Chaplains; LESSEE: William Maddock; RENT: 1s.

PREMISES: Late Perkins's; LESSEE: Christopher Chapman; RENT: 2s.

PREMISES: a cottage; LESSEE: Henry Phelps; RENT: 3s.

PREMISES: a house and gardens; LESSEE: William Way; RENT: 3s.

PREMISES: Late Chibbets; LESSEE: John Tucker; RENT: 2s.

PREMISES: Knights Mappleridge; LESSEE: Walter Coffin; RENT: 8s. 2d.

PREMISES: Hensleys Mappleridge; LESSEE: Walter Coffin; RENT: 7s. 3d.

PREMISES: Menners; LESSEE: Philip Taylor; RENT: 9s. 2d.

PREMISES: Hill Gate; LESSEE: John Eames; RENT: 3s.

PREMISES: Stoates Mappleridge; LESSEE: William Stoate; RENT: 5s. 6d.

PREMISES: Greenslades Mappleridge; LESSEE: John Bustin; RENT: 4s. 7½d

PREMISES: Dunkrey Close; LESSEE: Rachel Fish; RENT: 5s.

PREMISES: a plot of ground at Dunckrey called Long Close; LESSEE: Christopher Chapman; RENT: 6d.

PREMISES: Three acres at Dunkrey [Dunkery Beacon SS 892416]; LESSEE: Christopher Chapman; RENT: 8d.

PREMISES: Two acres of ground at Dunkrey near Hill Gate

[Dunkery Gate SS 896406]; LESSEE: Sarah Steer; RENT: 2s.

PREMISES: Green Hill or Chapple Hill; LESSEE: Reverend Robert Gould; RENT: 2s. 6d.

PREMISES: a plot of ground of two acres at Allerford Coomb; LESSEE: John Court; RENT: 1s.

PREMISES: a plot of ground called the New Barton containing six acres in Allerford Coomb; LESSEE: John Court; RENT: [blank]

PREMISES: half an acre under Luckham Coppice; LESSEE: Nicholas Snow; rent; 1s.

BARTON OF EAST LUCKHAM

PREMISES: Bryants Moor; LESSEE: William Stoate of Brandy Street; RENT: 13s. 6d

PREMISES: Three Acres; LESSEE: Francis Greenslade; RENT: 1s. 6d.

PREMISES: Cheese Lands alias West Field and Pit Close: LESSEE: John Ellis; RENT: 18s. 6d.

PREMISES: Higher Holt Ball [Holt Ball SS 918440]; LESSEE: William Gregory; RENT: 3s.

PREMISES: Gillhams Close; LESSEE: Abraham Clark; RENT: 4s.

PREMISES: Holthay; LESSEE: Abraham Clark; RENT: 4s.

PREMISES: Woods Plott Meadow, Rook Moor and vernage; LESSEE: Abraham Clark; RENT: 1s.

PREMISES: Rixham; LESSEE: John Beague; RENT: 12s.

PREMISES: Higher Clay Hill; LESSEE: William Way; RENT: 8s.

PREMISES: Pilchers and Langer; LESSEE: Mr John Snow; RENT: 1s. 6d.

PREMISES: Little Knowle; LESSEE: Thomas Hole; RENT: 5s.

PREMISES: The Pound Orchard; LESSEE: William Ellis senior; RENT: 1s.

PREMISES: Lower Cleyhill; LESSEE: Reverend Robert Gould; RENT: 4s.

PREMISES: Oakhams Croft, Guilliams Cleeve, Punck Crof[t] and Little Garden; LESSEE: Robert Birth; RENT: 9s.

PREMISES: New Park and Little Plot adjoining the Herring House; LESSEE: William Ellis senior; RENT: £4. 4s.

Premises; Whitemans Moor; LESSEE: Abraham Clarke; RENT: £1

PREMISES: Stonehay; LESSEE: Sarah Ellis; RENT: 13s.

PREMISES: Oakham Meadow; LESSEE: John Ellis; RENT: 17s.

PREMISES: West Knowle; LESSEE: Ann Ellis; RENT: 8s.

PREMISES: East Field; LESSEE: Abraham Clarke; RENT: 16s. 4d.

EASTCOTTS AND GOODWINS LANDS

PREMISES: A house and garden at Allerford [SS 905470]; LESSEE: Mary Gendle; RENT: 2s.

PREMISES: Lee House at Allerford; LESSEE: Francis Greenslade; RENT: 5s.

PREMISES: the moiety of Doverhay Down; LESSEE: Thomas Rawle; RENT: 13s. 4d.

PREMISES: The Hams; LESSEE: Thomas Rawle; RENT: 7s. 4d.

PREMISES: The Eastern Croft; LESSEE: William Stote; RENT: 2s.

PREMISES: a smith shop at Allerford; LESSEE: Robert Sully; RENT: 1s.

Devon

MANOR OF STOCKLEY LUCKHAM

CHERITON FITZPAINE PARISH

PREMISES: East Upham [Upham SS 884083]; LESSEE: John Parkhouse; rent; 9s. 8d.

PREMISES: Cotton and Stockley Meadow [Cottons SS 887080]; LESSEE: Augusta Kaye, 60 years, the senior life; RENT: 17s. 8d.

PREMISES: Lower Water House; LESSEE: William Sharland; RENT: 12s.

PREMISES: Lower Harsh; LESSEE: John Stone; RENT: 11s. 8d.

PREMISES: Higher Harsh; LESSEE: Samuel Wotton; RENT: 6s. 8d.

PREMISES: Redyates [SS 878073]; LESSEE: William Badcock junior; RENT: 16s.

PREMISES: Upper and Lower Herne [Hayne SS 887073]; LESSEE: Henry Stone; RENT: 11s. 4d.

PREMISES: Peach Hayne; LESSEE: Augusta Kaye; RENT: £1. 6s. 8d.

PREMISES: Marshay [Marshay Farm SS 884095]; LESSEE: John Melhewesh; RENT: 1s.

PREMISES: Marshay Cottage; LESSEE: John Melhewesh; RENT: 1s.

PREMISES: West Farley [SS 901073]; LESSEE: Betty Besley; RENT: 19s. 6d.

PREMISES: Smith Hayne; LESSEE: Augusta Kaye; RENT: 19s. 8d.

PREMISES: Higher Waterhouse [SS 889084]; LESSEE: Agnes Badcock; RENT: 6s. 8d.

PREMISES: Sellacks; LESSEE: William Badcock; RENT: 13s. 4d.

PREMISES: Water House, Short Park, Short Park Mead and Middle Waterhouse; LESSEE: John Parkhouse; RENT: £1. 1s. 10d.

PREMISES: Court Place [SS 881082]; LESSEE: Augusta Kaye; RENT: £4.

PREMISES: South Coombe [?SS 890087]; LESSEE: George Besley; RENT: 16s.

PREMISES: Moorhay; LESSEE: Betty Melhewish; RENT: 5s.

PREMISES: Keates Cottage; lessee; Margaret Row; RENT: 2s.

PREMISES: Cottage late Moxeys; LESSEE: William Sharland; RENT: 2s.

PREMISES: Cottage late Moors; LESSEE: [blank]; RENT: 3s.

PREMISES: Cottage late Coalmans; LESSEE: George Luxton; RENT: 2s. 6d.

PREMISES: Cottage late Fursdons; LESSEE: George Bradford; RENT: 2s. 6d.

High rents payable to the following manors

Cornwall

MANOR OF TRERISE

PREMISES: Hologllin in St Evel paid by Simon Lewellin Leach, 2s.

PREMISES: Hologllin in St Evel paid by Rachel Hawkins, widow, 2s.

PREMISES: Pentire Morgan paid by William Varco of St Columb, 2s. 6d.

PREMISES: Pentire Morgan paid by William Varco of St Columb, 2s. 6d.

TOTAL: 9s.

Cornwall

MANOR OF CRAGANTALLAN

PREMISES: Trevilson paid by Lord Falmouth, 1s. 3d.

PREMISES: Trevilson paid for as lands belonging to the poor of Newlyn, 1s. 3d.

PREMISES: Trevilson paid by Lord Falmouth ['now of Sir C. Vyvyan Vyvyan', written in pencil] 1s. 3d.

PREMISES: Trevarton paid by Richard Gulley, gent., 1s. 7d.

PREMISES: Trewinnion paid by Johnson Vyvyan esq., 2s. 4d.

PREMISES: Redowallesoe paid by Samuel Hill esq., 1s. 1d.

PREMISES: Trevithick alias Polwheele paid by Abel Angowe, gent. late Palamour, 2s.

PREMISES: Carvinack paid by Jon^n Vyvyan esq. late Tannis, 2s.

PREMISES: Ween Hoskyn paid by William Gully, gent., 1s. 9d.

PREMISES: Tresodren paid by Edward Hublyn, gent., 2s. 6d.

TOTAL: 17s.

Cornwall

MANOR OF DEGEMBRIS

PREMISES: Midcliose in Mitchell paid by Lady Arundell of Lanhern, 8s. 1d.

PREMISES: Woodley in Lanivet paid by Lady Arundell of Lanhern, 3s. 1d.

PREMISES: Skues Pridaux and Skues Dean, paid by George Hunt of Llanhedrock near Bodmin, esq., formerly the Earl of Radnors, 10d.

PREMISES: Bonderay Boscarn in Bodmin, paid by Mr Peterson, attorney in Plymouth, formerly Edward Hoblyns, esq., 3s. 4d.

PREMISES: Nancollath in Newlyn, paid by Lord Falmouth, late Sir William Carys and Sir Francis Vyvyans. 7s. 6d.

PREMISES: Treninick and Treverneck in Newlyn paid by Lord Falmouth, late Sir Wlliam Carys and Sir Francis Vyvyans, 7s. 6d.

PREMISES: Trevosa and Penscawen in St Enader (sic), paid by Lord Falmouth and Jonathan Rashleigh, esq., 7s. 3d.

PREMISES: Pencoss in St Enoder, paid by Arthur Fortescue. esq., of Manguisse, 8s. 0½d.

PREMISES: Ween Hoskin in St Enoder, paid by Mr Richard Gulley of Tresillion, 2s. 6d.

PREMISES: Gerlis in Newlyn, paid by the Reverend Mr John Trevenan of Camborn[e], 3s.

PREMISES: Nansmeer in Newlyn paid by John Ennis of Ennis, esq., near Penryn, 2s. 6d.

PREMISES: Tregare in Newlyn, paid by the heirs of Mr Thomas Prater, junior, of Tregare, 4s. 1d.

TOTAL: £2. 10s. 8½d

PREMISES: Polgraine in Newlyn, paid by the heirs of Mr Thomas Prater, junior, of Tregare, 2s. 4d.

PREMISES: Pentire Vean in Crantock, paid by Sir Edward Deering and Sir Rowland Wynn, 3s. 3d.

PREMISES: Eglose Cubert in Cubert, paid by John Hambly late Carters, 2s. 4d.

PREMISES: Trenhale in Newlyn, paid the heirs of Mr Thomas Prater, junior, of Tregare, late Sir Richard Vyvyan, 2½d.

PREMISES: Porth Glavian in Newlyn, paid by Richard Hussey of Truro, esq., late the Reverend Mr Tregeannas, 5s.

PREMISES: Trenhale in Newlyn, paid by the heirs of Mr Thomas Prater, junior, of Tregare, 5s.

TOTAL: £3. 8s.10d.

MANOR OF GOVILEY

(high rents)

PREMISES: Cammals, paid by William Trevanion, esq., 2s. 1d.

PREMISES: Cammals, paid by William Trevanion, esq., 2s. 1d.

PREMISES: Goviley Vean and Goviley Gove, paid by Lord Falmouth, 3s. 1d

PREMISES: Trencreek Vean, paid by Richard Hennah, 2s. 1d.

PREMISES: Forda, paid by Lord Falmouth, 1s. 1d.

PREMISES: Rose Vallen, paid by the Reverend Nicholas Trevanion, 2s. 1d.

PREMISES: Treworga, paid by Henry Double, 3s. 4d.

PREMISES: Hendra in St Dennis, paid by the heirs of the Earl of Radnor, 7s.

TOTAL: £1. 2s. 10d.

MANOR OF THURLIBEER

(high rents)

PREMISES: Treyeo, paid by John Jolly, 10s.

PREMISES: Burne, paid by Elizabeth Bullock, 1s.

'Thurlibeer 1pd of Cummin Seed'

TOTAL: 11s.

(and one pound of cummin seed)

MANOR OF EBBINGFORD ALIAS EFFORD

(high rents)

PREMISES: North Park and houses in Stratton Town, paid by Miss Mary Harris, 2s.

PREMISES: Burrocott, paid by the Reverend Mr Hammet, 8s.

PREMISES: Burn Jacobstow, paid by Mr William Nottle, 5s. 2d.

PREMISES: Heddon in Jacobstow, paid by Mr William Nottle, 1s. 10d.

PREMISES: Burracott late Dodges, paid by Thomas Torn, 5s.

PREMISES: Burracott late Dodges, paid by Thomas Torn, 5s.

PREMISES: Heddon in Jacobstow Foss, paid by the Earl of Radnor, 1s.

PREMISES: Lunestone, paid by Mr Welcth, late Blakes, 8d.

PREMISES: Lunestone, paid by Sir Francis Basset, Bart, 8d.

PREMISES: Lunestone, paid by the Reverend Mr Corey, 8d.

PREMISES: Crabb Hay in Stratton, paid by His Grace the Duke of Bedford, 1s.

PREMISES: Dodges, late Joan Tremble, paid by Jane Wallis, widow, 0½d.

PREMISES: Upton, paid by Mr John Phillips, 4d.

PREMISES: Upton, paid by the heirs of Granville and Barnfield, 4d.

PREMISES: Lunestone, paid by the heirs of Cook, 8d.

PREMISES: Jacobstow Town, paid by Richard Cory 'lost', 6d.

TOTAL: £1. 12s. 10½d.

Somerset

MANOR OF EAST LUCKHAM

(high rents)

PREMISES: Wood Stockley in Doverhay, paid by Nicholas Snow, 6d.

PREMISES: Cloutsham, paid by Isaac Clark, late Anolds, 1s.

PREMISES: Oven Holt, paid by the heirs of James Blackford, 6d.

PREMISES: West Linch, paid by John Clarke, 6d.

PREMISES: West Linch, paid by Isaac Clarke, 6d.

PREMISES: Dean in Timberscombe, paid by Mary Greenslade, 6d.

PREMISES: East Luckham, paid by James Darsh, 6d.

PREMISES: Witchanger, paid by Mr John Worth, 6d.

PREMISES: Allerford, paid by Joan Spurrier, 0½d.

PREMISES: East Luckham, paid by Joan Fish, 6d.

PREMISES: Manor of Neither Holt, paid by the heirs of James Blackford, 10s.

TOTAL: £0. 15s. 6½d.

Devon

MANOR OF STOCKLEY LUCKHAM

(high rents)

PREMISES: Furze in Cheriton, paid by the Feoffees of the Poor there, 7s. 4d.

PREMISES: East Trendle Moor in Cheriton, paid by John Patridge (sic), gent., 13s. 4d.

PREMISES: West Uphome, paid by Richard Melhuish, 8s. 5d.

PREMISES: East Farley in Cheriton, paid by Joseph Copplestone, esq., 7s.

PREMISES: East Hayne in Cheriton, paid by Edward Hiuish, esq., 3s. 4d.

PREMISES: North Coombe in Cheriton, paid by the Reverend Mr Modiston, 4s. 8d.

PREMISES: West Hayne in Cheriton, paid by John Read, gent., 8s.

PREMISES: Regiless alias Brendevil in Cheriton, paid by Edward Hewish, esq., 8s.

PREMISES: West Trundle Moor in Cheriton, paid by Stephen Davy, 1s. 6d.

PREMISES: East Hayne in Cheriton, paid by Edward Hewish, esq. for the late Elizabeth Moorish's widow (sic), 4s. 8d.

PREMISES: Gory Bushes, paid by Henry Pope, 6s. 8d.

TOTAL: £3. 12s. 11d.

Section II

Descriptive list of maps and surveys

Acland Maps and Surveys 1720–1840

DEVON

1. 1726 Survey	Manors of Riverton, Hackworthy, Nimet St George, Southmolton, Hacche, Romansleigh, Woolleigh Omer and Hunshaw, Essebeare alias Aishbeare, Leigh, Loxbeare, Collom:john (land in 40 Devon parishes)	DRO, 1148M add/6/11
2. 1739 & 1761 Surveys	High Bray	DRO, 1148M add/6/3
3. 1756 Atlas	Broadclyst	DRO, 1148M add 23/E1
4. 1757 Atlas	(4A) Chulmleigh and other parishes and maps separated from the atlas:–	DRO, 1148M add/6/11
	(4B) Barnstaple	DRO, 1148M add/10/1a
	(4C) Buckland, East	DRO, 1262M/E22/44
	(4D) South Molton	South Molton Museum
5. 1762 Map	Coomroy (Broadclyst)	PWDRO, 81/X25
6. 1765 Survey	11 Devon Manors as in 1726 Survey	DRO, 1148M add/6/11
7. 1766 Map	Killerton (Broadclyst)	DRO, 1148M add/10/5/1
8. 1767 Survey	Ashclyst (Broadclyst)	DRO, 1148M add/6/4
9. 1774 Map	Langacre (Broadclyst)	DRO, 1148M add/1/T8/168
10. 1775 Map	Broadclyst	DRO, 1148M add/10/5/2
11. c.1791 Map	Manor of Stockley Luckham	DRO, 1148M add/10/7
12. c.1801 Map	Broadclyst (Cliston Manor)	DRO, 1148M add/10/5/3
13. c.1802 Survey	Manor of Stockley Luckham	DRO, 1148M add/6/13
14. post 1804 Survey	Manors of Riverton, Hackworthy, Woolleigh, Leigh, Loxbeare, Romansleigh, Hacche, George Nympton	DRO, 1148M add/6/11

15. post 1804 Maps	Manors of Riverton, Leigh, Loxbeare, Romansleigh, Hacche, George Nympton	DRO, 1926B/A/E2/12
16. 1805 Atlas	Ashburton and other parishes	SRO, DD/AH/Box 14/5
17. 1807 Survey	South Tawton	DRO, 1148M add/6/10
18. 1807 Survey	High Bray (Oxenham)	DRO, 1148M add/6/3
19. 1809 Map	Manor of Wooleigh (Beaford)	DRO, 1148M add/10/1b
20. 1809–10 Survey	Manor of Hacche	DRO, 1926B/A/E1/95
21. 1811–25 Map	Higher & Lower Newland Farms (Broadclyst)	SRO, DD/WY/Box 121
22. 1812 Map	Broadclyst (road)	DRO, 1148M add/21/3/1
23. 1812 Map	Broadclyst (road)	DRO, DQS 113A/34/1
24. early 19th cent. Map	Aishclyst and Killerton (Broadclyst)	SRO, DD/SAS/c1540/12/1
25. c.1815 Map	Kenn	SRO, DD/AH/42/2/12
26. 1816 Map	St Giles in the Wood (Woolleigh Park)	DRO, 96M add/E18
27. 1819 Map	Broadclyst (road)	DRO, 1926B/A/E/3/2
28. c.1820 Map & view	Broadclyst	DRO, 1148M add/10/5/15
29. 1836 Map	Kenton	DRO, 484M/T4/37
30. 1839 Map	Whitedown (Cullompton)	DRO, 1148M add/1/T13/2
31. 19th cent. Map	High Bray	DRO, 1148M add/10/3/1

SOMERSET

32. c.1700 Map	Exmoor (diagrammatic)	DRO, 1148M add/10/13
33. 18th cent. Survey	North Petherton	DRO, 1148M add/6/17
34. 1720 Survey	Dulverton	DRO, 1148M add/6/14
35. 1720 & 1741 Surveys	Luccombe	DRO, 1148M add/6/15
36. 1720 Survey	Bossington	DRO, 1148M add/6/18
37. 1720&1755 Surveys	Manors of Banckland, Buckland, Cheadmeade & Auler and land in Lyng	SRO, DD/AH/65/15
38. 1746–7 Survey	Manors of Avil, Bossington, Wilmersham & West Luckham, West Luckham, Holnicote & Exbridge Ryphay	DRO, 1148M add/6/20
39. c.1760 Map	Lyng	SRO, DD/AH/65/13c/2252

40. 1761 Map	Manor of Auler (Aller)	SRO, DD/SAS/W51
41. 1767 Map	Stogursey and other Parishes	SRO, DD/AH/66/11
42. *c.*1770 Survey	Manor of East Luckham	DRO, 1148M/ Box 9/2
43. 1779 Survey	Manors of Newton Wroth and Newton Regis	DRO, 1148M add/6/17
44. 1795–1806 Atlas	Stogursey and other Parishes	SRO, DD/AH/65/12
45. *c.*1802 Survey	Manor of East Luckham	DRO, 1148M add/6/13
46. 1809 Map	North Petherton	DRO, 1148M add/10/23a
47. 1809 Map	North Petherton	DRO, 1148M add10/10/28
48. 1809 Survey	North Petherton	DRO, 1148M add11/1
49. 1809–12 Atlas	Holnicote	DRO, 1148M add/9/6/24
50. 1810 Map	Manor of Avil	DRO, 1148M add/10/20
51. 1820 Map	Winsford	DRO, 1148M add 6 (unlisted)
52. 1829 Map	Selworthy	DRO, 1148M add/21/3/3

CORNWALL

53. *c.*1770 Survey	Manors of Cragantallan, Degembris, Ebbingford alias Efford and Thurlibeer	DRO, 1148M/Box 9/2
54. *c.*1791 Map	Manor of Thurlibeer	DRO, 1148M add/10/19
55. *c.*1802 Survey	Manors of Cragantallan, Degembris, Ebbingford alias Efford, Goviley, Penstrase Moor, Thurlibeer, Trerise and Tresillian	DRO, 1148M add/6/13
56. 1817 Map	Bude Canal	Bude Museum, Budex 276
57. 1820 Survey	Manors of Efford and Thurlibeer	DRO, 1148M add/6/12
58. 1824 Map	Bude Canal	DRO, 1148M add/10/15/1
59. 1826 Maps	Bude Canal	CRO, DC/NC/15/37–39
60. 1828 Atlas	Manors of Efford and Thurlibeer	Private hands
61. 1833 Map	Bude Haven	DRO, 1148M/Box 20/7

SURVEY

| 1. 1726 | DRO, 1148M add/6/11 |

PLACES: Manors of Collom:john, Essebeare alias Aishbeare, Hacche, Hackworthy, Leigh, Loxbeare, Nimet St George, Riverton, Romansleigh, Southmolton, Woolleigh Omer & Hunshaw

PARISHES: East Anstey, Barnstaple, Beaford, Berrynarbor, Bickleigh, Bishop's Nympton, Bishop's Tawton, Broadclyst, East Buckland, Charles, Chawleigh, Chittlehampton, Chulmleigh, Creacombe, East Down, George Nympton, St Giles in the Wood, Huntshaw, Huxham, Knowstone, Landkey, Loxbeare, Marwood, North Molton, South Molton, Puddington, Rackenford, Rewe, Romansleigh, Roseash, Silverton, Stoodleigh, Swimbridge, Tedburn St Mary, Tiverton, Great Torrington, Little Torrington, Washfield, Witheridge, East Worlington

TITLE: 'A Survey of the Manors Farms Lands Tenements Hereditaments lying in the County of Devon of Sir Hugh Acland Bart Taken from former Surveys Rent Rolls and Counterparts of Leases in the year of our Lord 1726 by Mr Thomas Knott Steward'

SURVEYOR: Thomas Knott

FORMAT: volume, size 23.6cms x 37.5cms, with leather cover tooled in gold; this survey appears on pages 1–261

DETAILS: tenants' names; tenements' names; acreage; dates of leases and fines; names and ages of lives; Lord's rent; heriots; yearly value

NOTE: this survey is abstracted as *Survey 1* in this volume

For further details of the contents see *Introduction*, pp. 5–7

SURVEYS

| 2. A–B. 1739 &1761 | DRO, 1148M add/6/3 |

PLACE: Manor of High Bray PARISH: High Bray

(A) TITLE: 'A Rental of the Manor of High Bray in the County of Devon 1739'

SURVEYOR: not named

FORMAT: parchment sheet, 32.9cms x 60.3cms

DETAILS: tenants' names; names of estates; lives in possession; ages [all blank]; lives in reversion; ages [all blank]; yearly value; free tenants listed separately

(B) TITLE: 'Rental Michaelmas 1761'

SURVEYOR: not named

FORMAT: small book, parchment covers, size approx. 22cms x 32.5cms

DETAILS: as above

ASSOCIATED DOCUMENTS: rentals 1787–96 (2 vols) and Abstract of Leases, 1756, in the same bundle

ATLAS

| 3. 1756 | DRO, 1148M add 23/E1 |

PLACES: Manors of Killerton, Essebeare, Leigh, Loxbeare

PARISHES: Broadclyst, Loxbeare, Rackenford

Leather-bound volume of various Parishes, 40cms x 62.5cms. 12 maps listed below

SURVEYOR: Thomas Hodge

SCALE: 'Scale of Chains'; scale bars; scales on maps vary, see below

MATERIAL & ORIENTATION: parchment, coloured; direction indicated on each map

CONTENT: rivers, blue, named; some maps contain details of aspect indicated either by letter or in description; fields washed in various colours on Map 1; Maps 2–4 outlined in colour with alpha-numeric reference to table giving field names and content; Maps 5–11 give field names and content on each map; some hedges shaded yellow over hatching giving information regarding hedge ownership; alphabetic reference to land use and aspect, explained in note; fence; green tree symbols showing orchards, avenues and isolated trees; woods marked by tree symbols superimposed on a green wash; roads, fenced and unfenced; directions given; buildings in plan; peripheral owners named

DECORATION: title cartouches: simple frame, maps 5,9,11a,11b; simple scrolls, maps 1,2,3,6,19; delicate leaf design superimposed on title, maps 1,7,8; 4 point compass indicator, grey/white; north marked by fleur-de-lys

Map 1

'A Map of the Manor of Killerton & CulmJohn'

Double-page spread; 1"=9 chains; 1:7128

Areas of manor named, shown in more detail on subsequent maps 2–4; peripheral owners named, some in a later hand; title cartouche: ribbon and flowers; various areas identified as 'Sir Thomas Acland' to the east of the Silverton road and south of 'New Hole'.

Killerton SS 973001 Columbjohn SX 960997

Map 2

'A Map of the 'Barton of CulmJohn' With White's, Toswell's Jarman's And Gun's tents'

1"=6.25 chains; 1:4950

INSET: 'A Map of Budlake in Killerton Manour'; circular map; some field names erased, replaced by 'Sir Thomas Acland's' in a different ink and hand.

ACREAGE: Gunns 91.2.05; Barton of CulmJohn 425.2.03; Budlake 39.1.15

Budlake SS 984001

Map 3

'A Map of Killerton Dolbery Killerton Francis Killerton Mashes Bastions Cross Pimms Bridge Tents'

1"=6 chains; 1:4752; various areas with original names erased, now noted as 'in the Park'.

ACREAGE: Killerton Marshes 69.0.28; Bridge T'nt 31.0.12; Cross T'nt 16.0.25; Killerton Barton 152.3.10; Killerton Francis 37.3.25; Bastons T'nt 18.3.17; Croome Cott etc 1.1.29

Killerton Dolbery SS 974006 Killerton Francis SX977995 Killerton Mashes SS 965014

Map 4

'A Map of Francis Court New Hall and Great & Little Cutton'

1"=6.25 chains; 1:4950

ACREAGE: Great Cutton 194.2.27; MiddleCutton 55.2.38; Little Cutton 39.3.01; Francis Court 162.1.36; Newhall 85.1.20

Francis Court SX 977995 New Hall SX 981992 Cutton SX 972987

Map 5

'A Map of Canworthy Backstone Moor and Eastbackstone in ye Parishes of Rackenford and in the Manour of Leigh except Backstone Moor wch is Manour of Essebeare 1756 T. Hodge Fecit'

1"=7 chains; 1:5544

INSET: 'A Map of Lan[l]land in ye Parish of Rackenford and in Leigh Manour 1756' 'T H Fecit'

ACREAGE: Parish of Rackenford 361.2.19

Backstone SS 835191

Map 6

'A Map of ye Barton of Leigh, Leigh Town, Leigh Mill & Perry in ye Parish of Loxbeare & Manour of Leigh 1756 T H Fecit'

1"=3.5 chains; 1:2772

Notes give details of aspect and land use; 'Perry Situate on ye Side of an Hill Aspect East . . . Good Land very good for Barly'; 'Leigh Mill . . . (frequently in want of Slates)'; Leigh Town is divided into three Small Tents prettily Situated on ye South Side of an Hill of easy Ascent'.

ACREAGE: Parish of Loxbeare 198.1.25

Leigh Barton SS 909148 Leigh Town SS 914149 Leigh Mill SS 909149 Perry SS 920152

Map 7

'A Map of Sedborough & Ford Two Estates in the Manour of Leigh T H Fecit'

1"=3.25 chains; 1:2574

ACREAGE: Sedborough 76.0.18; Tiverton Parish (Ford) 67.2.10

Sidborough SS 901150 Ford Barton SS 913184 Ford in Tiverton Parish SS 900146

Map 8 'A Map of Buttermoors Great Little & Wester Winbow

Wood and pt of the Glebe 1756 T Hodge Fecit'
1"=3.25 chains; 1:2574
ACREAGE: Butter Moors 33.2.19; Great Winbow 40.0.01; Wester
Winbow 7.2.03; Wood T'nt 19.1.16
Buttermoors SS 917161 Winbow SS 919166

Map 9

'A Map of Churchill and Churchill Park Two Tenemts in ye
Parish and Manour of Loxbeare Thos Hodge Silverton Fecit
1756' 1"=3.5 chains; 1: 2772
ACREAGE: Loxbeare Parish 159.1.32
Churchill SS 904165

Map 10

'A Map of Loxbeare Barton Pantacrudge and part of ye Glebe in
ye Manour of Loxbeare 1756 T H Fecit'
1"=3.5 chains; 1: 2772
'Loxbeare Barton consists of a very good Stone built House'
ACREAGE: Loxbeare Parish 126.2.07
Loxbeare Barton SS 914159 Pantacridge SS 905158

Map 11a

'A Map of Ham and Venhay Two Tenemts in ye Manour of Leigh
T H Fecit 1756'
ACREAGE: Ham & Venhay 50.2.17
Ham SS 905154 Venhay now Ingrams SS 905156

Map 11b

'A Map of Lurlie in ye Manour of Leigh T H Fecit' [Parish of
Tiverton]
1"=3.5 chains; 1:2772
ACREAGE: Lurlie Parish of Tiverton 74.1.11
Lurley SS 924148

PUBLICATIONS: Todd Gray, *The Garden History of Devon* (Exeter,
1995), 130; Mary R. Ravenhill and Margery M. Rowe, eds,
Maps of Georgian Devon (Exeter, 2002), 18–9.
For further details of the maps see Introduction, pp. 11–12

1757 ATLAS

These maps were part of the same mapping exercise but subsequent events led to their appearance in different collections.
For convenience they are listed and described separately.

MAPS	
4A. 1757	DRO, 1148M add/6/11

PLACES: Manors of George Nympton, Hacche, Riverton and
Romansleigh
PARISHES: George Nympton, King's Nympton, Landkey, North
Molton, South Molton, Romansleigh This group of 21 maps
and accompanying terriers, were probably bound in atlas form;
not all have survived because they were stored in a boiler house
at Killerton prior to deposit in the Devon Record Office. A
burst boiler damaged the documents
Maps I–V are of Romansleigh with Terriers
Maps VI–IX not present [for IX see Map 4C, for VII see Map
4D]
Map X not present, Terrier present
Map XI of Hacche with Terrier
Maps XII–XIII not present
Maps XIV–XVI are of George Nympton with Terriers
Map XVI not present
Map XVII not present
Map XVIII, Rivaton Manor, but no Terrier
Maps XIX–XXI Terriers of 'Riverton Manor' but no maps. One
map with no title Terriers: similar in size to maps with title
indicating to which map each refers giving names of tenants
and tenements; field names with land use and content; value;
conditions on which land held Maps are signed 'John Bowring
of Chulmleigh Surveyor'

Map I

TITLE: 'A General Map of Romansleigh Mannor in the County
of Devon Belonging to the Honble Thomas Dyke Acland Bart
1757'
Romansleigh Church SS 727205

Map II

TITLE: 'Romansleigh Mannor The Church, The Glebe & The Barton. Map II'

Map III

TITLE: 'Romansleigh Mannor Horridge, Duxford, Oxen parks & Little ham, Church house, Waste, & Crockers Garden, Rumbelows Cottage & Garden'
Horridge SS 722195

Map IV

TITLE: 'Romansleigh Mannor Whitehouse & Droocombe, Duboundisland, and Dockworthy Map IIII'

Map V

TITLE: 'Romansleigh Mannor Hummacotts in Kings Nympton, & Coombe'; 2 maps on 1 page
Hummacotts SS 702194 Coombe SS 688179

Maps I–V

SURVEYOR: 'John Bowring of Chulmleigh Surveyor'

SCALES: 'A Scale of — Chains'; map I 1"=7 chains; 1:5544; maps II–V 1"=4 chains; 1:3168; map III scale for insets of Church House and Rumbelows Cottage 1"=2 chains; 1: 1584; north to top

MATERIAL, SIZE & ORIENTATION: parchment, coloured; 80cms EW x 57.5cms NS; north to top

CONTENT: streams, blue with one wide, one fine grey margin; arrows indicating direction of flow; pond, blue; bridges; fields outlined in various colours and washed in shades of green or buff; some field names; general names of various areas; some owners' names; alpha-numeric reference to Terrier; gates; green tree symbols showing orchards, woods coppices and isolated trees; additional symbol marking brakes [brushwood]; roads buff and named; where no actual name word 'Road' used to distinguish from narrow buff line indicating footpath, also named; buildings in plan, some light blue; church in elevation; peripheral owners named; letters marking various points on perimeter of some maps

DECORATION: title cartouches: rococo in style with acanthus, shaded grey; map III has elaborate rococo style with acanthus

decorating a frame of scrolls with 2 waterfalls and 3 cherubs, one with dividers, one with survey book, one holding map; also cartouche round scale of scrolls with masks and plants; 32 point compass rose on all maps in various colours with coloured outer circles; yellow borders to all maps

Map XI

Part only cut from a sheet similar in size to the other maps

TITLE: 'Hacche Mannor South Aller In South molton Scotts Tenement Withytheyeate, & Bere In North molton'

SURVEYOR: J Bowring

SCALE: not given on this part of the map

MATERIAL etc and CONTENT as in maps I–V

Hacche Barton SS 714278 South Aller SS 698273 Withygate SS 707346 Beara SS 706351

Map XIV

TITLE: 'George Nympton Manor The Church & Glebe, Little Hele Dower Land. Bury-slade, Martins Parks, & sundry small Tenements'

SURVEYOR: not named [John Bowring]

SCALE: 'A Scale of Chains'; scale bar; 1"=4 chains; 1:3168

MATERIAL etc and CONTENT as in maps I–V

DECORATION: title cartouche: rococo style with acanthus, shells, trees and wheat; 32 point compass rose, coloured as in maps 1–5

George Nympton SS 700229

Map XV

TITLE: 'Geo: Nympton Manor. Ford, West Stone, East Stone, & Newnham Parks'

SURVEYOR: not named [John Bowring]

SCALE: 'A Scale of Equal Chains'; 1"=4 chains; 1:3168

MATERIAL etc and CONTENT as in maps I–V

DECORATION: as in map XIV

George Nympton SS 700229

Map XVI

TITLE: 'George Nympton Manor Amory's, Kings, & Pearses Tenements, and Worthy in Comberew'

SURVEYOR: not named [John Bowring]

SCALE: 'A Scale of Equal Chains'; 1"= 4 chains; 1:3168

MATERIAL etc and CONTENT as in maps I–V

DECORATION: title cartouche: rococo, elaborate in style with acanthus and scrolls; 32 point compass rose, coloured as in maps I–V

Comberew SS 653262

Map XVIII

TITLE: 'Riverton Manor, Acland Barton, Westcott, East Bathey, West Bathey and a cottage at Newland in the Parish of Lankey 1758'

SURVEYOR: not named [John Bowring]

SCALE: 'A Scale of Equal Chains'; 1"=4 chains; 1:3168

MATERIAL etc and CONTENT as in maps I–V

DECORATION: title cartouche: elaborate rococo style with acanthus, field plants, lamb and winged putto drawing map; scale decorated with scrolls and cornucopias of fruit and flowers; 32 point compass rose coloured as in maps I–V

Rivaton SS 638300 Acland Barton SS 595325 Westcott SS 585328 Newland SS 597313

MAP

| 4B. 1757 | DRO, 1148M add/10/1a |

PLACE: Barnstaple

PARISH: Barnstaple

TITLE: not given; map shows Acland street properties; 7 small maps on one sheet of parchment each bordered with a wide yellow margin

SURVEYOR: not named; marginal style suggests John Bowring

SCALE: not given

MATERIAL, SIZE & ORIENTATION: parchment, coloured; irregular shape max. measurement 18.3cms x 47.5cms; no direction

CONTENT: shows location of houses and plots of land in relation to roads and river; river, blue; plots of land outlined in colour on green wash; alphabetic or alpha-numeric reference [to Survey Book]; tree symbols; roads, brown and named; houses in plan with gardens; peripheral owners named

Barnstaple Church, St Mary SS 558332

MAP

| 4C. 1757 | DRO, 1262M/E22/44 |

PLACE: Hacche Manor, West Brayley Barton

PARISHES: East Buckland, South Molton

TITLE: 'Hacche Manor, Snurridge In Southmolton, and West Brayley Barton In East Buckland. Map IX'

SURVEYOR: [John Bowring]

SCALE: 'A Scale of 12 Equal Chains; scale bar; 1"=4 chains; 1:3168

MATERIAL, SIZE & ORIENTATION: parchment, coloured; 80.6cms EW x 58.7cms NS; north to top

CONTENT: streams, grey lines; fields outlined in various colours and coloured with green or buff wash; alpha-numeric reference to terrier which is present; gates; tree symbols showing orchards, woods, coppices and isolated trees; roads, buff, directions given; buildings in plan, grey; peripheral owners named

DECORATION: title cartouche and scale cartouche rococo style with acanthus; 8 point compass rose, buff/grey, green/plain in green circle; north marked by fleur-de-lys, east by cross; yellow border and in centre separating the two maps

TERRIER: [torn in 2 pieces] entitled Hacche Manor, Map IX' is of similar size to the map and has columns headed: 'Tenements and tenants Names: Term of the Lease and Ages of Lives: . . . with Letters . . . in theMap: Letter & Number: Quality: Quantity: Yearly Value p. Acre: Yearly Value of Each Close: Fine & Consideration: RENT: Herriots: Duties: outbound Hedges: Maintain'd by'

The last two columns refer to perimeter letters

NOTE: the map and Terrier at one time formed part of DRO, 1148M add/6/11, which is listed as a group of 21 maps and accompanying terriers, not all present, by John Bowring of Chulmleigh, 1757. See 5A.

Brayley Barton SS 687302; Hacche Barton SS 714278; Snurridge SS 703283

MAP

4D. 1757   South Molton Museum
Details supplied from coloured scanned copy

PLACE: South Molton in the Manor of Hacche

PARISH: South Molton

TITLE: 'Burrough of South Molton within the Mannor of Hacche
Map VII'

SURVEYOR: [John Bowring]

SCALE: 'equal chains'; [illegible on copy]

MATERIAL, SIZE & ORIENTATION: ?parchment, damaged; coloured;
approx. 81cms EW x 58.5cms NS; north to top

CONTENT: River Mole and stream, blue; bridge; fields. green wash
and plain. outlined in dark green and brown, some with alpha-
numeric reference [to Survey] and some with owner's names;
gates; tree symbols, green, showing isolated trees; roads, plain;
buildings in plan and Church in elevation; peripheral estates
and owners named

PUBLICATION: Typescript by N. K. Swaine lodged with South
Molton Museum. Mr Swaine dates the map to *c*.1760 from
the topographical evidence

South Molton Church SS 714259

For further details of the maps see *Introduction*, p. 11

MAP

5. 1762   PWDRO, 81/X25

PLACE: Coomroy Farm

PARISH: Broadclyst

TITLE: 'A Map of Coomroy Farm in the Parish of Broadclyst
Devon by Wm Hayman & Robt Stribling Exeter 1762'

SURVEYORS: William Hayman and Robert Stribling

SCALE: 'A Scale of Chains'; scale bar; 1"=3.8 chains; 1:3010

MATERIAL, SIZE & ORIENTATION: parchment, coloured; 52cms EW
x 69cms NS; north to top

CONTENT: stream, blue; arrows indicating direction of flow; fields,
blue or yellow, outlined with simple green hedgerow symbols;

numeric reference to table giving field names and content;
gates; tree symbols showing orchards, woods and coppices;
isolated trees and density of woodland indicated; roads, paths,
buff, some marked by pecked lines; buildings in plan, grey;
peripheral owners named

DECORATION: title cartouche: delicate leaf and flower design in
green and gold in rectangular frame on yellow background;
similar frame to 'Refferences to the Map'; 16 point compass
rose, all points hatched and coloured in shades of grey; yellow
and black border

ASSOCIATED DOCUMENT: Advertisement for 'Combery Farm To
be Lett For 7, 14; or 21 Years from Lady-Day 1762'; *SM* 2, 9,
16 and 23 March 1761

PUBLICATION: Mary R. Ravenhill and Margery M. Rowe, eds,
Maps of Georgian Devon (Exeter, 2002), 24–5.

Higher Comberoy Farm ST 015005

For further details of the map see *Introduction*, p. 4

SURVEY

6. 1765   DRO, 1148M add/6/11

PLACES: Manors of Collom:john, Essebeare alias Aishbeare,
Hacche, Hackworthy, Leigh, Loxbeare, Nimet St George,
Riverton, Romansleigh, Southmolton, Woolleigh Omer and
Hunshaw

PARISHES: East Anstey, Barnstaple, Beaford, Berrynarbor,
Bickleigh, Bishop's Nympton, Bishop's Tawton, Broadclyst,
East Buckland, Charles, Chawleigh, Chittlehampton, Chulmleigh, Creacombe, East Down, George Nympton, St Giles in
the Wood, Huntshaw, Huxham, Knowstone, Landkey, Loxbeare, Marwood, North Molton, South Molton, Puddington,
Rackenford, Rewe, Romansleigh, Roseash, Silverton, Stoodleigh, Swimbridge, Tedburn St Mary, Tiverton, Great Torrington, Little Torrington, Washfield, Witheridge, East Worlington

TITLE: not given

SURVEYOR: not named

FORMAT: volume, leather cover tooled in gold, paper sheets

numbered 262–283 [preceded by 1726 Survey, see *Survey 1*]

DETAILS: tenants' names; tenements' names; acreage; details of leases and fines; names and ages of lives; Lord's RENT: heriots; yearly value

---

MAP

7. 1766   DRO, 1148M add/10/5/1

PLACE: Killerton

PARISH: Broadclyst

TITLE: 'A Plan of Part of the Estate of Sr Thos Dyke Acland at Kellerton in the County of Devon Bart Together with the Intended new Cut from the Leather Mill above Etherly Bridge to water ye Meadows and turn an Engine by Iohn Case Surveyor 1766'

SURVEYOR: John Case

SCALE: 'Chains', 'Feet'; scale bars; 1"=2 chains; 1:1584

MATERIAL, SIZE & ORIENTATION: paper, coloured; 103.5cms EW x *c.*73.5cms NS, paper torn; north to top

CONTENT: river, pale green, shoals in river; bridges, Etherly Bridge in elevation with 4 arches; relief shown by hill shading and coloured ochre and brown; fields outlined by hedge symbols and isolated trees, some coloured yellow and brown with pecked lines suggesting arable land; fences and gates; green tree symbols differentiating coniferous and deciduous copses and woodland; tree-lined road; alphabetic reference to leather mill and line of intended leat, also marked by double ink line

'NB the Leat will water 58 Acres Nearly and if took from the Corn Mill 12 Acres more'

DECORATION: 8 point compass rose, shaded grey cardinals, others simple lines

Ellerhayes Bridge SS 975021

For further details of the map see *Introduction*, p. 12

SURVEY

8. 1767   DRO, 1148M add/6/4

PLACE: Manor and Barton of Ashclyst

PARISH: Broadclyst

TITLE: 'The Contents of a Survey held this Thirtieth Day of October 1767 at the house of Mrs Deborah Cornish known by the Name of the Globe Tavern in Exeter by John Hole William Hole and Robert Wight Clerks and Wm Skinner Gent for Sale of the Fee Simple & Inheritance of the Manor Royalty and Barton of Ash Clist lying in the Parish of Broad Clist in the County of Devon and more particularly mentioned and described in the Survey or Particular thereof hereunto annexed'

SURVEYORS: John Hole, William Hole, Robert Wight and William Skinner

FORMAT: two paper sheets, 33.5cms x 42.4cms

DETAILS: properties are listed under 'Demesnes' and 'Reversions'

NOTE: the price is given as £7500 which is accepted by Sir Thomas Dyke Acland

---

MAP

9. 1774   DRO, 1148M add/1/T8/168

PLACE: Manor of Langacre

PARISH: Broadclyst

TITLE: 'A Map or Plan of all the Messuages Lands and Tenements (part of the Manor of Langacre in the Parish of Broadclyst and County of Devon) convey'd by Sir John Davie Bart by the Indenture of Release hereunto annex'd Wm Hole 1774'

SURVEYOR: William Hole

SCALE: 'A Scale of Chains, each containing Four Statute Perches'; scale bar; 1"=3 chains; 1:2376

MATERIAL, SIZE & ORIENTATION: parchment, coloured, water damaged; 61cms EW x 104cms NS; north to top

CONTENT: fields outlined in various colours; alpha-numeric reference to table giving names of tenements, tenants; field names and content; 'asterisms' indicating hedge ownership; gates; tree symbols showing orchards and isolated trees; roads; buildings in plan, outlined in purple; one in elevation; peripheral owners named, principally Sir Thomas Acland and Sir John Davie

Two tables:–

1: A Table of Particulars with References to the Map, listing Tenements and by whom held/ Referential Letters/ Names of the Fields or Parcels of Ground/ Measured Content/ Total Content of the Map – 160a: 2r: 4p.

2: A Survey of the Land delineated in this Map, Viz Tenants/ Tenements/ Measured Content/ Lives Subsisting thereon at Ladyday 1774/ Yearly Value as estimated in 1773/ Heriots Conl Rents Rates & Taxes to be received and paid in respect of the Premises *sold* and represented in this Plan, Viz/ Col Rents Rates & Taxes to be received and paid in respect of that Part of ye said Estates which remains Sir Jno Davie's

DECORATION: title cartouche: swag of drapery held back by tasselled cords; 8 point compass rose, shaded black/plain

ASSOCIATED DOCUMENT: map is attached to 'Release dated 29 March 1774 by Sir Thomas Dyke Acland of Killerton, Bt, William Mackworth Praed late of Warfield, Berks but now of the City of Exeter, Esq, Humphrey Mackworth Praed of Trewethow Hall, Cornwall Esq. & William Davie of Exminster, clerk to Sir John Davie of Creedy, Bt, and Catherine his wife of messuages in the manor of Langacre'

Budlake area SX 982996

For further details of this map see *Introduction*, p. 13

MAP

10. 1775   DRO, 1148M add/10/5/2

PLACE: illegible

PARISH: Broadclyst

TITLE: unreadable, scribed but not inked [or just faded]

SURVEYOR: 'M. Blackamore survey'd delin'd [delineated] 1775'

SCALE: 'A Scale of Chains'; scale bar; 1"=4 chains; 1:3168

MATERIAL, SIZE & ORIENTATION: paper, coloured; ½EW measurement 51cms x *c.*104cms NS; north to top

CONTENT: river, grey with stream lines; fields outlined in various colours with alpha-numeric reference [to Survey Book]; some field names; tree symbols; roads, brown; bridge across river in elevation with arches drawn; directions given; buildings in plan; gardens

DECORATION: title cartouche: elaborate rococo design, shaded grey with scrolls, acanthus, flowers and fruits; 32 point compass rose, coloured but damaged

Broadclyst Church SX 982973

For further details of the map see *Introduction*, p. 13

MAP

11. *c.*1791   DRO, 1148M add/10/7

PLACE: Manor of Stockley Luckham

PARISH: Cheriton Fitzpaine

TITLE: 'A Map of the Manor of Stockley Luckham in the Parish of Cheriton Fitzpeine and County of Devon The Fee of which is in Earl Strafford'

SURVEYOR: not named; David Palmer on stylistic evidence

SCALE: worm-eaten and illegible

MATERIAL, SIZE & ORIENTATION: parchment, 2 pieces badly worm-eaten and unfit for production; approx. 74cms x 120cms; no direction apparent

CONTENT: fields outlined in colour; numeric reference [to Survey Book]; asterisks indicating hedge ownership; tree symbols showing orchards; roads, buff; buildings in plan, grey; peripheral owners named

DECORATION: title cartouche: enclosed by fence and 2 trees

Cheriton Fitzpaine Church SS 867062

For further details of the map see *Introduction*, p. 14

MAP

12. *c*.1801	DRO, 1148M add/10/5/3

PLACE: Manor of Cliston

PARISH: Broadclyst

TITLE: not given [covers a large portion of Broadclyst Parish but not Killerton]

SURVEYOR: Robert Ballment

SCALE: no unit of measurement stated; 1"=2.5 ?chains; 1;?1980

MATERIAL, SIZE & ORIENTATION: paper, ink; approx. 267cms x 236cms [as repaired]; no direction

CONTENT: river, named, streams; arrows indicating direction of flow; fields outlined in ink, named, with content and numeric reference [to Survey Book]; asterisks indicating hedge ownership; gates; tree symbols showing orchards and isolated trees; roads, fenced and unfenced with directions given; buildings in plan with church and rectory in elevation; peripheral owners and estates named

ASSOCIATED DOCUMENTS: DRO, add 7 (unlisted) A Survey of the 'Manor and Hundred of Cliston in the Parish of Broadclyst and County of Devon, the Property of the Right Honourable Humphry Morice, deceased, from an Actual View of the Premises, Taken in the Year 1801, by William Hole.' Printed, 1802 *Sherborne Mercury*, 26 July 1802, has an advertisement for the sale of the Manor of Cliston

Broadclyst Church SX 982973

For further details of the map see *Introduction*, pp. 13–14

DETAILS: tenements' names; lives in being and their ages; lives added; conventional rent; capons; due days; the kind of heriots; the sum in lieu thereof; observations; the name of the present tenant has been added in another hand

NOTE: this survey is abstracted as part of *Survey 3* in this volume

For further details of the contents see *Introduction*, p. 9

SURVEY

14. post 1804	DRO, 1148M add/6/11

PLACES: Manors of George Nympton, Hacche, Hackworthy, Leigh, Loxbeare, Riverton, Romansleigh, Woolleigh

PARISHES: Barnstaple, Beaford, Berrynarbor, Bishop's Tawton, East Buckland, Charles, Chawleigh, Chulmleigh, East Down, George Nympton, St Giles in the Wood, Huntshaw, Landkey, Loxbeare, North Molton, South Molton, Rackenford, Romansleigh, Swimbridge, Tedburn St Mary, Tiverton, Great Torrington, Little Torrington, Washfield

TITLE: not given

SURVEYOR: not named

FORMAT: volume, paper, with leather covers (repaired), size 20.5cms x 25.5cms

DETAILS: alphabetical reference to map, names of tenements, acreage, rents and heriots

SURVEY

13. *c*.1802	DRO, 1148M add/6/13

PLACE: Manor of Stockley Luckham

PARISH: Cheriton Fitzpaine

TITLE: 'Manor of Stockley Luckham'

SURVEYOR: not named

FORMAT: small volume, size 19.3cms x 25.5cms , soft leather covers, paper sheets, affected by damp

MAPS

15. post 1804	DRO, 1926B/A/E2/12

This group of 13 maps, all in the same hand, is undated. However, the watermark on the paper of one has the date 1804 and so it is assumed that the maps are after this date.

Eight maps are of lands in the Manors of Leigh and Loxbeare. With the exception of the first all have been copied from maps in the Hodge Atlas of 1756 (see No. 3). The information entered is the same with minor modifications only, such as the absence of tree symbols on the map of the Barton of Leigh and the inclusion of figures in red.

i) PLACES: Manors of Leigh and Loxbeare
PARISH: Loxbeare
TITLE: 'Loxbeare and Leigh'
SURVEYOR: not named
SCALE: not given
MATERIAL, SIZE & ORIENTATION: paper, ink, damaged; 64.5cms EW x 58cms NS; north to top
CONTENT: fields outlined in ink, named; some with alphabetic reference to list headed Manor of Leigh with content and 4 areas noted as being 'Not in this Map'; roads, fenced; directions given; buildings in plan, black; peripheral owners named
Pencil annotations identifying various 'Lots'.
ENDORSEMENT: Leigh & Loxbeare General Map
Loxbeare Barton SS 914159 Leigh Barton SS 909148

ii) PLACE: Manor of Leigh
PARISH: Rackenford
TITLE: 'Manor of Leigh Canworthy East Backstone & Laneland in Rackenford' 3 separate areas mapped
SURVEYOR: not named
SCALE: not given
MATERIAL, SIZE & ORIENTATION: paper, ink; 38cms EW x 47.2cms NS; north to top
CONTENT: fields outlined in ink, named with content; alpha-numeric reference with upper and lower case letters; upper case indicate land use and aspect; rough tree symbols; roads, fenced and unfenced, directions given; buildings in plan (plain); peripheral owners named
ENDORSEMENT: Manor of Leigh Canworthy East Backstone & Laneland in Rackenford and Backstone Moor in Do [etc] Essebeare Manor
Backstone SS 835191

iii) PLACES: Barton of Leigh, Leigh Town, Leigh Mill, Perry
PARISH: Loxbeare
TITLE: 'The Barton of Leigh, Leigh Town Leigh Mill and Perry in Parish of Loxbeare'
SURVEYOR: not named
SCALE: not given
MATERIAL, SIZE & ORIENTATION: paper, ink; 43cms x 60.2cms; north west to top (pencil)
CONTENT: fields outlined in ink, named with content; alphabetic reference with upper and lower case letters with upper case indicating land use; garden; some figures in red (later additions); roads, fenced; where unfenced probably lanes across fields; buildings in plan, cross hatched
ENDORSEMENT: Manor of Leigh & Leigh Barton
Leigh Barton SS 909148 Leigh Town SS 914149 Leigh Mill SS 907149 Perry SS 920152

iv) PLACE: Manor of Loxbeare
PARISH: Loxbeare
TITLE: 'Sedborough and Ford in ye Manor of Leigh'
SURVEYOR: not named
SCALE: not given
MATERIAL, SIZE & ORIENTATION: paper, ink; 47.5cms EW x 38.3cms NS; west to top
CONTENT: fields named with content; upper (black) and and lower (red) case reference; upper case indicates land use and aspect; tree symbols; roads fenced, directions given; buildings in plan; garden plan suggested
ENDORSEMENT: Manor of Leigh Sedborough & Ford
Sidborough SS 901150 Ford SS 900146

v) PLACES: Manors of Leigh and Loxbeare
PARISHES: Loxbeare and Washfield
TITLE: 'Butter Moors Great Little & Wester Winbow Wood & pt of ye Glebe & Manor of Leigh and Loxbeare'
SURVEYOR: not named
SCALE: not given
MATERIAL, SIZE & ORIENTATION: paper, ink; 38.5cms EW x 48cms NS; north to top (pencil)
CONTENT: fields outlined in ink, named with content; reference in upper case letters indicating land use and lower case letters indicating tenement; some rough tree symbols; roads, fenced, directions given; buildings in plan (no peripheral owners)

ENDORSEMENT: Manor of Leigh & Loxbeare Butter Moors
Buttermoors SS 917161 Winbow Wood SS 919166

vi) PLACE: Manor of Loxbeare
PARISH: Loxbeare
TITLE: 'Churchill and Churchill Park in Parish and Manor of Loxbeare'
SURVEYOR: not named
SCALE: not given
MATERIAL, SIZE & ORIENTATION: paper, ink; 23.5cms x 80.8cms; north-west to top (pencil)
CONTENT: fields outlined in ink, named with content; some with upper case T or M (land use); some tree symbols, roads, fenced and unfenced, directions given; buildings in plan, cross hatched; 2 peripheral owners
ENDORSEMENT: Loxbear(sic) Great and Little Park
Churchill SS 904165

vii) PLACE: Manor of Loxbeare
PARISH: Loxbeare
TITLE: 'Loxbeare Barton Pantacrudge and pt of ye Glebe in the Manor of Loxbeare'
SURVEYOR: not named
SCALE: not given
MATERIAL, SIZE & ORIENTATION: paper, ink; 38.5cms x 57cms; no direction
CONTENT: fields outlined in ink, named with content; alphabetic reference with upper and lower case letters; upper case refer to land use; some numbers in red (later additions); garden; rough tree symbols; roads, fenced and unfenced (probably lanes across fields); 1 direction given; buildings in plan, cross hatched (no peripheral owners)
ENDORSEMENT: Loxbear (sic)
Loxbeare Barton SS 914159 Pantacridge SS 905158

viii) PLACE: Manor of Loxbeare
PARISHES: Loxbeare and Tiverton
Two maps
TITLE: 'Ham and Venhay in Manor of Leigh Lurlie in Manor of Leigh'

SURVEYOR: not named
SCALE: not given
MATERIAL, SIZE & ORIENTATION: paper, ink; 38.7cms EW x 47.8cms NS; north to top – fletched arrow
CONTENT: fields named with content; alphabetic reference with upper and lower case letters; upper case letters refer to land use; no trees; roads, fenced, directions given; buildings in plan, cross hatched; 2 peripheral owners named
ENDORSEMENT: Manor of Leigh Ham & Venhay & Lurlie
Ham SS 905154 Venhay now Ingrams SS 905156 Lurley SS 924148

Five maps of land in Manors in mid Devon have much of their information derived from maps by John Bowring in the Chulmleigh Atlas of 1757 (see No. 4). Unlike the first group neither the scale nor the arrangement of the material is close to the earlier work.

ix) PLACES: Borough of South Molton, Manors of Hacche, George Nympton, Riverton, Romansleigh
PARISHES: Barnstaple, Bishops Tawton, George Nympton, Landkey, Swimbridge and South Molton
TITLE: 'Riverton manor'
SURVEYOR: not named
SCALE: not given
MATERIAL, SIZE & ORIENTATION: paper, ink; watermark 1804; 51.7cms x 40.5cms; no direction
CONTENT: stream; fields outlined in ink with alpha-numeric reference; letters keyed to list giving names of tenements and their content; some rough tree symbols; roads, fenced and unfenced, named; footpaths, broken lines; buildings in plan; peripheral owners named
Map also shows small properties in Barnstaple
ENDORSEMENT: Riverton Manor
Riverton SS 638300

x) PLACE: George Nympton
PARISHES: George Nympton and South Molton
Two pieces of paper stuck together showing 6 separate maps oriented in different directions

TITLE: 'General Map of George Nympton Manor'

SURVEYOR: not named

SCALE: not given

MATERIAL, SIZE & ORIENTATION: paper, coloured; 60cms x 38cms; direction varied

CONTENT: River Bray and River Mole named; arrows indicating direction of flow; fields outlined in various colours, two washed in green; alpha-numeric reference with letters keyed to list giving names of tenements and their content; tree symbols, green showing orchards, woods, hedgerow and isolated trees; roads, fenced, directions given; buildings in plan; peripheral owners named

ENDORSEMENT: Manor of George Nympton

George Nympton Church SS 700229

xi) PLACE: not identified

PARISHES: East Buckland, North Molton, South Molton

5 separate areas mapped

TITLE: not given

SURVEYOR: not named

SCALE: not given

MATERIAL, SIZE & ORIENTATION: paper, coloured; 100.5cms x 40.5cms; south west to top (pencil)

CONTENT: rivers, some blue, one named; arrows indicating direction of flow; fields outlined in colour; alpha-numeric reference; letters keyed to list giving names and content of tenements; roads, fenced; no trees; buildings in plan; peripheral owners

ENDORSEMENT: Manor of Hacche excling(sic) of S. Molton Town

acres within	1190.3.39	
S. Molton Town	181.–.30	1372.–.29
G. Nympton	991.3.39	
Romansleigh	1113.3.16	
Riverton	574.3.29	

Hacche Barton SS 714278 South Molton Church SS 714259 George Nympton Church SS 700229 Romansleigh Church SS 727206 Riverton SS 638300

xii) PLACE: Manor of Romansleigh

PARISHES: Chawleigh, Chulmleigh and Romansleigh

Map shows 4 separate areas roughly copied

TITLE: 'Manor of Romansleigh'

SURVEYOR: not named

SCALE: not given

MATERIAL, SIZE & ORIENTATION: paper, coloured; 71cms x 38.4cms; no direction

CONTENT: areas named, Coombe, Humacotts, Docworthy and in Romansleigh Glebe, Romansleigh Barton, Horridge, Duboundisland, Whitehouse; river; fields outlined in various colours; alpha-numeric reference with letters keyed to list identifying Glebe Land and areas named with content; rough tree symbols; other rough symbols marking ?waste or marsh; roads, fenced; footpaths, broken lines; buildings in plan (plain); peripheral owners named

ENDORSEMENT: Manor of Romansleigh

Romansleigh Church SS 727206

xiii) PLACES: Manor of Hacche and Borough of South Molton

PARISH: South Molton

TITLE: 'Burrough of South Molton Manor of Hacche'

SURVEYOR: not named

SCALE: not given

MATERIAL, SIZE & ORIENTATION: paper, coloured; 81cms EW x 59.5cms NS; north to top

CONTENT: stream, river, grey; Mole Bridge named; arrows indicating direction of flow; fields outlined in colour, some washed green or buff; gates, black; alpha-numeric reference with letters keyed to list giving field names and content; other landowners named within the town and on periphery of Acland town lands; tree symbols, green; roads, buff, named; footpaths, broken lines; church in elevation

ENDORSED: Manor of Hacche

South Molton Church SS 714259

ASSOCIATED DOCUMENTS: A Survey Book, DRO, 1148M add/6/11, which lacks Referential Letters A-D at the beginning of the Manor of Riverton, has some notes in the same hand as are found on the above maps, and covers all the Manors listed above. It also refers to the Manors of Hackworthy and Woolleigh, for which no maps have been found in the above collection.

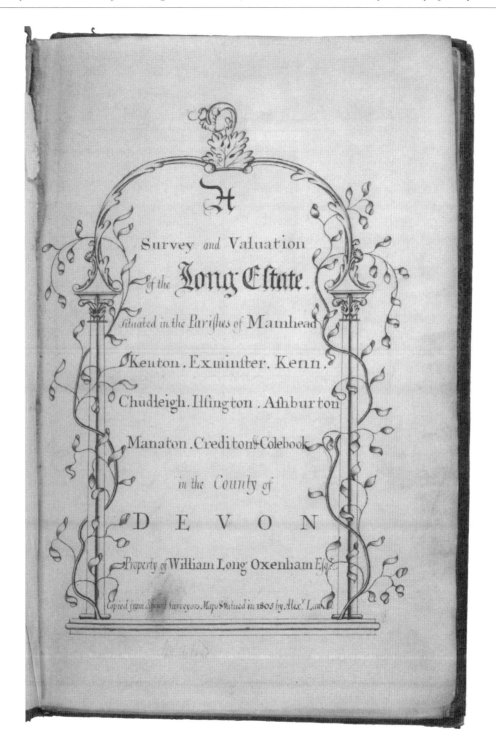

ATLAS

16. 1805	SRO, DD/AH/Box 14.5

PLACES: 'The Long Estate'

PARISHES: Ashburton, Chudleigh, Colebrooke, Crediton, Exminster, Ilsington, Kenn, Kenton, Mamhead, Manaton

Leather-covered volume, 17.5cms x 27cms, tooled in gold of 7 maps; 'J Acland 1805' in ink on end paper

TITLE OF VOLUME: 'A Survey and Valuation of the Long Estate situated in the Parishes of Mamhead Kenton. Chudleigh. Ilsington. Ashburton Manaton. Crediton & Colebook[sic] in the County of Devon Property of William Long Oxenham Esqr Copied from different Surveyors Maps & valued in 1805 by Alexr Law'

SURVEYOR: Alexander Law

SCALE: 'Scale of Statute Chains each containing 66 Feet'; scales vary

MATERIAL, SIZE & ORIENTATION: parchment, slight colour; sizes vary; direction indicated on each map

GENERAL CONTENT: streams with headwaters, ponds, outlined in blue; relief shown by hill shading; fields, named, outlined in ink with boundaries of estates in colour; alpha-numeric reference to lists on facing or following pages giving names of parcels, field names, land use ('Arable & Pasture, Furse and Waste, Hedges & Ditches'), content and total content; note at bottom explaining use of asterisks on boundaries of estates to indicate fence ownership; some fence symbols; gates, red; tree symbols showing orchards, avenues, hedgerow and isolated trees; and with stippling, woods; stippling only, waste; roads, buff, fenced and unfenced; directions given; Turnpike roads; buildings in plan, black; peripheral owners and manors named

DECORATION: title cartouche: simple rococo; 8 point compass rose, plain/shaded grey; north marked by fleur-de-lys, east by cross

MAPS:

'Map of the Lands in the Parishes of Mamhead and Kenton Taken 1805'; 42.5cms EW x 47cms NS; 1"=6 chains; 1:4752
Mamhead Church SX 931807; Kenton Church SX 958833

'Map of the Lands in the Parish of Exminster Taken in 1805'; 51cms EW x 49.2cms NS; 1"=9 chains; 1:7128; inset of Luccombe's Estate; River Exe, green, showing 'Low Water Mark, High Water Mark of Spring Tides, High Water Mark at Ordinary Tides', 'Fishing Post' and marshes
Exminster Church SX 946877

'Map of the Lands in the Parish of Kenn Taken from Surveys made in 1796 & 1805'; 54.5cms EW x 65.5cms NS; 1"=11 chains for Haldon Hill and some estates, 1:8712; others 1"=16 chains; 1:12672
Kenn Church SX 922857

'Map of the Lands in the Parish of Chudleigh Taken in 1805'; 27cms EW x 25.8cms NS; 1"=6 chains; 1:4752
Higher Upcott SX 890806

'Map of the Lands in the Parish of Ilsington Taken 1805'; 1"=9 chains; 1:7128
Lounstone SX 786751, Higher Sigford SX SX 782744

'Map of the Lands in the Parish of Manaton Taken 1805'; 29cms EW x 31cms NS; 1"=7.5 chains; 1:5940
Manaton Church SX 749813

'Map of the Lands in the Parishes of Crediton and Colebrook Taken in 1805'; 27cms EW x 34.2cms NS; 1"=6 chains; 1:4752
Lower Wotton SX 762981, Great Wotton SX 755984

ABSTRACT AT THE END OF THE VOLUME: 1 page giving High and Chief Rents payable to the Long Estate followed by 2 pages giving names of occupiers, tenements, terms of lives, content etc Value as given by A. Law £1487. 16s. 9½d

For further details of the maps see *Introduction*, pp. 18–19

SURVEY

17. 1807	DRO, 1148M add/6/10

PLACE: South Tawton

PARISH: South Tawton

TITLE: 'Survey & valuation of certain Lands in the Parish of South Tawton. Property of William Long Oxenham Esqr. by Alexr Law in 1807'

SURVEYOR: Alexander Law

FORMAT: one sheet, paper, size 39.5cms x 66cms

DETAILS: names of tenants, tenements, measured content (statute), 'Lives existing thereon or Number of Years unexpir'd 1807' (no., names, ages), conventionary rents, heriots reserved, yearly value as entered in former surveys, yearly value as estimated in 1807 by Alexr Law, 'Outgoings *communibus annis* viz:' poor rates and chief rents, Church rates, Land Tax redeemed, repairs, total of Outgoings, clear yearly value as estimated in 1807 by Alexander Law, value of the lessees interest, value of the fee simple under its present contingencies and observations. Under the last heading is a note under Addicoats that the lime rock and waste is to remain the joint property of Thomas Acland and Wroth Palmer Acland Esqrs.

ASSOCIATED DOCUMENT: South Tawton Rental for 1784–1795

For further details of the contents see *Introduction*, p. 4

SURVEY

| 18. 1807 | DRO, 1148M add/6/3 |

PLACE: Manor and Advowson of High Bray

PARISH: High Bray

TITLE: 'A Survey and Valuation of the Manor and Advowson of High Bray – Property of Willm. Long Oxenham Esq. by Alexr Law in 1807'

SURVEYOR: Alexander Law

FORMAT: paper sheet, size 39.4cms x 63.5cms

DETAILS: names of tenants, tenements, measured content (statute), lives existing (number, names and ages), conventionary rents, heriots reserved, yearly value as entered in former surveys, yearly value as estimated by A. Law in 1807, outgoings (poor rates, church rate, land tax and repairs), total of outgoings *communibus annis*, clear yearly value entered in former surveys, clear yearly value estimated in 1807 by Alexander

Law, value of the lessees interest, value of the fee simple under its present contingencies and Observations

NOTE: the Survey is signed by Alexander Law in August 1809 and witnessed by Ralph Barnes on 22 Sept. 1809

MAP

| 19. 1809 | DRO, 1148M add/10/1b |

PLACE: Manor of Wooleigh

PARISHES: Beaford, St Giles in the Wood, Little Torrington

Map originally on rollers

TITLE: 'Map of the Manor of Wooleigh in the Parishes of Beaford, St Giles [in the] Wood, and Little-Torrington Devon Property of Sir Thomas Dyke Acland Baronet by Alexander Law and Thomas Bradley'

SURVEYORS: Alexander Law and Thomas Bradley

SCALE: 'Scale of Statute Chains'; scale bar; 1"=4 chains; 1:3168

MATERIAL, SIZE & ORIENTATION: parchment, slight colour; badly water-damaged; 190.5cms EW x 140.5cms NS; north to top

CONTENT: river Torridge, stream lines; tributary; relief shown by hill shading; fields outlined in various colours; alpha-numeric reference [to Survey Book]; gates, red; asterisks indicating hedge ownership; tree symbols showing orchards and woodland; roads, some directions given; buildings in plan, grey; peripheral owners named

DECORATION: 16 point compass rose, line shaded; north marked by fleur-de-lys; dividers above scale

Woolleigh Barton SS 532168

For further details of the map see *Introduction*, pp. 20–21

SURVEY

| 20. 1809–10 | DRO, 1926B/A/E1/95 |

PLACE: Manor of Hacche

PARISHES: Bishop's Nympton, East Buckland, South Molton

TITLE: 'A Survey and Valuation of the Manor of Haache (sic) in the County of Devon, Property of Sir Thomas Dyke Acland Bart. Taken in the Years 1809 &1810 by Alexr Law.'

SURVEYOR: Alexander Law

FORMAT: 3 paper sheets, size 40.6cms x 30.8cms

DETAILS: alpha-numeric referential letters to map (not present), tenants' names, tenements' names, measured statute content, Parishes wherein situated, lives exising thereon or number of years or number of years unexpired at Lady Day 1814 (no., names and age), conventionary rents, heriots reserved, yearly value as entered in former surveys, yearly value as estimated in 1809 by Alexander Law, outgoings (poor rates, church rate, land tax redeemed, repairs), total of outgoings communibus annis, clear yearly value as entered in former survey, clear yearly value as estimated in 1809 by Alexander Law, value of the fee simple under its present contingencies

MAP

21. 1811/25   SRO, DD/WY/Box 121

PLACES: Higher and Lower Newland Farms

PARISH: Broadclyst

TITLE: 'Map of Higher and Lower Newland Farms in the Parish of Broadclyst; in the County of Devon. 1811'

SURVEYOR: not named

SCALE: 'Scale of Chains'; scale bar; 1"=6 chains; 1:4752

MATERIAL, SIZE & ORIENTATION: paper, mounted on linen, coloured; 34.6cms EW x 46cms NS; north to top

CONTENT: river, buff; fields, green (Higher Newland Farm), yellow (Lower Newland Farm), red (free hold lands), outlined in ink; numeric reference [to Survey Book]; roads, buff; buildings in plan, red or grey; peripheral owners and Glebe named

Explanation to use of colour:- 'Higher Newland Farm green; Lower Newland Farm yellow; Farm Houses red; Outhouses grey'

DECORATION: 8 point compass rose, shaded-line decoration; north

marked by fleur-de-lys

The map seems to be 1811 in date and the signature, lower right, 'Thomas Hawkes 1825' is an endorsement

Newlands SY 003979

For further details of the map see *Introduction*, p. 4

MAP

22. 1812   DRO, 1148M add/21/3/1

PLACE: intended new road at Killerton

PARISH: Broadclyst

TITLE: 'Plan of the intended new Road at Killerton'

SURVEYOR: not named

SCALE: not given

MATERIAL, SIZE & ORIENTATION: parchment, slight colour; 44cms x 21.5cms; no direction

CONTENT: river, blue; fields outlined in ink; gates; tree symbols showing isolated trees; old roads, buff, fenced and unfenced; directions given; new road, yellow; buildings in plan, grey; Killerton House named

ASSOCIATED DOCUMENT: Agreement by Sir Thomas Dyke Acland for the exchange of land for the new road with that of the old road

NOTE: part of the old road east of Columbjohn remains

See also DRO, DQS 113A/34/1, No.23.

Columbjohn SX 960997; Killerton House SS 973001

For further details of the map see *Introduction*, p. 21

MAP

23. 1812   DRO, DQS 113A/34/1

PLACE: as in 22

PARISH: Broadclyst

TITLE: 'Plan of the intended new road at Killerton'

SURVEYOR: [Alexander Law on stylistic grounds]

SCALE: not given

MATERIAL, SIZE & ORIENTATION: parchment, slight colour; 38cms x 22.4cms; no direction

CONTENT: river and stream outlined in ink; fields outlined in ink but not named; gates, red; tree symbols, black, marking clumps of trees; roads, buff, including 'Road from Stoke Canon', 'Turnpike Road from Exeter', 'Turnpike Road to Cullompton' ['Bradninch' substituted in pencil], 'Road to Broadclist'; line of new road, yellow; limits of the road to be diverted and the new road shown by the letters A, B and C; key to Intended New Road and Old Roads; buildings in plan, grey, including Killerton House; part of drive to Killerton House, dotted line

ENDORSEMENT: note of enrolment at Adjourned Sessions 8 May 1812

ASSOCIATED DOCUMENT: statement by Sir Thomas Dyke Acland that he is the owner of the lands described in the Plan which the new road, delineated by a yellow line, as being intended to be diverted, is to pass, agrees that in consideration of the Old Road also described in the Plan, being vested in him by way of exchange, and gives the new road to the public forever, 23 March 1812.

The old road is described as 'frequently impassable on account of floods'

The hand is that of Alexander Law and the map is almost the same as DRO, 1148M add/21/3/1 but with slight differences:-

1) drive to Killerton House not present on Map 22
2) turnpike road to Bradninch correct on Map 22 map but on DQS has Cullompton erased and 'Bradninch' substituted in pencil
3) gates on Map 22 are in black but on DQS are in red (typical of AL' style)
4) writing on 1148 is not in AL's hand

Columbjohn SX 960997; Killerton House SS 973001

For further details of the map see *Introduction*, p. 21

MAP

24. Early 19th cent.　　　SRO, DD/SAS c/1540/12/1

PLACE: 'Manors of Killerton & Aishclyst'

PARISH: Broadclyst

TITLE: 'Manors of Killerton & Aishclyst'

SURVEYOR: not named

SCALE: 'Chains'; scale bar; 1"=10.2; 1:8078

MATERIAL, SIZE & ORIENTATION: paper, coloured; 82cms EW x 61.8cms NS; north to top

CONTENT: rivers, double black lines, smaller streams with headwaters, ponds; fields, various colours distinguishing holdings; alpha-numeric reference [to Survey Book]; fence symbols; gardens; tree symbols indicating orchards, woods, plantations, isolated trees; deciduous and coniferous trees distinguished; roads, fenced and unfenced; road from Columbjohn 'stopped up'; footpaths, pecked lines; buildings in plan, black; quarry Inset of detached areas

DECORATION: 4 point compass indicator; north marked by fleur-de-lys

Area between Killerton and Ashclyst surveyed in detail but without names etc and uncoloured; shows river, fields, roads and buildings in plan

Killerton House SS 973001, Ashclyst Forest SY 003995

For further details of the map see *Introduction*, p. 21

MAP

25. *c*.1815　　　SRO, DD/AH 42/2/12

PLACE: 'A Plan of Lisles's Estate, in the Parish of Kenn, Devon, the Property of Wm. Long Oxenham Esqr.'

PARISH: Kenn

TITLE: 'A Plan of Lisles's Estate, in the Parish of Kenn, Devon, the Property of Wm. Long Oxenham Esqr.'

SURVEYOR: not named

SCALE: 'A Scale of Chains'; scale bar; 1"=4 chains; 1:3168

MATERIAL, SIZE & ORIENTATION: paper, ink; field references only , red; 53.2cms EW x 37.8cms NS; north to top

CONTENT: relief shown by hill shading; fields outlined in ink, named with content; alpha-numeric reference, red, [to Survey Book]; land-use notes in pencil; 'old Hedges' named; gates; asterisks indicating hedge ownership; tree symbols on Penn Hill, also marking copses and orchards; roads, fenced and unfenced, directions given; footpaths, broken lines; 'halter path' named; garden named; buildings in plan, hatched black; 'Castle' (Haldon Tower) in plan; peripheral owners named

ENDORSEMENT: Map of Lisles & Commins's

Kenn Lisles & Commins's

NOTE: in Alexander Law's hand:

1816   18 Beech cut in the Plantation belonging to Lyle & Commins's and 14 Firs

13 Firs in Penhill Plantation and one Ash

6 Timber Trees and 16 Saplings of Fir for the Repairs of the Premises where the Game Keeper lives and carried from the plantation adjoining and part of Haldon Hill u.8

Kenn Church SX 922857

MAP (rough sketch)

26. 1816   DRO, 96M add/E18

PLACE: Woolleigh Park

PARISH: St Giles in the Wood

TITLE: 'A Plan & Admeasurement of 3 Waste Spots on the North side of Woolleigh Park, belonging to Sir T.D. Ackland, in the Parish of St. Giles'

SURVEYOR: not named

SCALE: not given

MATERIAL, SIZE & ORIENTATION: paper, ink; 23.5cms EW x 18.6cms NS; north to top (NSEW spelt out)

CONTENT: river, black lines, arrows showing the direction of flow, ox-bow lake; fields, numbered 1–3; gate across road; tree symbols showing ?orchard; roads, named; house in elevation;

peripheral estates

Note that 'In the sd. Plot there is an Old Water Course full of water'

Woolleigh Barton SS 532168

MAP

27. 1819   DRO, 1926B/A/E3/2

PLACE: turnpike road

PARISH: Broadclyst

TITLE: 'Map of a Road near Broad Clist Village to be cut thro' Sir Thos. Dyke Aclands lands'

SURVEYOR: not named

SCALE: not given but notes 'Length of the old line of the Road is 140 Poles. Length of the Intended new line of Road 117'

MATERIAL, SIZE & ORIENTATION: paper, coloured (torn); 40.1cms x 32.2cms; no orientation

CONTENT: river, black; bridges; fields outlined in green and orange and arable, meadow and orchards specified; line of old road, plain, intended new road shown by dotted lines; 'Old Turnpike Road to Cullompton' and 'Old Turnpike Road to Exeter' named; buildings in plan, black; School Room and Rev. Mr Barton's house named

ASSOCIATED DOCUMENTS: (a) an account of land taken of Sir Thomas Dyke Acland Bart by the Cullompton New Road, 1815 (b) Stopping Up Order, 1819 (c) estimate by William Wright for making the new road, n.d., all at the same DRO reference SX 983975

MAP & VIEW

28. Early 19th cent.   DRO, 1148M add/10/5/15

PLACE: Killerton Park

PARISH: Broadclyst

2 sheet perspective view of proposed new approaches to Killerton, based on scaled plan

Sheet 1

TITLE: not given

SURVEYOR: not named

SCALE: not present on this sheet

MATERIAL, SIZE & ORIENTATION: paper, ink; 74.8cms x 54.5cms; no direction

CONTENT: river; fence symbols; tree symbols marking mixed woodland, isolated trees in various stages of maturity; detailed plantings screening mill, granary and to lesser extent church-yard; proposed new line of drive and sunk fence (shown by shaded lines ///), superimposed on tree symbols; road from Rewe named; footpaths, dotted lines; Church, Granary, Mill in plan, hatched

Sheet 2

TITLE: not given

SURVEYOR: not named

SCALE: in feet, scale bar; 1"=65 feet; 1:780

MATERIAL, SIZE & ORIENTATION: paper, ink, slight colour; 166cms x 67cms; no direction

CONTENT: ponds, parallel lines; symbols marking hedgerows; tree symbols marking mixed woodland, and with shading suggesting open woodland; orchards; isolated trees as in sheet 1; open fields/pasture shown by ... ...; shaded lines /// marking sunk fence; roads from Exeter and Broadclyst named; unfenced road, gated, leading to 'Mansion'; footpaths, pecked lines; 'Proposed Line of Approach' leading to Mansion, gated and additional road, red, superimposed on tree symbols; buildings in plan, hatched; Mansion and Stables named

ENDORSEMENT: William Gilpin

Killerton House SS 973001

For further details of the map see *Introduction*, pp. 15–16

MAP

29. 1836   DRO, 484M/T4/37

PLACES: Brickhouse, Cofford Mill, Mowlish and Newhouse (farm)

PARISHES: Kenton and Mamhead

TITLE: 'The Schedule referred to by the above written indenture'

SURVEYOR: not named

SCALE: 'Scale of Chains'; scale bar; 1"=5 chains;1:3960

MATERIAL, SIZE & ORIENTATION: parchment, coloured; 97.4cms EW x 70cms NS; north to top

CONTENT: streams, pond, blue; fields coloured with boundaries of estates in deeper colour; numeric reference to lists giving field names, land use and content, grouped by estates; asterisks indicating fence ownership; tree symbols showing orchards, brakes and avenues; roads, buff; buildings in plan, red; parish boundary between Kenton and Mamhead shown; peripheral owners named

DECORATION: 8 point compass rose, shaded-line decoration; north marked by fleur-de-lys

ASSOCIATED DOCUMENT: map is bound in with Conveyance dated 23 March 1836 from Sir Thomas Dyke Acland of a mansion house and farm called Newhouse in Mamhead and Brickhouse, Mowlishes and Cofford Mill in Kenton to the use of Sir Robert William Newman

Mowlish SX 951811

For further details of the map see *Introduction*, p. 31

MAP

30. 1839   DRO, 1148M add/1/T13/2

PLACE: Whitedown

PARISH: Cullompton

TITLE: ' Whitedown in the Parish of Cullompton Devon'

SURVEYOR: not named; 'Surveyed March 1839'

SCALE: 'chains'; scale bar; 1"=2 chains 1:1584

MATERIAL, SIZE & ORIENTATION: paper, mounted on linen, coloured:

40.8cms EW x 20.3cms NS; north to top

CONTENT: fields, green; numeric references to table giving field names and content; hedge ownership indicated by fence symbols; tree symbols showing coniferous plantations; roads, buff; directions given; buildings in plan, red, grey and hatched; peripheral owners and estates named

DECORATION: 4 point compass indicator; north marked by fleur-de-lys

ASSOCIATED DOCUMENT: map is attached to a Conveyance (by way of Lease and Release) of 19 and 20 July 1840 by R.C. Campion to Lord Courtenay and S.T. Kekewich as trustees of the property. Sir T. D. Acland is a party to the Release only, presumably as a trustee and the map shows that he was a 'peripheral owner' of the property conveyed.

Whitedown Cross ST 010015

MAP

31. 19th cent.   DRO, 1148M add/10/3/1

PLACE: Kedworthy

PARISH: High Bray

TITLE: 'Kedworthy in the Parish of High Bray in the County of Devon'

SURVEYOR: not named

SCALE: 'A Scale of 10 Chains'; scale bar; 1"=4 chains; 1:3168

MATERIAL, SIZE & ORIENTATION: paper, coloured; 65cms EW x 45.8cms NS; north to top

CONTENT: river, named 'Kentaway Water', blue; fields, green yellow or pink wash with numeric reference to table giving field names and content; gates; dotted lines indicating fence ownership; fence symbols; tree symbols, green, showing woods; roads, grey; footpaths, pecked and broken lines; court[lage], grey; house in elevation; peripheral estates named, also Rockley Wood, Lidacott Down and Kedworthy Cleave

DECORATION: 8 point plain compass rose, inner circle, dots; north marked by a symbol

ACREAGE: 106a.0r.35p.

Kedworthy SS 707370

For further details of the map see *Introduction*, p. 5

MAP

32. *c*.1700   DRO, 1148M add/10/13

PLACE: Exmoor

PARISHES: Brendon, Challacombe, High Bray, Lynton, Molland, North Molton, Twitchen (all Devon), Exford, Oare, Porlock, Stoke Pero, Withypool (all Somerset)

TITLE: not given

SURVEYOR: not named

SCALE: not given

MATERIAL, SIZE & ORIENTATION: parchment, discoloured and damaged, ink; 38.4cms x 29.5cms, no direction

CONTENT: circular map with details shown within 3 concentric circles as follows:-

inner circle, diameter 12.1cms; Rivers Exe, Barle and Kinsford; tree symbol showing 'Hore Oake' at division of Lynton Common and Brendon Common segments; stone symbols marking 'Sadlerstone, Wadborow, Edgerley Stone, Settaborow, Two borow' and other stones; 'Kensford Cross' marked by a cross

middle circle, diameter 24cms; segments divided by dotted lines named as 'Hawkeridge Common, Whithipoole Common, Exford Common, Larkborow, Stoke Pero Common, Porlock Common, Oare Common, Badgeworthy, Brendon Common, Lynton Common, Challacombe Common, High Bray Common, Five borow North Molton (shown by stone symbols), North Molton Common, Twitchin Common, Molland Common'

outer circle, diameter 28cms; churches in elevation (not completely stylised) – 'Withipool, Exford, Stoke Pero, Porlock, Oare, Brendon, Lynton, Challacombe, High Bray, North Molton, Twitchin, Molland'

ASSOCIATED DOCUMENT: there are no documents in the Acland collection (1148M) to indicate a date for making this map but

'The Map of Exmore' of 1675 in the Public Record Office (PRO, Excheq. B &A Chas. II, Devon 269) reproduced in Edward T. MacDermot, *The History of the Forest of Exmoor* (Newton Abbot, 1973), frontispiece, is similar. This volume also mentions that several similar maps of Exmoor were made at this time.

For further details of the map see *Introduction*, p. 2, n9

SURVEY

33. 18th cent.	DRO, 1148M add/6/17

PLACE: North Petherton
PARISH: North Petherton
TITLE: 'North Petherton' on front cover
SURVEYOR: not named
FORMAT: volume, paper sheets, much damaged, size 18.7cms x 24cms
DETAILS: number on map, premises, quality, measure, price per acre and annual value

---

SURVEY

34. 1720	DRO, 1148M add/6/14

PLACE: Manor of Exbridge Riphay
PARISHES: Bampton (Devon); Brushford, Dulverton, Hawkridge, Winsford (all Somerset)
TITLE: 'A Survey of the Mannor of Exbridge Riphay near Dulverton in the County of Somerset'
SURVEYOR: not named
FORMAT: paper sheet, size 38.7cms x 30.7cms
DETAILS: names of tenants, tenements, lives, reserved rents, heriots, yearly value and remarks
NOTE: Lists 'Estates in hand in Brushford'

SURVEYS

35. A–B. 1720 & 1741	DRO, 1148M add/6/15

PLACES: Manor of West Luckham, Wilmersham and West Luckham Manor
PARISHES: Luccombe, Stoke Pero

(A) TITLE: 'A Survey of the Mannor of West Luckham Entirely Mr Blackfords 11 Oct 1720'
SURVEYOR: not named
FORMAT: paper, much damaged, size 41.8cms x 31.5cms
DETAILS: names of tenants, number of tenements held by each tenant, number of lives on each tenement, reserved rents, heriots and yearly value

(B) TITLE: '1741 Survey of the Mannor of West Luckham 10 Feb 1741'
SURVEYOR: not named
FORMAT: paper, damaged, size as above
DETAILS: lives by lease, names of tenements, heriots, high rent and yearly value
ASSOCIATED DOCUMENTS: 3 undated surveys, all appear to be 18th cent., two headed 'Mannor of West Luckham' and the third 'Wilmersham and West Luckham Manor'. Similar details to 35A–B. Damaged.

SURVEY

36. 1720	DRO, 1148M add/6/18

PLACE: Manor of Bossington
PARISHES: Luccombe, Minehead, Porlock, Selworthy, Timberscombe
TITLE: 'A Survey of the Mannor of Bossington'
SURVEYOR: not named
FORMAT: large paper sheet, size 47.8cms x 37cms
DETAILS: names of tenants, premises, number of lives, reserved rents, heriots, yearly value

SURVEYS

37. 1720–1755   SRO, DD/AH/65/15

PLACES: Manors of Banckland, Buckland alias Buckland Sororum, Cheadmead and Auler (Aller)

PARISHES: Aller, Lyng, North Petherton

TITLES: 'November 1st 1720 The Mannors of Cheadmead Banckland and Buckland Sororum'; 'Mannors of Chedmeade Banckland and Buckland Soror' 1752/1755'; 'A Survey of the Manours of Buckland alias Bankland Chadmead and Buckland alias Buckland Sororum with the rights members and appurtenances in the County of Somerset formerly in the tenure of Sir Coplestone Warwick Bampfylde Bar[t]. since of Thomas Wroth Bart deceased and now of Arthur Acland, Esq. in the right of Elizabeth his wife taken in the year 1755 by Jer. Dewdney Steward'

SURVEYOR: Jere[miah] Dewdney

FORMAT: volume, size 20.5cms x 32cms, with parchment covers

DETAILS: tenants' names; tenements' names; tenures; rents; heriots; yearly value; lives in being

NOTE: most of the volume is taken up with the 1755 Survey; land in the Parish of Lyng is also listed

For further details of the contents see *Introduction*, pp. 16–17

SURVEY

38. 1746–47   DRO, 1148M/6/20

PLACES: Manors of Avil, Bossington, Exbridge Ryphay, Holnicote, West Luckham, Wilmersham and West Luckham

PARISHES: Bicknoller, Brompton Regis, Brushford, Carhampton, Crowcombe, Cutcombe, St Decumans, Dulverton, Dunster, Exford, Hawkridge, Luccombe, Minehead, Old Cleeve, Porlock, Selworthy, Stoke Pero, Timberscombe, Winsford, Withicombe (Somerset); Bampton (Devon)

TITLES: General title: 'Holnycote Surveys 1747 Avill Bossington Holnycote West Luckham Exbridge Ryphay'; titles to individual manors: 'A Survey of the Manor of Avil near Dunster & Lying in the severall Parishes of Bicknaller Crocombe Carhampton Cutcombe Old Cleave Dunster St Decumans & Timberscombe'; 'Survey of the Manor of Bossington lying in the several Parishes of Porlock, Selworthy, Minehead, Timbersombe and Luckham'; 'A Survey of the Manor of Wilmersham and West Luckham Lying in the several Parishes of Luckham Stoke Pero Exford and Selworthy'; 'A Survey of the Manor of Holnicote Lying in the several Parishes of Selworthy, Luckham, Minehead, Porlock, Dulverton, Brompton Regis and Exford'; 'A Survey of the Manor of Exbridge Ryphay lying in the several Parishes of Brushford, Dulverton, Winsford, Hawkridge and Bampton'

SURVEYOR: not named

FORMAT: volume, size 23cms x *c*.35cms, paper, with limp parchment covers

DETAILS: number of tenement within the manor [each manor is numbered separately], dates of original leases and who granted them, lessees and fines, premises, lives and their ages, present tenants, Lord's rent, heriots, yearly value, notes and remarks

NOTES: this survey is abstracted as *Survey 2* in this volume; the 1747 survey is preceded by rental for one year to Lady Day 1746 for the manors. There are columns for dates of leases [all blank], number in survey, premises and rents

For further details of the contents see *Introduction*, pp. 7–8

MAP

39. *c*.1760   SRO, DD/AH 65/13 c/2252

PLACE: Lyng Farm

PARISH: Lyng TITLE: 'A Map of Ling Farm an Estate of Arthur Acland Esq. T.H. Fecit.'

SURVEYOR: 'T H'; Thomas Hodge

SCALE: 'Scale of Chains of 4 Perch'; scale bar; 1"=3.5 chains; 1:2772

MATERIAL, SIZE & ORIENTATION: parchment, slight colour; 71.2cms EW x 55.7cms NS; south to top

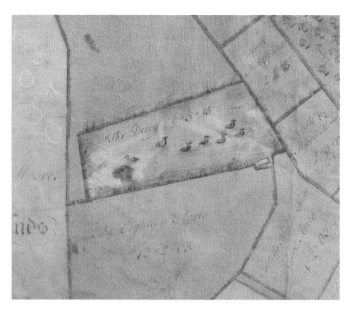

Duck decoy shown on map/survey 40 (SRO, DD/SAS/W51)

MAP

40. 1761	SRO, DD/SAS/W51

PLACE: Aller Manor

PARISH: Aller

TITLE: 'Aller Manor in the County of Somerset the Lands of Arthur Acland Esq. 1761'

SURVEYOR: [John Bowring, on stylistic grounds]

SCALE: 'A Scale of Equal Chains'; scale bar; 1"=4 chains; 1:3168

MATERIAL, SIZE & ORIENTATION: parchment, very faded and crumpled, coloured; approx. 91.5cms x 71cms; north to top

CONTENT: 'River Perrot', blue; fields, green wash outlined in darker green; named with content; tree symbols, green, showing some hedgerow trees, and an orchard; gates, black; gardens in detailed plan; drove roads, green, named; 'Decoy' with ducks shown, grey; Church in elevation; peripheral owners named

DECORATION: cartouche: surrounded by scrolls, with flowers and leaves; 8 point compass rose, north marked by fleur-de-lys and east by a cross

Aller Church ST 396288

For further details of the map see *Introduction*, p. 17

CONTENT: river, ponds, grey-blue; fields outlined with hedge symbols, green; numeric reference to list giving field names and content; field names and content inserted in a later hand; gateways; 'rick yard' named; 'Common Meadow' named; tree symbols, green showing isolated trees; roads, directions given (Road to Taunton, Road to Barrow Bridge); buildings in plan, grey, including church and 'Smith's Shop'

Note below scale:- 'N B All ye Boundery's colour'd green belong to ye Estate'

Pencil construction grid

DECORATION: title cartouche: scrolls with diaper pattern below and garlands of flowers above; 4 point compass indicator, plain/shaded grey; north marked by fleur-de-lys

Lyng Church ST 333289

For further details of the map see *Introduction*, p. 17

ATLAS

41. 1767	SRO, DD/AH 66/11

PLACES: Manors of Auler and Oath, Bankland, Buckland, Currill, Durborow, Fairfield, Huntspill Verney and Woolmerston

PARISHES: Aller, Durborow, Glastonbury, Holford, Lyng, Mear, North Petherton, Nether Stowey, Over Stowey and Stogursey

Map 1

TITLE: 'A Plan of the Manor of Fairfield the Seat of Arth^r Acland Esqr Situate lying and being in the Parish of Stokcoursy Somerset by W Fairchild 1767' The maps are not numbered in the volume but are numbered here for convenience.

SURVEYOR: William Fairchild

Volume (rebound) with no introductory sheet, size 36.5cms x

52cms, paper, coloured; scales vary but mostly 1"=5 chains (1:3960); most have compass roses, shaded black/plain, north marked by fleur-de-lys

GENERAL DESCRIPTION OF CONTENT: rivers, black; bridge; some relief shown by hill shading; fields outlined in various colours, named, some content shown and with land use distinguished; written survey on facing and contiguous pages gives names of lands, computed acres, measured acres, woods and furzy land, arable, meadow, pasture, value per acre, value of each piece and old rent, all arranged under tenement; gateways; meadows, stippled; other owners named in cursive script; tree symbols, black, showing orchards; tree symbols, black, arranged in clumps, indicating woods; roads, plain, some named and some directions given; buildings in plan, hatched black or red; peripheral owners and estates

DECORATION: cartouche (map 1): urn on plinth, swags, leaves, flowers, acanthus and scrolls, grasses
Fairfield House ST 187430

Map 2 'A Plan of detached Pieces in the Parish of Stokecursy set on Lease for Lives to John Hawkins'

Map 3 'Plan of the Manor of Durborow Belonging to Arthur Acland Esqʳ WF' Cartouche: acanthus, shell/ruched fabric, leaves
Durborough ST 192414

Map 4 'A Plan of detached Pieces belonging to the Manors of Durborow and Currill'

Map 5 'A Plan of Durborrow Common, part of five Lords Wood and Catsford Marsh Detached pieces in the Parishes of Durborow, Holford and Stokecursy'
Holford ST 158414

Map 6 'A Plan of Cock Farm in the Parish of Stokecursy'
Cock Farm ST 230434

Map 7 'A Plan of the Manor of Auler and Oath belonging to Arthur Acland Esqʳ 1767 by W Fairchild' Decoy marked and 'The great Drove from Auler to Bridgwater'; River protected by an embankment

Aller Court Farm ST 395288 Oath ST 384275

Map 8 'A Plan of Ling Farm in the Parish of Ling Belonging to Arthur Acland Esqʳ Copied from a Plan Signed TH by W Fairchild 1767' Cartouche shows a sun behind clouds, scrolls, leaves, a quiver of arrows and a mythical beast with an arrow through it
Lyng Church ST 333289

Map 9 'Manor of Bankland and Parish of North Petherton'
Bankland ST 316300

Map 10 'Manor of Buckland in the Parish of North Petherton'
Buckland Farm ST 300281

Map 11 'A Plan of Lands Lying in the Parishes of Mear and Glastonbury'
Glastonbury Church ST 497388

Map 12 'A Plan of a Farm Situated at Haydon Green called Taunton Dean Land belonging to Arthur Acland Esq Copied by WF' Cartouche of acanthus leaves, scrolls, a basket of fruit below a tree and a shepherd's crook

Map 13 'A Plan of the Manor of Huntspill Verney'
Huntspill ST 312454

Map 14 'Plan of Aller Allotment in King's Sedgmoor' (Acland allotments inclosed with a red line)
Note: this map does not appear to be by W. Fairchild

Map 15 'Manor of Woolmerston, in the Parish of North Petherton'
Woolmersdon ST 284336

Map 16 Ditto

Map 17 'Lands in the Parishes of Nether and Over Stowey' (2 scales)
Nether Stowey Church ST 196396 Over Stowey Church ST 185385

Maps have annotations in pencil
Some 'Lands on Lease for Lives' listed
2 Pages headed 'Somerset Amounts Collected' in columns

under:- Names of Farms and Tenants / Computed Acres / Measured Acres / Waste Com or Heath / Furze Woods or Orchard / Arable / Marsh or Meadow / Present Value

2 pages headed 'References' in columns under Tenants & Tenements / Parcels / Measured Content / Yearly Value

ASSOCIATED DOCUMENTS: There is a map of the Manor of Auler and Oath belonging to John Acland Esq., undated, at SRO, DD/AH 66/12

There is a similar volume of maps made by W. Fairchild c.1770 of lands of the Slade family at SRO, DD/SLM C/1795, much of the land being in the Parish of North Petherton. On page 7 of this volume are 'Plans of Spitgrove etc. part of the Manor Lands, also Ashes, etc. part of Acland lands, with references thereto' and a note on a Plan of lands at Bankland states that 'this was purchased off Sir John P Acland Bart'

For further details of the map see *Introduction*, p. 17

SURVEY

42. *c.*1770	DRO, 1148M/Box 9/2

PLACE: Manor of East Luckham

PARISHES: Carhampton, Dunster, Luccombe, Selworthy

TITLE: 'A Rental of the Arundell Estate A Survey of the Manor of East Luckham'

SURVEYOR: not named

FORMAT: volume of 12 paper sheets, size 17cms x 26.8cms, no covers

DETAILS: tenants' names; tenements' names; the sum paid. The amounts are totalled at the bottom of each page

NOTE: the survey also lists lands, etc. in four Cornish manors, see no.53 in this list

For further details of the contents see *Introduction*, p. 9

SURVEY

43. 1779	DRO, 1148M add/6/17

PLACES: Manors of Newton Wroth and Newton Regis

PARISH: North Petherton

TITLE: 'A Survey of the Manors of Newton Wroth and Regis settled in April 1779 by Mr John Bailey Steward to Sir Thomas Dyke Acland Barrt. the Proprietor'

SURVEYOR: John Bailey

FORMAT: paper sheets of different sizes, in parchment cover

DETAILS: names of tenants, ages, tenements, tenures, rents, heriots, yearly value, fines

---

ATLAS

44. 1795–1806	SRO, DD/AH 65/12

PLACES: 'Manors of Fairfield and Durborow with detached estates'

PARISHES: Holford, Littlestoke, Kilton, Stogursey, Stringston

Leather-bound vol. 33.5cms x 47.7cms

Title gold on red leather 'Fairfield Survey Book 1795'

TITLE PAGE: 'A Survey of the Manors of Fairfield and Durborow with the detached Estates in the several Parishes of Stogursey, Littlestoke Stringston Holford & Kilton in the County of Somerset belonging to John Acland Esq. 1795 by C. Chilcott Land Surveyor'

44 numbered pages, paper, containing plans, mostly slight colour. Plans preceded by:-

1. 'Remarks' '1806 Many new purchases & exchanges having been made by the aforesaid Jno Acland Esqr since this Survey was mde & arranged in 1795; it is therefore entered and corrected down to the present year 1806 Chas Chilcott';
2. page entitled 'Numerical Reference' giving numerical reference and page number;
3. 'Index';
4. 'Explanation' of the signs and symbols used on the maps.

Each map is followed by page[s] of Reference listing the 'Premises' (field names), 'Measure' – compd and Statute, 'Qual[ity]' – arable, meadow

SURVEYOR: Charles Chilcott

SCALE: varies from map to map

MATERIAL, SIZE & ORIENTATION: paper, slight colour on most maps; directions indicated, north marked on some by fletched and decorated arrowhead

GENERAL CONTENT: relief shown by hill shading; fields, distinguishing arable and meadow and with numeric reference to Survey which lists premises, field names, quality indicated by letter – P, A, M, O – and computed and statute measure; boundaries shown by hedge symbols; gates; gardens; tree symbols showing orchards; tree symbols and stippling indicating plantations, woods and coppice; roads, plain; footpaths, shaded lines – ////; buildings in plan, black

Each map is followed by a Reference Table

Maps: [not numbered in the volume]

Map 1. Plan of Fairfield House, Plantations, Farm &c: including the alterations made by F Acland Esqr. down to the year 1806; Parish boundary between Stogursey and Lilstock noted as fixed by a perambulation of Lilstock Commissioners in 1803
Fairfield House ST 187430

Map 2. Lands in Demesne &c 1795; garden shown in detail; pencil annotations showing new road

Map 3. Water Farm
ST 194432

Map 4. Honibere Farm
ST 182435

Map 5. Peadon
Peadon Farm ST 202413

Map 6. Cock Farm
ST 230433

Map 7. Chalcot Farm 1796; purchases of 1806 noted
Chalcot Farm ST 234448; map includes Woolstone Farm ST 238443, Idson Farm ST 226443, (Upper) Cock Farm ST 230435, Catsford Marshes (Catsford Common) ST 237456

Map 8. Farringdon-Hill; water mill noted
Farringdon Farm ST 213434

Map 9. Bullen Farm 1794; cornucopia below title (?Benhole) ST 197457

Map 10. Hurfords Rowes & Hartrey's

Map 11. North Gound and Cole Land
Culls Farm ST 193444

Map 12. Durborow Leaseholds; including mill
Durborough ST 192414

Map 13. Durborow Leaseholds

Map 14. A plan of Detach'd Lands in Stringston
Stringston Church ST 176424

Map 15. A Plan of the Town & Borough of Stogursey; Acland properties coloured
Stogursey Church ST 204428

Map 16. A Plan of Sundry Lands

Map 17. Fairfield Leaseholds

Map 18. North & South Week Moors and Nedham
North Moor & Wick Moor ST 215455

Map 19. Stolford Field & Broad Hill
Stolford near North Moor ST 233458

Map 20. Plan of Old Peadon
Kilton ST 164439

For further details of the atlas see *Introduction*, p. 17

SURVEY	
45. *c.*1802	DRO, 1148M add/6/13

PLACE: Manor of East Luckham
PARISHES: Luccombe

TITLE: 'Manor of East Luckham'

SURVEYOR: not named

FORMAT: small volume, size 19.3cms x 25.5cms, soft leather covers, affected by damp

DETAILS: tenements' names, lives in being and their ages, lives added, conventionary rents, capons, due days, the kind of heriots, the sum in lieu thereof, observations. The name of the present tenant has been added in another hand.

NOTES: this survey is abstracted as part of *Survey 3* in this volume; the survey also covers eight manors in Cornwall and one in Devon

For further details of the contents see *Introduction*, p. 9

MAP

46. 1809   DRO, 1148M add/10/23a

PLACE: Petherton Park and Manors of Newton Roth and Regis

PARISH: North Petherton

Map originally on rollers

TITLE: 'Map of Petherton Park and Manor and Tithes of Newton=Roth & Regis situated in the Parish of North Petherton and County of Somerset. Property of Sir Thomas Dyke Acland Baronet Survey'd and Mapped in 1809 by Alexander Law and Assistants'

SURVEYOR: Alexander Law and Assistants

SCALE: 'Scale of Statute Chains each containing 66 Feet'; scale bar; 1"=4 chains; 1:3168

MATERIAL, SIZE & ORIENTATION: parchment, coloured; 152.5cms EW x 131.5cms NS; north to top

CONTENT: river, blue; fields outlined in ink or colour; asterisks indicating ownership; gates, red; in Petherton Park alpha-numeric reference using upper case letters, referring to 'Table of Particulars' listing tenants, tenements and 'Measured Content Statute; alpha-numeric reference using lower case letters referring to Newton Manor in the 'Table of Particulars'; fields coloured green with double lower case letters and figures referring in 'Table of Particulars' to 'Lands Titheable to but

not belonging to the Manor of Newton'; other owners named in fields; tree symbols, black, showing orchards and isolated trees; roads, buff, directions given; buildings in plan, back; peripheral owners named

'Note 1st The Property of the Out Fences bounding the Premises delineated in this Map is distinguished by * Asterisks Viz.

Where the Asterisk is placed on the inside of the Hedge or Fence there it belongs to the Premises Mapped but Where they are placed Outside the Fence there it belongs to the adjoining Lands. Also the Asterisks placed on both sides of the Fence divides it to be equally kept.'

'Note 2nd Those Fields couloured all over are Titheable to but not belonging to the Manor. The Titheable Lands in and part of the Manor are distinguished by having an Asterisk placed after the Referential Letters thus a.6* &c. &c.'

DECORATION: title cartouche: simple scrolls with acanthus leaves, flowers and ruched fabric; 8 point compass rose, plain/black, north marked by fleur-de-lys

North Petherton Church ST 291330

MAP

47. 1809   DRO, 1148M add10/10/28

PLACE: Petherton Park and Manors of Newton Roth and Regis

PARISH: North Petherton

TITLE: 'Map of Petherton park and Manor and tithes of Newton=Roth & Regis taken in 1809'

SURVEYORS: Alexander Law and Thomas Bradley (named in Survey Book)

SCALE: 'Scale of Statute Chains each containing 66 Feet'; scale bar; 1"=12 chains; 1:9504

MATERIAL, SIZE & ORIENTATION: parchment, coloured; 50cms EW x 48cms NS; north to top

CONTENT: canal, blue, locks; arrows indicating direction of flow; fields outlined in ink or colour; alpha-numeric reference to Survey Book; asterisks indicating fence ownership; Petherton Park outlined in yellow with alpha-numeric reference (upper

Case Letters) and these fields not included in Survey Book; titheable fields marked with red asterisk; fields 'coloured over' titheable to but not belonging to the manor; gates, red; tree symbols showing orchards and isolated trees; roads, directions given; buildings in plan, black; peripheral owners named

Note: The Property of the Outhedges or Fences bounding the Premises delineated in this Map is distinguished by * Asterisks Viz where the Asterisks are placed on the inside of the Hedge or Fence there it belongs to the premises Mapp'd but where they are placed outside the Fence there it belongs to the adjoining Lands.

Those Fields coloured over are Titheable to but not belonging to the Manor. The Titheable Lands in and part of the Park or Manor are distinguished by having a red asterisk placed after the Referential Letter thus a.3.*

Decoration: title cartouche: simple frame of scrolls with acanthus leaves; 8 point compass rose, plain/black; north marked by fleur de lys, east by cross

North Petherton Church ST 291330

The map is folded in such away as to imply that it was originally held inside the Survey Book, No.48.

Content'; arranged by tenement. Indication of which lands titheable

2ND PART: 'Abstract of Newton Manor'
'Referential letters; Tenants; Tenements; Measured Content Statute; Lives existing thereon or Number of Years unexpired Lady Day 1809; Conventionary Rents; Heriots reserved; Yearly Value as entered in former Surveys yearly Value as estimated in 1809 by Alex. Law Outgoings *Communibus Annis* viz (Poor Rates, Church Rate, Land Tax, Repairs) Total outgoings *communibus annis*; Clear Yearly Value as entered into former Survey; Clear Yearly Value as estimated in 09 by A Law

TOTAL:	A	R	P
	468:	2:	12'

3RD PART: Lands Titheable to, but not belonging to the Manor, arranged by owner
'Referential Letters; Names of Parcels; Arable and Pasture; Furze and Waste; Hedges & Ditches; Total Content'

'Totals Collected	A	R	P
Manors of Newton Wroth and Regis	468:	2:	12
Titheable but not belonging to Do	128:	1:	15
Petherton Park	1234:	3:	19
Total Content of Map	1831:	3:	6'

For further details of nos 46–48 see *Introduction*, p. 21

SURVEY BOOK

48. 1809	DRO, 1148M add11/1

PLACE: Petherton Park and Manors of Newton Roth and Regis
PARISH: North Petherton
SURVEY BOOK, TITLE: 'A Survey and Valuation of Petherton Park and manors and Tithes of Newton Wroth & Regis situated in the Parish of North Petherton and County of Somerset Property of Sir Thos Dyke Acland Bart. Surveyed and mapped in 1809, by A. Law, & T. Bradley' Leather-bound volume tooled in gold, 15cms x 21.9cms with decorated title page common to all Law's bound volumes
1ST PART: 'Referential Letters; Names of Parcels; Content of Arable & Pasture; Furze & Waste; Hedges & Ditches; Total

---

ATLAS

49. 1809 & 1812	DRO, 1148Madd 9/ 6/24
	Photo copies at SRO, T/PH/ac/1–2c/3253

PLACES: Manors of Blackford, Bossington, East Luckham, Holnicote, Stock Pero, West Luckham, Wilmersham
PARISHES: Carhampton, East Luccombe, Exford, Minehead, Porlock, Selworthy, Stoke Pero, Timberscombe
Leather-covered volume tooled in gold with brass clasps, 22cms x 27cms, entitled 'Part of the Manor of Holnicote The Manors of Bossington Wilmersham West Luckham Stock Pero East Luckham & Blackford Also The Barton of East Luckham & Eastcotts & Goodwins Lands'

This title is superimposed on red leather and tooled in gold with the same design as on the whole volume.

TITLE PAGE: 'A Survey and Valuation of Part of the Manor of Holnicote the Manors of Bossington, Wilmersham, West-Luckham, Stock Pero, East Luckham & Blackford Also the Barton of East Luckham, & Eastcotts & Goodwins Lands. situated in the several Parishes of Selworthy, Porlock, Stock Pero, Exford, East Luckham, Timberscombe, Minehead, & Carhampton in the County of Somerset Property of Sir Thos Dyke Acland Bart. Surveyed and Mapped in 1809 & 1812, By Alexr Law & Messrs Bradley & Summers'

General Map opposite title page

TITLE: not on map; see above

SURVEYORS: Alexander Law, Thomas Bradley & William Summers; Alexander Law 'set the work in train' but the maps would appear to be the work of Bradley and Summers (with Wm Shillibeer being responsible for mapping the country adjoining Holnicote) – see correspondence

SCALE: 'Scale'; scale bar shows chains ands furlongs; 1"=25 chains; 1:19880

MATERIAL, SIZE & ORIENTATION: parchment, coloured; 65.5cms EW x 68cms NS; north to top

CONTENT: shore line, form lines; beach, stippled black; cliffs in profile, black; Porlock Bay named; rivers, some named, black outlines; 'Decoy' named, outlined by form lines; relief shown by hill shading; fields outlined in ink and various colours identifying the individual manors, described in Reference List; moors and commons named; tree symbols, black, marking woods, and with stippling waste; roads, fenced and unfenced; buildings in plan, black; settlements named; some archaeological features named, also Beacons, Mill, Chapel, Porlock Quay; peripheral owners named

Adjoining areas also surveyed and shown in some detail but with no colour. This was probably the work of William Shillibeer. See Summers letter of April 15th 1813 (DRO, 1148M add 36/181)

Rivers, some named; relief shown by hill shading; commons, moor named; roads, fenced and unfenced; tree symbols, black; settlements in plan, black; archaeological features named

especially Burrows (barrows) marking the boundary of the Acland estates

DECORATION: 8 point compass rose; north marked by fleur-de-lys; 4 principal cardinal points in leaf design with flower in centre; the style is not typical of Law's work

The following 8 maps are all by Alexander Law, Thomas Bradley & William Summers; all have a scale bar showing chains and furlongs although the scales used vary; the topographical features, the reference lists and the abstracts are common to each map and each shows a compass rose of common design. Individual features are noted in the separate entries.

Map 1

Parishes of Luccombe, Timberscombe, Minehead, Selworthy and Exford

TITLE: 'Part of the Manor of Holnicote'

SURVEYORS: Alexander Law, Thomas Bradley & William Summers

SCALE: 'Scale'; scale bar shows chains and furlongs; 1"=12 chains; 1:9504

MATERIAL, SIZE & ORIENTATION: parchment, coloured; 55cms EW x 69.5cms NS; north to top

CONTENT: river, black outlines; relief shown by hill shading; fields washed in colour and outlined in deeper shades, each parcel in different colour; alpha-numeric reference to lists on following pages under 'Names of Parcels, Gardens & Orchards, Arable & Pasture, Furze & Waste, Hedges & Ditches' each with content, and 'Total Content'; this is followed by an Abstract listing names of 'Tenants, Tenements, Parishes where situated, Content'; followed by various terms of leases, 'Values in former Surveys and by Alexr Law in 1809, Outgoings, Clear Yearly Value in former Surveys and Clear Yearly Value made in 1809 by Alexr Law'; black tree symbols showing orchards and plantations; roads, fenced and unfenced; buildings in plan, black; peripheral manors and owners named

2 insets showing detached parts of the manor

Pencil grid.

NB Where the date 09 is not included in the Yearly Value columns this is noted in the individual map entries

DECORATION: title cartouche: medallion of leaves with 2 sprays

of oak leaves tied with ribbon at base; 16 point compass rose; north marked by fleur-de-lys; shaded-line decoration on 8 principal points
ACREAGE: 1917:1:18
Luccombe Church SS 911445

Map 2

Parishes of 'Poorlock', Selworthy and Luccombe
TITLE: 'Manor of Bossington'
SCALE: 1"=12 chains; 1:9504
MATERIAL, SIZE & ORIENTATION: parchment, coloured; 43.5cms EW x 43.5cms NS; north to top
CONTENT: cliffs in profile; beach stippled black; Bristol Channel named; original strips clearly shown
DECORATION: title cartouche: medallion of leaves and flowers tied with ribbon at base; fishing vessel and larger ship shown in channel
ACREAGE: 799:0:1
Bossington Village SS 898180

Map 3

Parishes of Luccombe and Stoke Pero
TITLE: 'Manors of Wilmersham West Luckham & Stock Pero'
SCALE: 1"=16 chains; 1:12672
MATERIAL, SIZE & ORIENTATION: parchment, coloured; 69cms EW x 54.8cms NS; north to top
CONTENT: commons shown in detail; barrows named; some pencil annotations showing roads
2 insets: West Luckham Village and Horner Village; these on a larger scale which is not stated
DECORATION: title cartouche: 'mirror' frame with garland of flowers below
Abstract has tenants' names in pencil
ACREAGE: 4853:3:33
Wilmersham SS 874437 West Luccombe SS 899462 Stoke Pero Church SS 878435 Horner Village 899454

Map 4

Parish of Selworthy
TITLE: 'Manor of Blackford'
SCALE: 1"=8 chains; 6336

MATERIAL, SIZE & ORIENTATION: parchment, coloured; 48.5cms EW x 43cms NS; north to top
DECORATION: title cartouche: simple medallion of scrolls, leaves and ruched fabric
No date in Yearly Value columns
ACREAGE: 589:3:15
Blackford Village SS 924453

Map 5

Parishes of Luccombe and Selworthy
TITLE: 'Manor of East Luckham'
SCALE: 1"=12 chains; 1:9504
MATERIAL, SIZE & ORIENTATION: parchment, coloured; 49cms EW x 72.2cms NS; north to top
CONTENT: barrows named
DECORATION: title cartouche: medallion of oak leaves entwined with ribbon
Abstract has tenants' names in pencil
ACREAGE: 1100.1.10
Luccombe Church SS 911445

Map 6

Parishes of Luccombe and Selworthy
TITLE: 'Barton of East Luckham'
SCALE: 1"=8 chains; 1:6336
MATERIAL, SIZE & ORIENTATION: parchment, coloured; 37.5cms EW x 54.5cms NS; north to top
DECORATION: title cartouche: as Map 1 and Map 5
Abstract has tenants' names in pencil
No date in yearly Value columns
ACREAGE: 274:0:14
Possibly SS 921445

Map 7

Parishes of Selworthy, Porlock, Luccombe and Carhampton
TITLE: 'Eastcotts, Goodwins Lands'
SCALE: 1"= 12 chains; 1:9504
MATERIAL, SIZE & ORIENTATION: 35.5cms EW x 35.7cms NS; north to top
CONTENT: 2 insets, each showing 2 fields; 1 showing land in Selworthy Combe, the other unidentified

DECORATION: title cartouche: medallion of leaves and flowers tied with ribbon at base

Abstract has tenants' names in pencil

No date in Yearly Value columns

ACREAGE: 260:1:8

Eastcott SS 857469

Map 8

TITLE: 'Dean's Ground'

SCALE: scale bar shows no unit of measurement; 1" = 4 ?chains

MATERIAL, SIZE & ORIENTATION: paper, slight colour; 20.5cms EW x 26.3cms NS; north to top

CONTENT: fields outlined in ink with hedge symbols; numeric reference to list on opposite page, but not followed by Abstract

ACREAGE: 20:0:39

Unidentified; 4 fields east of the Manor of Holnicote

TOTAL ACREAGE: 9820:0:2

For further details of the maps see *Introduction*, pp. 19–20

MAP

50. 1810	DRO, 1148M add/10/20

PLACE: Manor of Avil

PARISHES: Carhampton, Dunster, Timberscombe

2 sheets of probably a 4 sheet map showing separate farms

TITLE: 'Map of the Manor of Avil in the Parish of Dunster, Carhampton and Timberscombe Somerset Property of Sir Thomas Dyke Acland Baronet By Alexander Law & Thomas Bradley 1810'

SURVEYORS: Alexander Law, Thomas Bradley

SCALE: not indicated on these sheets

MATERIAL, SIZE & ORIENTATION: parchment, coloured; damaged; each sheet, 88cms EW x 68.5cms NS; original map *c.*176cms EW x 137cms NS; north to top

CONTENT: rivers, ponds; bridges; relief shown by hill shading; fields outlined with hedge symbols showing ownership; total holdings outlined in colour; asterisks indicating boundary

ownership; fence symbols; gates, red; alpha-numeric reference [to Survey Book]; some other owners named; variety of tree symbols showing Oaktrow Wood and ?coppice, orchards, isolated trees and with stippling waste; formal gardens in detailed plan; Commons, light green, named, including Dunster Common Marsh; roads with hedgerow trees, some named; directions given; footpaths, pricked lines, one red; buildings in plan, black; peripheral estates and owners named

The town of Dunster, the wide main road with the shambles and market building are shown lower right. St Georges, the dedication of the church, confirms this identification.

INSET MAP:

TITLE: 'Oaktrow Farm in Timberscombe & Cutcombe'

DECORATION: 16 point compass rose, ink-line decoration at base of cardinals; north marked by fleur-de-lys; border, 1 fine and 1 broad black line

NOTE: The lower part of the original map, still on its roller, is also to be found at the above reference. Unfortunately it is in too poor a condition to describe or produce for examination.

Avil Farm SS 977431 Dunster Church SS 991436 Carhampton ST 009427 Oaktrow SS 942404 Timberscombe SS 956420

For further details of the map see *Introduction*, pp. 20–21

MAP

51. 1820	DRO, 1148M add 6(unlisted)

PLACE: Estates in Winsford and West Nethercott

PARISHES: Winsford and Dulverton

TITLE:

Map 1 'Plan of West Nethercott in Winsford Somerset'

Map 2 'Plan of Estates called Liscombe and Spire in Dulverton and Hobbs in Winsford Somerset 1820'

SURVEYOR: 'John Easton Surveyor'

SCALE: scale bar; 1"=6 chains; 1:4752

MATERIAL, SIZE & ORIENTATION: parchment, coloured; 85cms EW x 50.5cms NS; north to top; map is on rollers

CONTENT: rivers, blue; River Exe named; fields outlined in green with hedge symbols; numeric reference to tables listing field names, 'Kind' (land use) and content in statute measure; gates, black; tree symbols, green; roads, fenced; footpaths, broken lines; buildings in plan, red; peripheral owner (Sir Thomas Dyke Acland) named, Parishes named; Knaplock Farm, Nethercott Farm and Winsford Hill named.

ASSOCIATED DOCUMENT: 'Valuation of Higher Naplock Farm in the Parish of Winsford in the County of Somerset The Freehold Property of Mr Robert Leigh by Charles Chilcott' with a copy of his letter to Mr Day advising purchase by the 10th Bart is dated 16 May 1823, three years later than the map. This seems to be an attempt to consolidate the Winsford Estate. (DRO, 1148M/Box 21(iv)/19).

Nethercote SS 874362 Spire SS 883328 Knaplock SS 867331 Liscombe SS 877325 Hobbs unidentified

MAP

52. 1829	DRO, 1148M add/21/3/3

PLACE: Bakers Garden and Village Meadow

PARISH: Selworthy

TITLE: 'This is the Plan referred to in the order and Consent respectively hereunto attached'

SURVEYOR: not named

SCALE: scale bar with no unit of measurement stated; 1"= 100 unnamed units but a measured distance on the map suggests a scale of 1"=50 yards; 1:1800

MATERIAL, SIZE & ORIENTATION: parchment, slight colour; north to top

CONTENT: tree symbols marking boundary of old road, Holnicote Shrubbery and Long Orchard; 'Proposed new Road' marked by broken line, red; Bakers Garden named; 2 Linhays, Bakers Cottage in plan and named

ASSOCIATED DOCUMENT: Map attached to Agreement by Sir Thomas Dyke Acland to the realignment of the road between Porlock and Minehead to pass through Bakers Garden and Village Meadow; receipt from Sir Thomas Dyke Acland for

the payment of £50

NOTE: 'Old Road From the South West corner of Baker's Garden to the South East corner of Village Meadow Length 231 Cloth Yards Breadth 13 feet upon a medium

Proposed New Line Same termini Length 212 Cloth Yards Breadth 20 feet'

Selworthy Church SS 920468

SURVEY

53. c.1770	DRO, 1148M/Box 9/2

PLACES: Manors of Cragantallan, Degembris, Ebbingford alias Efford and Thurlibeer

PARISHES: Bodmin, Bridgerule, St Clement, St Columb Major, St Columb Minor, Crantock, Cubert, St Enoder, Gorran, Jacobstow, Lanivet, Launcells, Mawgan-in-Pydar, Newlyn East, Poundstock, Stratton, St Wenn, Withiel

TITLE: 'A Rentall of the Arundell Estate'

SURVEYOR: not named

FORMAT: volume of 12 paper sheets, size 17cms x 26.8cms, no covers

DETAILS: tenants' names, tenements' names and the sum paid. The amounts are totalled at the bottom of each page

NOTE: the survey also lists land in the Manor of East Luckham, Somerset. See no. 42.

For further details of the contents see *Introduction*, pp. 8–9

MAP

54. c.1791	DRO, 1148M add/10/19

PLACE: Manor of Thurlibeer

PARISH: Launcells

TITLE: 'A Plan of the Manor of Thurlibeer in the County of Cornwall The property of Fred.^{k} T:^{s} Wentworth Esqr Survey'd & Delineated by David Palmer'

SURVEYOR: David Palmer

SCALE: 'A Scale of Statute Chains'; scale bar with dividers super-imposed; 1"=3 chains; 1:2376

MATERIAL, SIZE & ORIENTATION: parchment, coloured; 186cms EW x 98.5cms NS; north to top

CONTENT: rivers, black lines; fields, plain and outlined in green and yellow, and hedge symbols; with numeric reference [to Book of Particulars] and to an inset summary; hedge symbols showing boundary ownership and 'asterisms' indicating out-boundary ownership only with explanatory note at bottom of map; black tree symbols showing ?woods and isolated trees; roads, plain, directions given; buildings in plan, pink and grey; peripheral owners and estates named and 'Part of the River Tamar'

Details of Bude Canal added later; stream acting as feeder to canal; Thurlibeer Inclined Plane with buildings in plan, 2 pits and 1 halfway up the Plane, Reservoir, Waste Drain, Road and Bridge; Aqueduct, Bridge and Towing Path; near Red Post, Wharf, Thorn Bridge (over canal) Puddle Pit, Waste Weir; on canal to the east, Layby, Bridge, Layby, Towing Path, Sher-nick Bridge (over canal); Wharf; on canal to the south, Puddle Pit, Bridge (over canal) with approach path, Towing Path, Bridge with aproach paths

Two insets of parts of the estate, with the line of the Bude Canal added later

INSET: 'A Brief account of this Plan for a fuller Explanation see the Book of Particulars'

Additional information in pencil

			A	R	P
Cobthorn	No. 1	to 26	84	1	1
Groves	27	63	76	1	7
Lower Shirnick	67	94	112	0	23
Higher Shirnick & Sudarans	95	125	138	2	18
Heards Pitton	126	139	08	3	31
Rowoo Pitton	140	163	73	1	3
Saunders Pitton	165	172	36	3	39
Thurlibear	174	195	65	1	35
Mead Parks	196	203	44	1	30
Thorn	205	241	94	0	13

Mabyn's Butspur	243	256	23	0	38
Norcott's Do.	257	270	31	3	7
Darts Do.	272	289	39	0	19
Browns Do.	290	302	26	0	36
Banbury's Do.	304	319	16	3	34
Hobbicott Downs	320	326	89	0	29
Hobbicott	327	346	81	1	14
Lower Underwood	347	360	12	1	22
Higher Do.	362	368	8	1	25
Church Park	370	372	12	0	32
Windmill Park	373	383	40	0	12
Mills's Do.	384	387	15	1	23
Scorsham & Woodhouse	388	409	63	2	27
North Harbour	440	443	25	2	11
South Do.	414	424	37	0	37
Little Bridge	426	431	14	3	26
Rows Cottage	432		0	0	27
Roads & Hedges belong.ng to the Manor			49	0	22
		Total	1403	2	7

DECORATION: title cartouche: medallion with frame of acanthus leaves. other leaves and scrolls; scale: dividers, yellow and grey, superimposed; 8point compass rose, black/plain, in circle, north marked by fleur-de-lys

Launcells Church SS 244057 Launcells Cross SS 264060

For further details see *Introduction*, pp. 22–23

SURVEY	
55. *c.*1802	DRO, 1148M add/6/13

PLACES: Manors of Cragantallan, Degembris, Ebbingford alias Efford, Goviley, Penstrase Moor, Thurlibeer, Trerise and Tre-sillian

PARISHES: Bridgerule, St Columb Major, St Columb Minor, Cran-tock, Cubert, Cuby, ?St Dennis, St Enoder, St Eval, Jacobstow, Kenwyn, Ladock, Lanivet, Launcells, Mawgan-in-Pydar, St Merryn, Newlyn East, Poundstock, Stratton, Veryan

TITLE: no general title; titles of manors given

SURVEYOR: not named

FORMAT: small volume, size 19.3cms x 25.5cms, soft leather covers, affected by damp

DETAILS: tenements' names, lives in being and their ages, lives added, conventionary rents, capons, due days, the kind of heriots, the sum in lieu thereof, observations. The name of the present tenant has been added in another hand.

NOTE: this survey is abstracted as part of *Survey 3* in this volume. It also covers the Manors of East Luckham in Somerset and Stockley Luckham in Devon

For further details of the contents see *Introduction*, pp. 8–9

MAP	
56. 1817	Bude Museum (Budex 276)

PLACES: Bude Canal

PARISHES: various, Devon and Cornwall

Note that this map covers a wide area of Devon and Cornwall and more parishes than those through which the canal was cut

TITLE: 'Map of the Proposed Lines of Canal, from Bude-Haven into the Interior of Cornwall and Devon, Surveyed under the direction of James Green, Civil Engineer by Thomas Shearm, Land Surveyor. 1817.'

SURVEYOR: Thomas Shearm (under the direction of James Green)

SCALE: scale bar, covering 2 miles; 'Scale'; 1"= approx. 17 chains; 1:13464 (approx.)

MATERIAL, SIZE & ORIENTATION: parchment, coloured; 338cms EW x 140.5cms NS, framed; north to top

CONTENT: Bristol Channel, named, blue; shore, buff; cliff edge and entrance to Bude Harbour marked by rocks; rivers, reservoirs, blue; Tamar and Torridge rivers named; Compass Point, Great Chapel Rock, Little Chapel Rock, lime kiln, marked; line of proposed canal, red, but from Bude Haven to Hele Bridge, dark blue; planes, pink; plots adjoining the canal numbered; stippling on a green wash, marking woodland; moorland, named; roads, fenced and unfenced, brown; sandhills;

barrows; farms and villages named; churches in elevation (including Black Torrington, Holsworthy, Pancrasweek, Buckland Filleigh, Petrockstow, Hatherleigh, Exbourne, Meeth, Dowland, Iddesleigh (all Devon) and Stratton, Kilkhampton, Marhamchurch and North Tamerton in Cornwall; windmill and beacon at Holsworthy in elevation; other buildings in plan, black; reference list gives mileage, distances between the 3 inclined planes, and summit level

EXPLANATION: Full red lines denote the Intended Course of the Canal. Dark blue line shows the Canal from Bude Haven to Hele Bridge, as connected with the improvement of the Haven The dotted line from Moreton Mill to the reservoir on Langford Moor shews the line of the feeder supposing the Canal not to be carried eastwards of the River Tamar There appears to have been originally an extension of this map further south

DECORATION: 8 pt compass rose (plain), north marked by fleur-de-lys

ASSOCIATED DOCUMENTS: Bude Museum, *c.*1818, 'Map of the Bude Canal from Bude to Marhamchurch Incline Plane. No. 1'; DRO, DP 36, Devon Quarter Sessions Deposited Plans series: printed map dated 1818 (certificated 1819) and four small notebooks dated 1817–18 which served as a Book of Reference to the printed and manuscript maps; CRO, QS/PDH/1/1–2, PDH/1/3/1–2, PDH/1/5, Cornwall Quarter Sessions Deposited Plans series: two small Reference Books dated 1817, plans 1817 and copy of a printed plan

Bude Canal sea lock SS 203064

For further details of the map see *Introduction*, p. 24

SURVEY	
57. 1820	DRO, 1148M add/6/12

PLACES: Manors of Efford and Thurlibeer

PARISHES: Bridgerule, Jacobstow, Launcells, Poundstock, Stratton

GENERAL TITLE: 'Manors of Thurlibeer and Efford. Rental 1820'

TITLES TO MANORS: 'Manor of Thurlibeer'; 'Manor of Ebbingford alias Efford'

SURVEYOR: not named

FORMAT: book, paper covers, size 25.8cms x 41.4cms

DETAILS: number, dates of leases, by whom granted and fines paid, lessees, present tenants, premises, parishes, quantities, lives in being in 1820, ages, yearly rents, capons, due days, heriots, when due and observations

MAP

| 58. 1824 | DRO, 1148M add/10/15/1 |

PLACE: Bude Canal

PARISH: Launcells, Marhamchurch, Stratton

TITLE: 'Bude Canal Sketch Map from Bude to Heale Bridge Incline Plane 1824 (No. 1)'

SURVEYOR: 'Thomas Shearm Landsurveyor 1824'

SCALE: 'Scale of Chains'; scale bar; 1"=4 chains; 1: 3168

MATERIAL, SIZE & ORIENTATION: paper, coloured (fragile) watermark; 50cms EW x 115cms NS; east to top

CONTENT: Bristol Channel named; coastline, blue; low water and high water marks shown; cliffs shaded with cliff edge clearly marked; breakwater, yellow with rocks beside it; Little Chapel Rock at end of breakwater; Great Chapel Rock, Compass Point named; areas of sea sand indicated; river and canal, blue; old river course, blue, new river line, plain; river embankment, shaded; bridge over river; canal details:- bason; locks including sea lock, intended entrance lock; swivel bridge; waste wear; wharves indicated including sand wharf, 'Private Wharf Sir T D Acland', 'Company's Wharf', yellow; towing paths with 'Slope', yellow and orange; rail road including those extending on to sea sand leading to sand wharf; Pier Head named; principal bridges named; roads, orange, directions given including 'Ancient Road to Marhamchurch' and road to Stratton and Launceston also marked as Sand Road; Efford stone quarry; Heale Mill; Marhamchurch Incline Plane and wharf, yellow; fields outlined in ink, numeric reference to inset; buildings in plan, grey; Lime Kiln Cottage named; 'Othello Buildings' named but back extension, yellow and named 'Company's Lease'; peripheral Parishes and villages named; note explaining use of colour

INSET: 'Reference to Corners and Strips of Land, situate between Bude and Marhamchurch incline Plane . . . The Land of Bude Harbour and Canal Company'

No. on Plan	Description	Quantity			Annual Value			Remarks
		A.	R.	P.	£.	s.	d.	
	Parish of Stratton							
22	Part of Eastern Town Marsh							
	(Late Sir T.D. Acland Bart.)	0	0	28	0	2	0	Company to pay Taxes
31	Corner of Coarse Marsh (Late Chings)	0	9	16	0	1	0	
36	Corner of Little Meadow (Late Chings)	0	0	7	0	0	6	Parish of Marhamchurch
3	Part of Pope Tree Meadow, (between							
	canal and river (Late Lord Clinton)	0	1	0	0	1	0	
	Do. Do. Corner at South End	0	0	13	0	7	0	
4A	Part of Great Hill							
4B	(Late Lord Clinton & Kingdon)	0	1	34	1	5	0	Rogers's
6	Part of Marshalls Great Hill							
	(Late Lord Clinton)	0	1	11	0	15	0	
5	Part of Curtis's Close, adjoining							
	the Wharf (Late Messrs Harwood & Co.)	0	3	0	2	10	0	
	Total	**2**	**0**	**29**	**6**	**0**	**6**	Occupier to pay Tythe

DECORATION: 4 point compass indicator, north marked by fleur-de-lys Note describing use of colour

Bude Canal sea lock SS 203064

For further details of the map see *Introduction*, p. 24

MAPS

| 59. 1826 | CRO, DC/NC/15/37–39 |

PLACE: Bude Canal

PARISH: Launcells, Marhamchurch, Stratton

Series of 9 maps of the Bude Canal by Thomas Shearm showing the canal company's land, the canal with its associated roads, bridges and buildings etc. Of these numbers 37, 38, and part of 39 show where the canal passed through Sir Thomas Dyke Acland's land, and the information may be compared with that added to the Palmer map.

TITLE: 'No. 1 A Map of the Bude Canal from Bude to Marhamchurch Incline Plane By Thomas Shearm Landsurveyor Launceston'

SCALE: 'A Scale of Chains'; scale bar; 1"=4 chains; 1:3168

MATERIAL, SIZE & ORIENTATION: parchment, coloured; 67 cms EW x 127cms NS; east to top

CONTENT: Bristol Channel named with lines in 3 shades of blue following coast; off-shore rocks with Great Chapel Rock, Little Chapel Rock and Muscle Rock named; cliffs; areas of sea sand, buff; low water mark; river and ponds, blue; 'Old River Course' and 'New Channel' shown and named; breakwater, yellow with red path on top, Pier Head at end; hill shading with East and West Shalder Hill named; fields, some with hedge symbols; numeric reference to Survey Book; tree symbols showing mixed woodland and orchards, marsh; company's land, green and TDA's land marked

CANAL DETAILS: (moving inland from the sea) rail roads on to the sand; Sea Lock and bridge; Sand Wharf with landing stage; Company's Wharf; Bason; 'Sir T.D. Aclands New Road' to swivel bridge; Private Bason with Wharf; Tow Path; Lay by; Efford Stone Quarry; embankment beside river; Company's

Land; Swivel Bridge; Lock, Lock; Swivel Bridge; Waste Weir; Heale Bridge, Heale Bridge Wharf; Marhamchurch Incline Plane; buildings – Othello Buildings with Canal Office; yellow strip where labourers cottages now are; possible Efford Cottage by Lime Kiln; Falcon Hotel named with possible houses beside it

'Explanation' describing use of colour:-

The Company's Lands are Coloured as follows

The Canal	coloured	Blue
Towing Path Banks Slopes etc	"	Red
Strips of lands corners	"	Yellow
Public & Private Roads	"	Brown

TITLE: 'A Map of the Bude Canal from Marhamchurch Incline Plane to the Red Post No. 2 By Thomas Shearm Landsurveyor Launceston'

SCALE: as above

MATERIAL, SIZE & ORIENTATION: parchment, coloured, 160.4cms EW X 73.2cms NS; north to top

CONTENT: as above plus roads some with hedge symbols, unfenced, broken lines; directions given; some detailed garden plans; distance from Bude indicated; settlements and Parishes named; Parish boundaries, green;

CANAL DETAILS: Marhamchurch Incline Plane, yellow with red margins and blue resevoir; towing paths red; weir; company's land identified; Thurlibeer Incline Plane yellow with red margins; Mouth of Adit, Pit; Reservoir; Engine House; Pit; Company's Road; plane 4½ Miles From Bude; 'Aqueduct' over road; TDA's land named; Company's Land, yellow; Thorn Bridge with canal to Holsworthy with waste Weir and branch canal to Druxton Bridge

TITLE: 'No. 3 A Map of the Bude Canal from Red Post to Junction at Brendon Moor 1826 By Thomas Shearm Landsurveyor Launceston'

Only one third of this is relevant to TDA's land, that is as far as Shernick Bridge; details as above

Bude Canal sea lock SS 203064 Canal at Red Post SS 264050 Shernick SS 274048

For further details of the maps see *Introduction*, p. 24

ATLAS

60. 1828   Private hands;
photocopies in Bude Library and CRO

PLACES: Manors of Efford and Thurlibeer

PARISHES: Launcells, Jacobstow, Poundstock, Stratton

Leather-bound volume, 20.5cms x 28.5cms, with some evidence of original gold decoration. 5 coloured maps and terrier on parchment. Title on cover ' Manors of Efford and Thurlibeer. By S. T. Coldridge Exeter. 1828.'

Acland arms in colour facing title page; title 'Maps and Particulars of the Manors of Efford and Thurlibeer in the Parishes of Stratton, Jacobstow, Poundstock and Launcells Cornwall The Property of Sir T: D: Acland, Bart:

Map 1

TITLE: 'Lands at Efford and Lunstone'

SURVEYOR: not named [S T Coldridge]

SCALE: 'Scale of Eight Chains to One Inch'; scale bar; 1:6336

MATERIAL, SIZE & ORIENTATION: parchment, coloured;35.2cms EW x 51.6cms NS; north to top

CONTENT: Bristol Channel, blue, shaded at shoreline; sand, buff and Bude Harbour named on sand (covered at high tide), cliffs and offshore rocks grey with slate-like symbols; Breakwater with Pier Head, pink; Company's Quarry beside it, brown; Little Chapel Rock, Great Chapel Rock and Compass Point (also marked by symbol) named; Bude River with Old Course and New Course named, blue; direction of flow indicated; relief shown by hill shading; fields, some with hedgerow symbols, coloured green or buff; alpha-numeric reference to Survey Book listing field names and content; other landowners named, land pale green; tree symbols, green, marking woods, orchards and with stippling waste; roads, buff, directions given; buildings in plan, red; Bude named, buildings, grey; peripheral owners including the 'Poor of Stratton' named; peripheral Manor of Binamy named

Canal Works: Breakwater, Sea Lock, Rail Road, Companys Wharf and Basin, Swivel Bridge, Towpath, brown, Layby and Quarry all named

DECORATION: title inscribed on rock with some leafy tree decoration and grass at base; 4 point compass indicator, WE marked by fletched arrow; north-south line shown by mast supported by shrouds; anchor, anchor chain and mast also with shrouds and penant

ACREAGE: 611a: 1r: 2p

Efford Beacon SS 201059 Lynstone SS 206053

Map 2

TITLE: 'The Manor of Thurlibeer'

SURVEYOR: 'Saml. T Coldridge Land Surveyor and General Draftsman Exeter'

SCALE: 'Scale of Nine Chains to One Inch'; scale bar; 1:7128

MATERIAL, SIZE & ORIENTATION: parchment, coloured; 72.5cms EW x 51.4cms NS; north to top

CONTENT: River Tamar, stream, blue; relief shown by hill shading; fields coloured buff, light and dark blue, with alpha-numeric reference to Survey Book listing field names and content; asterisks indicating boundary ownership with explanatory note below scale; tree symbols, green marking mixed woodland, orchards; roads, buff, directions given; Red Post named; buildings in plan, red or grey; peripheral owners and estates named; County of Devon named

Canal Works: Thurlibeer Inclined Plane, brown; Steam Engine Resevoir, 2 Pits named; canal shown to Red Post with Canal Company's Land named; towing path, buff; branch to south with bridge and principal route to east with 2 laybys

Two areas some distance from principal area mapped shown with sections of Bude Canal named

DECORATION: title inscribed on rock with some leafy tree decoration and grass at base; compass indicator with north-south line only; north marked by fleur-de-lys and south by letter and symbol, the whole encircled by sheaf of corn, seed dispenser, sickle, scythe and pitchfork; border, running design

ACREAGE: 1418a: 3r: 12p

Thurlibeer SS 252047 Red Post SS 263052 (present position)

Three maps interleaved in Survey Book

Map 1

TITLE: 'West Down' (Jacobstow); 'The Two Penleans' (Poundstock) SX 202981

SURVEYOR: not named [S T Coldridge]

SCALE: 'Scale of 20 Chains'; scale bar; 1"=9.5 chains 1:7524

MATERIAL, SIZE & ORIENTATION: parchment, coloured; 15cms EW x 24cms NS; north to top

CONTENT: parts of stream, blue; relief shown by hill shading; fields, blue or pinky-buff with alpha-numeric reference to Survey Book listing field names and content; tree symbols, green showing orchards; roads, buff, fenced and unfenced; directions given; buildings in plan, red; on de Dunstanville land, grey

DECORATION: 4 point compass indicator, north and south marked by symbols with feathers on line below north; WE indicated by letter

Poundstock Church SS 202995

Map 2

TITLE: 'Heale and Tower Hill' (Jacobstow)

SURVEYOR: not named [S T Coldridge]

SCALE: 'Scale of 20 Chains'; scale bar, 1"=9.5 chains, 1:7524

MATERIAL, SIZE & ORIENTATION: parchment, coloured; 18cms x 25cms; north west to top

CONTENT: stream, blue; relief shown by hill shading; fields, pale green or brown with alpha-numeric reference to Survey Book listing field names and content; tree symbols, green, marking mixed woodland; roads, buff; buildings in plan, red; peripheral owners named

DECORATION: title hanging from branch of tree trunk with leaves and grass below; 4 point compass indicator with NSEW marked by letter with additional symbols at north and south with feathers below north point

Jacobstow Church SS 198958

Map 3

TITLE: 'Lands Near the Town of Stratton'

SURVEYOR: not named [S T Coldridge]

SCALE: 'Scale of Chains'; scale bar; 1"=8 chains; 1:6336

MATERIAL, SIZE & ORIENTATION: parchment, coloured; 29.5cms x 53.5cms; north east to top

CONTENT: streams, blue; relief shown by hill shading; fields outlined in colour with alpha-numeric reference to Survey Book;

other landowners named; tree symbols; roads, buff, directions given; buildings in plan, black

Stratton Town mapped on a larger scale (not stated); river, blue; roads, buff, directions given; buildings in plan, red or grey

DECORATION: 8 point compass indicator, north marked by fleur-de-lys and all marked with shaded line decoration

Stratton Church SS 232065

SURVEY

1828

TITLE: as above

SURVEYOR: [S T Coldridge]

FORMAT: as above

DETAILS: tenants' names; tenements' names; alpha-numeric reference to maps; acreage; total acreage of manors in statute and customary measure; 'aggregate' giving these details and listing existing lives on leases in 1828, ages on lives, conventionary rents, heriots and when due, 'Observations' and chief rents due to the manors

For further details of the atlas see *Introduction*, pp. 24–25

MAP

61. 1833   DRO, 1148M/Box 20/7

PLACE: Bude Haven

PARISH: Launcells, Stratton

TITLE: 'Design for laying out certain ground for Building at Bude-Haven, Cornwall: The Property of Sir Thos Dyke Acland, Bart. George Wightwick Archt.'; at top 'for Sir T D Acland Bart'

SURVEYOR: 'Geo. Wightwick Archt. Plymouth 1833'

SCALE: scale bar with no figures or unit of measurement stated

MATERIAL, SIZE & ORIENTATION: paper, coloured; 69.1cms x 52.5cms; no direction

CONTENT: 'The Sea' named; shore line, shades of blue; sands, buff; cliffs, dark brown; breakwater named; off-shore rocks; 'Bude harbour' named; river and canal, blue with darker margins; 2 basins and lock indicated on canal; bridges over river and canal; 'Compass Point', red; 'Bude-Haven Down' and meadow, pale green; relief shown by deeper green and ink shading; trees shown by green shading with 'Plantation' named (this probably the 'Shelter Belt' planted by Sir Thomas to protect the houses from the prevailing wind); roads, buff, direction 'To Stratton' given; buildings in plan, red, shown in numbered plots; 'Labourers Cottages' named; some houses, an inn and cottage (Efford Cottage) indicated as 'built'; one large house in plan, grey, 'built', [this probably Goldsworthy Gurney's Castle]; 'Ware House' named; 'Old Village of Bude'

Bude Canal sea lock SS 203064

For further details of the map see *Introduction*, p. 25

Section III

Letters of Alexander Law, Surveyor

Letters

Letters from Alexander Law are to be found in the Devon, Somerset and Cornwall Record Offices. They not only chart the journeys made when working for various landowners but also the business Law conducted on their behalf as agent, steward, surveyor and map-maker. In addition these letters provide an insight into the private life and interests of one of the most prolific independent professional men of the late eighteenth and early nineteenth centuries. Selected references to the Aclands and the maps and surveys of their estates are included below following brief notes introducing the collections.

Devon Record Office

It is hardly surprising that the largest collection of Acland papers, which is in the care of the Devon Record office, provides the most detailed record of the family, their life, their travels and all their interests. Information about estate management, the surveys and the maps form only a part of these documents and it is from this source that the following extracts are taken. Where desirable, parts of the letters have been paraphrased.

For convenience Sir Thomas Dyke Acland 10th Baronet is hereafter referred to as TDA, Alexander Law as AL and Charles Prideaux Brune as PB.

DRO 1148M add/36/

---

144 AL TO TDA Nov. 5TH 1810 FROM OXENHAM HOUSE

'I am very much in oppinion(sic) with you (*as I have been inform'd*) that you wish to have the whole of your Lands at and near Holnicote and those at or near Winsford put on one General Map. I have no doubt, but we can reduce the whole so as to come into one Plan for general purposes without being cumbersome and should wish for my own Part to adopt that plan, and my not having any Order either from you or Mr Weech how it should be done, have deferr'd mapping any part of that Property'

154 JOHN CAREW TO TDA 24 FEB. 1811 FROM EXETER ?LOCK

James Green is very busy and the 'unforseen occurrence on the Bude Canal delayed him' but he is 'going seriously to work on your plans & will probably dispatch them at no very distant period. Green is an enthusiast, & enthusiasm is infectious, but do not calculate on those immediate Returns, which you may have been induced to suppose would be made. The Canal will be navigable 10 miles in one direction, & 9 miles in another by next Season' Details regarding the profitability of the Canal. Plans of houses should be ready.

171 AL TO TDA 25 FEB. 1813 FROM LITTLEHAM

Writing at the suggestion of Dr Drury 'which I do now, rather reluctantly, feeling you may suppose, I have some End of my own to serve, which I trust you will not think so, when I say, that it is my fix'd determination to decline great part of my Business, and to attend only to that of a few Employers where an Attorney is not concern'd. My wish is to recommend you to sell off all your scatter'd Tenemts and connect your Property as near together as possible, and if you were to sell all your Lands in the Town of South Molton together with Brayley Barton which Lord Fortescue hath declin'd purchasing I think it would be much to your Interest, and I think those Gentlemen who hath obtain'd your promis'd accomodation(sic), ought in justice to pay the Expense of a Second Survey, which his Lordship hath refus'd – If I can render you any assistance in this respect I hope you will freely command me'

181 WILLIAM SUMMERS TO TDA 15 APRIL 1813

'Ashill April 15th 1813

Respected Sir I feel I am taking a great liberty in troubling you, but from your known Character as a lover of justice I am led to hope that you will take my case which I have the honour of submitting to you into your consideration & that you will interfere on my behalf if you should be of opinion that I deserve it. On the completion of the out door Surveys of your Property I went into partnership(sic) with Mr Bradley and the fair Mapping of the Estates was given up to us by Mr Law – since which we parted before the Broadclist Lands being quite finished; & by the most scandalous treatment have now a great balance due to me from Bradley on account of your work; to secure a part of which I was under the necessity of taking into my possession the rough and fair Maps of the Lands in Broadclist Ashclyst & Killerton – The Book is now ready for your inspection & I am anxious that you should have it as soon as possible & I trust I am not too sanguine in hoping you will not pay over the amount of this work untill I am settled with – A statement of my Account together with the Book, I will do myself the honour to present to you at any time your leisure may admit of, & at any place you may appoint – If I am fortunate enough to have your kind interference in causing justice to be done me, you will be the means of enabling me as a young Man just entering into business to go on in the support of my Wife & Children by honest industry and without which I fear I shall be so materialy(sic) injured as to make it a work of time to recover myself again

I have the honour to be

with great respect
Your devoted
Humble servt
Wm Summers'

227 WILLIAM SUMMERS TO MR DAY SOLICITOR AT MILVERTON 4 NOV. 1816 FROM ASHILL

'Dear Sir I regret that you could not conveniently remain at Honiton to hear the whole of the business between Mr Law and myself gone thro' Still I think you heard sufficient of it to be convinced of the justice of my claim on Mr Law on my own Account, and of his illiberal (not to say unjust) conduct towards me. You will recollect that he disclaimed any knowledge of the Maps of the new and old Road at Holnicote, and my charge of 10s/6d for making a sketch of Mr Crangs Estate for Mr Weech, which sums he stated he had omitted in his account (and which you will find are omitted) as he had no claim on Sir Thos for them and that as the order was given to me I was bound to look to Sir Thos for payment of . . . – [illegible.]

I satisfactorily proved to the Arbitrators Mr Laws agreemt to pay me 5d per acre for my labour in his imploy, but had unfortunately for myself under Mr Laws directions made out my account for the Commons above 100 acres at 3d with a memorandum at the bottom thereof that the additonal 2d was to be paid to me if Sir Thos would allow it (which Mr Law admitted before the Arbitrators), which has deprived me of 45l [45£] at the time I delivered my account to Mr L as before described. I considered him my friend and was bound to comply with his directions but he has now taken advantage of my credeility(sic) and robed(sic) me of my just due.

You recollect in the case of myself and Bradley against Law, that he denied his liability to pay me the £96 . 19s . 0d for the business done by me at Holnicote and Killerton and it was . . . that I was not his agent in doing that work, Sir Thos having given us the order thro Shillibeer, as I could not prove any order or direction from Mr L that sum is to be paid to me by Sir Thos and Mr Law has relinquished all claim on Sir Thos for the same so that I am to apply to him for the before mentioned several sums amounting together to £102 . 14s . 6d and I have inclosed you the particulars of my bills for that amount

Mr Law produced before the arbitrators in this action, two agreements between himself and Bradley which I was not aware had ever been made, and as these agreements existed between them the arbitrators are of the opinion under the authority of the case of Lucas and others against Dalacome reported in the 1st Vol of Marl & Salwins Reports page 249 that the joint action could not be supported against Mr Law and that he had a right to pay Bradley the money to my predjudice, which by documents produced by Mr Ford before the Arbitrators it appeared he had done, not withstanding that Mr Law well knew that I had paid the expenses of doing the work to a considerable amount and which in fact amounted to upwards of £200 of which sum I have been completely defrauded besides the time I gave up to the business and it clearly appeared that Mr Law had paid Mr Bradley £126. 19s after he knew that I ought to have been paid that sum as well as the £102 . 14s . 6d for the business transacted for him by Bradley & myself

I will thank you to write to Mr Ford to be satisfied that Sir Thos is to pay me the above mentioned sum and to fix a day for me to call on you for the business I shall have occasion to be at Taunton on Saturday next and should you be there also we can arrange it; if not I will ride to your House in the morning if you will be at home when I shall be able more fully to explain the business

An early answer will oblige

Your obt servt

Wm Summers

Ashill Nov 4th 1816

Mr Bawdon sent yr Papers by Shillibeer to the Castle Taunton'

234 AL TO TDA 19 DEC. 1816 FROM STURMINSTER NEWTON

'I am to inform you I have not recd half the Money which you were so good as to order me last Xmas; and am sorry to say for want of assistance, I was unable to finish the Valuations of your Property which I fully purpos'd last Summer. I have sent a letter to Mr Day from this place on the 17th which I would wish you

to see – I have done Business for many years with great pleasure for several Branches of the Acland Family, and am sorry I have not been so fortunate in serving you'

235 LETTER SENT BY JOHN DAY TO TDA 27 DEC. 1816, COPY OF AN ORIGINAL SENT TO A L

Deduced from text 'I have received yours of the 17th inst., and although I am not surprised on hearing from you, yet I must confess that I was greatly astonished at the contents of your Letter; for really I am not aware that I have given you any cause to be offended.

It has ever been my wish to fulfill the intentions of Sir Thomas Acland and Lord Carnarvon by paying you handsomely for what you have done for them; but his Lordship and Sir Thomas conceiving that you have overcharged them, and having Commissioned me to pay what you are justly entitled to; you cannot I think, on cool reflection, be offended at my having acted honestly towards my honorable employers by objecting to and endeavouring to moderate such charges as appeared to me to be unreasonable and unjust.

For instance; the charge of 5 per cent for marking and valuing the Timber estimated at £5112 on Sir Thomas's Estates exchanged with Lord Carnarvon, notwithstanding your positive engagement with Sir Thomas to charge for all your valuations at the rate of two Guineas a day including all expenses. But when you stated to me that in agreeing with Sir Thomas to make your valuations at two Guineas a day, you did not intend that it should extend to the valuation of Timber, and believing what you said; I thought it my duty to satisfy myself by enquiring what would be a reasonable per centage for marking and valuing Timber for sale or exchange: and I was informed by respectable and bred surveyors that upon £1000 and upwards, one and half per cent was the usual Charge; and a very handsome remuneration for a Surveyors trouble, so that instead of £255. 12 you oght to have charged £/. 4s only.

I will not impose upon myself the task of enquiring how you can consistently with a due regard for your Character, charge me with preventing you from completing the valuation of Sir

Thomas Acland's Property; but will rest satisfied with the conviction that I shall be acquitted by your cooler judgment. When Mr Carew and myself met you at Killerton in August last, I told you how anxious Sir Thomas was that you should complete the valuation of his Leasehold Estates – you then said that, you should have completed your valuations had not your Books been withheld by Mr Weech. But the fact is, that you never applied to Mr Weech for them; as your letter of the 29th of May last clearly shows: in that letter you thus express yourself "I wish to inform you that I have sent to Sir Thomas Acland the whole of the Survey complete, excepting the valuation of some of his Leasehold Property which I have not yet been able to attend to from my other engagements".

Thus Sir you see the dilemma created by your intemperate feelings

You are also pleased to say that it was generally believed that it was my wish to have saddled you with the Costs in Summers's Action. All that I said at the Meeting which could by any possibility have induced a prejudiced mind to have drawn such a conclusion, was (in answer to a question put to me) that Sir Thomas never supposed himself to have a seperate(sic) dealing with Summers, but considered him merely as an Agent employed by you to take his directions as to the manner in which you were to perform his Commission; and this Sir Thomas in his Letter to me of 22nd June 1816 informed me was the case; surely then I did not do wrong in stating this fact when asked the question on my Oath.

You have also insinuated that I have laid your Bill on Sir Thomas before Mr Abraham for his Opinion and remarks. In assuring you that I have not had the least communication with that Gentleman on the subject; I am actuated by the hope that a mature consideration will not only destroy your present animosity; but make you more anxious to confess that the whole of your Charges against me are extremely illiberal and unjust

As I am most anxious that the Matter between you and Sir Thomas should be closed; I will instantly recommend him to refer your Bill to some respectable Gentleman, and which I have no doubt he will most readily do. But with regard to your demand on Lord Carnarvon (his Lordship being out of the Kingdom) I can on no account agree to pay you more than one and half per cent for valuing his Timber.'

241 WILLIAM SUMMERS PROBABLY TO JOHN DAY 10 JAN. 1817

'Mr Shillibeer being in London I cannot obtain from him his bill for Sketching the adjoining Country on the Holnicote Map, but the Account stands on my Book of having paid him for that work £65:12s:6d which I believe include the expense of Mudges Map which I know was considerable, should Shillibeer return in a few [days] I will obtain from him the necessary particulars and forward them to you, in the meantime should you see Sir Thos Acland you will have the goodness to lay this letter before him, as I wish to leave it to him to pay me what he thinks proper, if he consider it in the least an overcharge, for I am ready to acknowledge that I did but very little with the making of the Maps as Bradley took that department to himself while I was engaged out and the charge for this work was made by him, but unfortunately for me the work was principally done by Shillibeer to home(sic) I have paid for this and for the other Maps of Sir Thos Aclands & others upwards of 300l of which I have never recd one Shilling and its decided I cannot recover anything from Mr Law, I must therefore set down content with the loss excepting what Sir Thos will be pleased to pay me on this acct which will be most thankfully recd by

Your obt Servt
Wm Summers'

243 J DAY TO TDA 18 JAN. 1817

'I enclose a correspondence between Mr Law and myself and it will appear that I have given offence without ever intending to do so – the Charges contained in his last Letter I will explain most satisfactorily when I have the honor(sic) of seeing you. Mr Law proposes to refer his demands on you to certain Surveyors named in his Letter of the 30th of December. But I submit that it would be better to refer the Business to some Private or Professional Gentleman who can if he should think it necessary or advisable avail himself of the Evidence of Surveyors. Mr E–

–ton of Bradford near Taunton a man of great eminence as a Surveyor informed me some little time since that he always charges two Guineas a day for valuing Timber and never more that he marked valued and sold 17500£ worth for Mr Luttrell last Spring and charged only at that rate – and that in his opinion even one and half per cent upon such an amount so the present is too much by a great deal.'

244 WILLIAM SUMMERS PROBABLY TO JOHN DAY 19 JAN. 1817

'I hope that by this time you have seen Sir T D Acland, and that he has come to some determination respecting the settlement of my Bill, and I trust you will be able to make me a remittance by the Bearer, for I assure you in consequence of the disappointments I have met with, I am at present in great <u>distress</u>, or I would not trouble you at this time, relying that you will comply with my request if it is in your power

Wm Summers'

245 J DAY TO TDA 3 FEB. 1817 FROM MILVERTON

'I am rather short of Cash and as it is certainly much to be wished that Mr Law should have remitted to him the remainder of the 500£ promised him last year' (send me some money!)

246 J DAY TO TDA 4 FEB. 1817 FROM MILVERTON

A L produced evidence that Summers was employed by TDA independently of AL the 'work was done without his direction or knowledge at the time, and proving by —— that he had not made any charge to you for it – the Arbitrator determined that he was not liable to pay Summers, and consequently that Summers must look to you for payment'. Summers leaves it to TDA to pay what he thinks proper for 'the Sketch of the Country adjoining Holnicote'; he says he is out of pocket £65-12-6

262 G B KINGDON TO TDA 18 AUG. 1817 FROM STRATTON

Information about resolutions entered into concerning Bude Canal. Mr Green was appointed to make a survey and report.

Principal object 'conveyance of sea sand for manure' At present roads much damaged by use of carts and wagons and if goods were brought back to Bude and the harbour was improved 'to make it safe and commodious' all would benefit. In 1774 an Act was proposed to make a canal but was not carried into execution; the present scheme is different and requires a new Act; does TDA think it feasible to get Government help; dues would benefit TDA as well as the whole district; would benefit the agriculture of the area – export of corn important and an improved harbour would help.

266 G B KINGDON TO TDA 18 OCT. 1817 FROM STRATTON

Enclosure concerning Bude Canal and Harbour 'The Charges and Expenses of the Engineer Surveyor &c to the 4th Novr 1817 549£-10s-0d' List of Subscribers and sums subscribed

281 AL TO J DAY 1817 LITTLE BRAY ESTATE

282 A L TO J DAY 30 DEC. 1816 FROM LITTLEHAM

'I have recd your letter of the 27th, and it is needless to enter into its contents, farther than to say; you have from time to time promised me remittances, both on Acct of the Earl of Carnarvon and Sir Thos Acland to no purpose' See letter no. 235

315 G B KINGDON TO TDA 18 APRIL 1818 – BUDE CANAL

Describes meeting about improvements to the haven at Bude and the proposed canal. 'Mr Green, the engineer, read his Report and shewed his Plans and Estimates of the Expenses. He also exhibited an admirable Model, on a large Scale . . .'

316 JOHN CAREW TO TDA 18 APRIL 1818 FROM STRATTON

Report on proceedings at the meeting. Estimate 'for improving Bude harbour & of cutting the Canal nearly to Okehampton, with lateral branches, is about 120,000£ & if it be carried to Launceston, so as to connect it with the Tamar about 30,000£

more'. Carew concerned about the profitability for TDA and over the loss of land – the best

362 Ld Carnarvon to James Brown 1821 copy signed J P Peters sent to Mr Day 19 Oct. 1827 from Crigmurrion near Tregony

Mentions Cornish business naming Corgurrul – to be conveyed to Miss Martin; rating of TDA's estates at Treluckey Major, Pencoose, Resparven

373 J Carew to TDA 1 April 1826

Trouble over possible building on North Down (Bude) – undesirable

381 J Tricker to TDA 7 Oct. 1827

Noting TDA owns 1/4 Cuby Parish

382 G B Kingdon to TDA 15 Oct. 1827 – Bude Harbour

Dealing with stone and the quantity taken. Wants amount due to him left by Mr Carew with Mr Shearm of Stratton and he will call for it. Settlement promised 2 years ago – forgotten. In 1800 he purchased property, spent money seeking quiet enjoyment but since 1819 'I can scarcely call it quiet enjoyment'

432 James Randolph to TDA 7 Dec. 1830

Bound stones on Penstrase Moor removed – lately fixed on the disputed parts; 'One field in particular in Cragantallan, called Willis's (No 9 on your map)', mention of Gwills Mill, Skarrier Gate, Kenwyn and Trencreak

434 J Day to TDA 20 Dec. 1830 from Wellington – Cornish estates

Sending copy of letter written by Mr Collins to Mr Tremaine of Trerise(sic) and sent on by him, i.e. Tremaine. Says he does not

expect TDA to accept lower offer (for Goviley) than price given 'some time since'

Enclosure: from Thurston Collins to Mr Tremaine Trerise 10 Dec. 1830 from St Columb His client Mr Collins wishes to invest in land and asks for his letter to be sent to Mr Day and asks that he (JD) should name his price; prices of land and stock have been falling!

441 Edward Collins to TDA 21 Jan. 1831

'In consequence of learning from your tenant at Trerice, that you are still desirous of disposing of your Manor of Goviley which was offered for sale about a year ago for which I was then in treaty, through my agent with Mr Day – That letter I addressed to you at Killerton but not having received any reply, and finding that you are now residing in Somersetshire it is possible that you have not received it . . .' if TDA still wishes to sell send a line to Collins at Trutham nr Truro

444 J Carew to TDA 1831

'The Langacre purchase will I trust be settled next week' TDA sold other property to pay for Langacre

445 J Carew to TDA 23 Feb. 1831 from Wellington

Discussing leases for buildings at Bude; Robert Birmingham was concerned with preparation of plans

1148M/Box 17/1 Letters 1808–9 30 Nov. 1808

J Weech to 'Mr Law has not furnished me with any valuation other than those of the Killerton and Marsh estate'

1148M/Box 17/6

Series of letters dealing with matters between Lord Rolle and TDA and behaviour of Weech and AL

26 Oct. 1813 Copy of letter from TDA to Lord Rolle

'I believe the valuation in 1808 by Alexander Law for the letting of the estates in 1809 not according to their true value but such as would enable all the old Tenants to retake their Farms certainly easily. Principle taken further than was intended, through a misunderstanding.' AL asked by TDA to give a fair price for the estate (to be sold to Rolle) – Stevenstone – but he declined

19 Nov. 1813 J Weech to TDA from Milverton

'Mr Law has a happy knack of shifting or rather endeavouring to shift every ——— or blame in conduct from himself to another, and so long as he escapes he cares not who is the sufferer — That he has not in the present instance assigned his primary reason for declining a secondary valuation is evident from a Letter of his to us on the 4 Augt last in which he says "In the matter betwixt Lord Rolle and Sir Thomas I hope I shall be excused from giving my Opinion – I never did any business for Lord Rolle but which was much animadverted upon by his agents" It is then he goes on to say "You will please to recollect in your first letter to me on that subject, there was something in it which I conceiv'd was not what I had usually been accustomed to in business of that kind"' – Weech goes on to describe conflict with Law

Somerset Record Office

Ten letters from John Palmer Acland (JPA) to Alexander Law and 197 from Law to Acland contain much detail of the day-to-day problems associated with managing widely-scattered estates. Many of these letters refer to those belonging to John Palmer Acland and some, of equal importance, to lands belonging to Sir Thomas Dyke Acland, 10th Bart. The items extracted are principally, though not entirely, those recording Law's responsibilities for surveying and map-making.

Bundle 1 DD/AH/Box 24/FT9/1

1807 Nov. 23 AL reporting a discovery at Lower Sigford and advising JPA to secure Mr Hodge's services; included is a letter from Hodge which concluded , You will please present my best respects to Messrs Bradly(sic) & Summers'.

1808 Jan. 20 dealing with mine business; Mr Hodge prevented from going down the mine – AL suggests this implies the mine either very rich or very poor – AL has sketched the surface.

Jan. 28 'I have been at Killerton at the request of Sir Thomas Acland who hath given me full direction to Survey Plan and value the whole of his Property'.

March 14 (from North Petherton) 'I came here last evening to make a begining)sic) on the Survey of Sir Thomas Aclands Lands in this Neighbourhood. For the past Fortnight I have been at Kilerton(sic) and put that business in such Train as can with safety be proceeded on during my absence . . . I have applied to Mr Symes for the Particulars of the Estates of Sir Thomas Acland with which he hath the management'.

April 14 'I will thank you if you could send me the Book Maps of Mr Oxenhams Lands' . . . before I return [I] shall in all probability see Sir Thomas Acland which is my only reason for wishing to have it'.

Oct 22 going to look over property at North Petherton 'which you take from your sister'; AL states he has sent a bill to Mr Short for extra business for Mr Oxenham but 'as I am engaged to Mr Oxenham with a certain salary I really wish when you see it as it will be sent to you that you will draw your pen through every part you think wrong'.

1809 Jan. 7 includes plan of a house to be built at Sigford Farm.

March 5 Barnes has struck off items from AL's bill on Mr Oxenham 'I consider it as a strong proof of what I have long suspected that he is not my Friend . . . I find in almost every instance that Sir Thomas's Property hath been let without the least degree of Judgement and I think I may venture to say that by means of the Survey having been put off till Sir Thomas Acland became of age instead of its having been done when you Propos'd it that Sir Thos for this one Year will loose(sic) 3000l [3000£]' AL lists the business Barnes has deducted –

journey to Sigford, Exeter, Ashburton where he 'measured Ground where mine Workings are, and made plan'.

March 30 AL says he has been over the greater part of Mr Oxenhams lands this spring.

April 25 AL concerned with repairs at Oxenham. Also says 'I am consider'd by Mr Weech as one in his way and that Sir Thomas Acland shall suffer, sooner then(sic) I shall carry my wishes into effect ..In all the sales which hath taken place for Sir Thomas I was never consulted on any one point and I never knew the day or Hour the Property was to be disposed of, but by the public Paper. This is what I have not been accustomed to . . .'.

Aug. 17 Information regarding Mr Oxenham's tenants.

BUNDLE 2 DD/AH BOX 24/FT9/2

1812 Feb. 9 problem over dealing with drainage on the Newhouse estate; concerning AL not paying an account above a previously agreed figure, a case has been brought against AL =, the Attorney must be one of the meanest Scoundrels existing, to act in such a manner . . . I have been nearly 40 Years in Business on my own Acct . . . In short I am surrounded with a set of Sharks . . .'.

March 5 'I have gone over all your estates' – Mamhead, Kenton, Kenn.

April 8 Queries regarding Oxenham property.

June 2 AL has visited estates on the other side of the Exe. 'On Monday I set out for Dulverton to value an exchange betwixt the Earl of Carnarvon and Sir Thos Acland'.

July 8 'On Monday I go to Great Torrington for Lord Rolle and from thence to South Tawton for the Dean and Canons of Windsor'; trouble over money and Mr Barnes 'I wish I had never known him, he has been a great enemy to me. My Valuations of the Dean and Chapters property he hath put into the Hands of an Ironmonger in Exeter and made him their Surveyor in my place. In fact he is the only Man on Earth that I could not do Business with – with Pleasure'.

Oct. 15 'My Father was a Builder & Architec(sic) in an extensive Line with whom I lived till I was 18 years of Age and by which means I had an insight into that Business which few of my Profession ever had'.

BUNDLE 1 DD/AH BOX 11/15/1

1818 Feb. 20 AL pleased JPA coming to visit his property.

March 20 AL been all over JPA's property in Mamhead, Kenton and Kenn – damaged in gales.

May 9 Queries over Sir Lawrence Palk's rights on land owned by JPA ofter the death of Mr Oxenham.

July 28 AL selling property for JPA in Exminster – sold Anchor Inn for £775 and the cottage for £220, both bought by Cartwright, Steward at Haldon House; 'This is a dear purchase, but I suppose his money comes in easy I employed this Man many years ago when he was not worth Sixpence; but since he hath been Agent for Sir Lawrence Palk he hath purchased more property than I ever could; who have done six times the Business; This is a mystery to me'.

Aug. 2 AL says Sir Lawrence Palk's agents deliberately trying 'to lessen your property in value as much as possible'.

Sept. 8 refers to tenement at Black Aller; 'You or Mr Symes must have Maps or other Surveys of Aller or North Petherton Lands which would be highly requisite for me to have'.

Oct. 10 House in Gandy Lane [Exeter] sold for £240 – 'the most disgraceable part of your property is here got rid of'.

Nov. 13 'I have for many years past endeavour'd to get my Accounts settled to no purpose'; asks JPA to examine the charges he has made (TDA & E of C) and hopes this will be the 'means of frustrating the injury which Mr Day hath long attempted to do me . . . I have had nothing but trouble from the Agents ever since, and instead of following my advice; acted contrary to everything I recommended and in the affair of Seaton, suffer'd the Tenant Otten to pocket at least 3000£ At Holnicote Sir Thomas has a Footman for his Bailif(sic) and who is now the greatest Farmer in all that Country and possessed of Property above anything which I can boast of and Mr Pearce who was a Country Carpenter, and Bailiff to the Earl of Carnarvon, keeps a better House than I could afford, yet these men are in full confidence, but if they had not been better paid than I have, they would not have been in the affluence they are now.

Dec. 5 I have this moment had two Letters put into my Hands, One from Sir Thos. Acland informing, that he had given an Order to Mr Day to get my Account settled as soon as possible, the other from Mr Day saying, that he would fix for Monday the 14th Inst if you should be at Dawlish to meet you and me there. I have by this post writ him that if I am alive and in Health, I will be there . . . The means which hath been taken to injure me, by Sir Thos. Aclands Agents hath been most cruel, and in my oppinion(sic) most infamous; purporting to get me discharged from Sir Thos. Aclands service to his ultimate loss; but I thank God that I never wanted Business, and that in the most respectable kind and from the first connections'.

DD/AH Box 11/15/2 Bundle 2

1819 Feb. 17 'If you are really determined to sell your estates in Kenn, Chudleigh Manaton Ilsington and Colebrook this Summer'; complains of treatment by TDA's Agents, by Mr Barnes for the Dean and Chapter and says he will '*increase my Farm* or go near Exeter perhaps Heavitree and shorten my Business'.

May. includes list of properties for sale; mentions estates in Kenn and Exminster, praising their location, lime rock at Upcott and copper mine at Lower Sigford; see *Sherborne Mercury* Oct. 19 1819

June 9 AL says he is tired of business 'I have not been liberally dealt with and if I had not been prudent I should not have been able to retire with a sufficiency but thank God that is not the case'.

Oct. 11 'Would it not be more convenient for you to come to my House during your Stay here. I can insure(sic) you a good bed and Batchelors(sic) Fare. I cannot now make it quite so comfortable as when Mrs Law was living'.

Oct. 17 dealing with sale fixed for Nov. 8th and 9th; has asked for price on rights of Common attached to estates in Kenn.

Dec. 4 encloses a letter from Charles Chilcott stating 'I can furnish you with the Plan and particulars of Sir J P Aclands Lands and Tithes in North Petherton'; says he never mapped Aller.

Bundle 3 DD/AH Box 11/15/3

1820 Feb 15 Asks for maps and papers dealing with property at North Petherton and Aller.

Feb. 17 Al going to Cornwall to settle disputes between proprietors of lands through which the Bude Canal will pass.

April 19 'You have no doubt been informed by Mr Ford that I sent him my valuation of the Lands which I went over at the request of Mr Templer and which I found to be worth about £18000 besides the Timber which is not more then(sic) about £500 and the Canal from which Mr Templer anticipates a great profit, runs through the Grounds, on the whole, I think you can with safety advance from 12 to £15000'.

'I am sorry to say that the Account which I have received differs so widely from the printed particulars of Mr Symes that I really know what not to do. I have requested the favour of Chilcott to meet me on Wednesday next, at N Petherton where I have left all the particulars to be made acquainted with them, and have such explaination(sic) as I can venture to treat for the Tithes. On Emses Tenmt there is 5 acres difference in the measure and I believe there is a difference in every Tenmt far beyond anything I was ever met with before and the whole of your property is not inserted in the map which he hath sent me'.

April 20 Chilcott did not keep the appointment. AL says he will wait to give him time to come from Crowcombe but 'if he does not come, I will put all the particulars I have of the property here with his own rough map into a parcel for him, to put it into some order that I may understand it; in its present shape it is impossible for any one to'.

Bundle 4 DD/AH Box 11/15/4

1821 March 3 AL going to Cornwall to Stratton to value lands taken up by Bude Canal.

April 7 trouble with Ford (solicitor) 'I hope Sir John you will pardon me if I here say anything wrong. I have not been consulted in the management of your Affairs as I was in the beging(sic) of Mr Fords acting and I think he now takes upon him, some parts of the Business which certainly not, as I conceive, in his department, and I have no hesitation in saying that I *think* he looks forward to my place at no very distant period; but thank God I have always found you my Friend; ever since I had the pleasure of knowing you; and I have that firm reliance on your goodness; that if I do my Duty, I shall not be cast off'.

June 1 AL says he has gone beyond JPA's orders and told his clerk to write to the tenants stating that all who attend the Audit and paid their rents regularly would have 20% reduction. 'They are all pretty much of tillage Farmers and require easily the greatest assistance'; returns are now a half what was made in the war; suggests gradation would help – all tillage 20% – 30%, corn, sheep, dairy and a little grazing about 20%, wholly or nearly all dairy 15%, wholly grazing or nearly 10%.

The Prideaux Brune Collection in the Cornwall Record Office

This archive contains some 1700 letters covering the period 1796–1829. Of these about 440 were written by Alexander Law, principally between 1800 and 1820. Eight letters merely inform the Rev. Charles Prideaux Brune of Law's intention to visit Killerton, Holnicote or John Acland whilst working on behalf of Prideaux Brune. Others are more detailed.

The letters are filed in separate bundles each containing a miscellaneous group of documents. This means that some examples of different dates have the same reference.

1802 May 30 'I spent a few days at Killerton with Mr Hugh Acland on some business for Sir Thomas Acland and on findg I did business for you, I never in my life saw any Man express so much Happyness on such an occasion.' PB/6/6

1803 Sept 11 '. . . what adds to her affliction our Young Man (Thomas Bradley) hath withdrawn himself from my protection, gone to London on a frolic, spent all his money and does not know he writes where to find a Shilling. I will take care he shall not absolutely want, but his Pittance shall be a scanty one, till he can help himself . . .' PB/6/7

1804 Jan. 27 'My Nephew hath got a good situation at Sea and I have reason to think that he will soon be made a Purser which I think will equal any Situation he could have had in my Line and I have an offer of an experienced Young Man to take the Survey off my hands.' PB/6/8

June 30 'I have engaged a young man who was regularly bred to the Surveying and has been surveying great part of the Oxenham (Devon) property for which I am concerned and the manner in which he does business is in general correct but not in that particular manner in which I have been accustom'd to adopt and what I have brought my Nephew to follow, and from the pressing manner in which he solicits to be again admitted to my House and employ I shall be induced to reinstate him'. PB/6/8

1805 20 Jan. 'The late Act of Parliament disqualifying Agents not being Attorneys from drawing Deeds is a most untoward circumstance to me as it will deprive me at least of 50 l (£) a year of my Income'. PB/6/12

Sept. 30 'I have now to return you my sincere thanks for the favor(sic) you have done me in procuring Mr Agars Interest in my Case which will without any difficulty get me admitted a Member of one of the Inns of Court'. PB/6/12

1807 Sept. 15 'but not being myself born in England . . .' PB/6/20

Nov. 14 'I was engaged to spend the Week at Mr Shorts with Mr John Acland to view the Condition of the Oxenham Estate.' PB/6/20

1808 April 9 '. . . I have some thoughts of spending a day or two at Mr John Aclands at Fairfield'. PB/6/22

1809 June 24 'On Monday I go for Sir Thomas Aclands Seal at Holnicote near Minehead Somerset where I purpose remaining just one Month.' PB/6/23

July 6 (from Holnicote) 'I cannot possible leave this place for some weeks'. PB/6/23

Sept. 23 '. . . unfortunately Sir Thos Acland has fixed for my being at Holnicote next Tuesday and fear he will detain me some time.' PB/6/23

Dec. 3 'I have again got my Nephew with me he appears sensible of his late imprudencies and if I can be the means of making him a useful Member of Society I shall think my trouble and expence well bestow'd'. PB/6/23

1810 Sept. 18 from Littleham '. . . here until 27 when I go to Tiverton to attend a Sale of some property of Sir Thos Acland.' PB/6/27

1812 May 19 'I will do my untmost to serve Lord de Dunstanville I have always found him a generous Employer, and a pleasant Man; but how I am to accomplish it I am rather at a loss from so many prior Engagements I have no less than the Parishes of Great Torrington, St Giles and Chittlehampton to survey for Lord Rolle. The Parishes of South molton(sic) South Tawton and Plymstock for the Dean and Canons of Windsor. A large Property to value in exchange betwixt the Earl of Carnarvon and Sir Thos D Acland Bart and the Lands of the Revd Mr Hallett of Stadcombe near Axmouth to arrange and lot . . .' PB/6/31

Sept. 16 'I am here on an exchange of property between the Earl of Carnarvon & Sir Thos Acland Bart.' PB/6/31

1813 July 14 'It would be a great pleasure to me if Lord de Dunstanville would employ Bradley, he might render his Lordship considerable service in many respects as to his Lordships property, few men are more capable, but he certainly does not love work like most of your Cornish Attorneys more shew than substance but I think if he could get into some Office under some Land Steward of great practice he might render many services and be extremely useful which would not require so much real hard labour as surveying Lands.' PB/6/31

Aug. 28 AL mentions the fact that he and Barnes could never agree 'like many others of his profession, [he] would be glad to see matters go wrong than otherwise . . .'.

1814 July 20 'I started on Monday Morning the 11th and went to Dulverton to finish an exchange betwixt the Earl of Carnarvon and Sir Thos Acland.' PB/6/32

1816 Jan. 25 complaining he has done work for Sir Thos Acland for which he has only been partially paid. '. . . Sir Thomas Acland considers me as one in his way.' PB/6/34

March 10 'P.S. Mr Barnes in my oppinion(sic) dug a pit for me, but at last he is got into it himself for I now have the entire management of Mr [John] Acland's Affairs this Quarter and of course I have nothing more to do with that Gentleman, [i.e. Mr Barnes] and for the future I never want to act with him.' PB/6/34

Dec. 18 '. . . I have many Friends in Devonshire, whom I cannot desert particularly John Acland Esqr, for whom I hve fought many hard Battles betwixt some of his Tenants and Mr Barnes his former Agent and I have now on my hands, a more serious Business for him . . .'. PB/6/34

1817 March 9 'Sir Thomas Aclands Steward hath at last sent me a remittance which may render it unnecessary for me to call on Mr John Acland as soon as my return from Hants; as Sir T's Acland may think I ought to be satisfied with what I have got for the present.' PB/6/34

March 10 'I am at this moment confin'd to a severe Fit of the Gout. I was never before so severely attacked.' PB/6/34

March 17 'I am able to get about again . . . Sir Thos Acland has sent me a part of my bill on him and the £700 which I was disappointed in some time ago was paid me last Monday.' PB/6/34

May 21 I hope to finish here which will complete the whole of my engagement with Sir Thomas Acland; and I go from hence to arrange some Business for John Acland Esq. and his son at Fairfield near Stowey' a letter will find AL at 'John Symes Esq. Stowey near Bridgwater Somerset.' PB/6/34

June 28 John Acland has asked Alexander Law to manage his Somerset estates as well as his Devon estates. PB/6/34

1818 Feb. 24 You see Sir Thomas Acland have brought in the Bill to disqualify all persons but regular Attorneys from drawing

Conveyances. Sir T Aland (sic) is not aware of the Curse (?) he will intail on the Landed Interest if the Bill should pass into a Law. It certainly cannot hurt me, for I am certain I shall not get this Year, with all my trouble, the amount of my Certificate . . .' PB/6/40

May 17 'It cannot in the common and ordinary course of events be many years longer that I can continue in this Service, and therefore, I would recommend you to look out some person who not only understands receiving your Rents, holding your Courts, which by the bye, is but a small part of the Business of an Agent, but the nature and management of Lands Woods and Buildings and Tenants suitable to the Farms which in my oppinion (sic) as difficult a part as any to find out, and to secure that Person.' PB/6/40

1819 June 2 from Prideaux Brune to his solicitor, Edward Coode, speaking of Alexander Law: 'I know his nature well, having frequently experienced his perverse obstinacy of temper . . .' PB/6/26

Sept 5 from Prideaux Brune to Edward Coode 'Mr Law has always unfortunately for his own Candour at least made his blunder concur with his own Interest.' PB/6/26

Dec 18 from Prideaux Brune to Edward Coode, says Alexander Law 'not exempt from Cunning and Chicanery.' PB/6/51

Index of Personal Names

Index of Manors and Parishes

Selective Bibliography

Acland, Anne, *A Devon Family* (London & Chichester: Phillimore, 1981).

Acland, Arthur H.D., *Memoirs and Letters of the Right Hon. Sir Thomas Dyke Acland* (London: Chiswick Press, for private circulation, 1902).

Adams, I.H., *Agrarian landscape terms; a glossary for historical geography* Special Publication Number Nine (London: Institute of British Geographers, 1976).

Ballard, Richard, *The Priory Church of St Andrew, Stogursey* 2nd ed., (Exeter: Papyrus Printers, 1992).

Bendall, A. Sarah, *Dictionary of Land Surveyors and Local Map-Makers of Great Britain and Ireland 1530–1950* (London: The British Library, 1997).

Bere, Rennie & Bryan Dudley Stamp, *The Book of Bude and Stratton* (Buckingham: Barracuda Books Ltd, 1980).

Beswetherick, Kathleen, *The Aclands and Bude Haven* (Bude: K. Beswetherick, 1995).

Boase, George Clement, *Collectanea Cornubiensis* (Truro: Netherton & Worth, 1890).

Boase, George Clement, and William Prideaux Courtney, *Bibliotheca Cornubiensis* 3 vols (London: Longman Green, 1882).

Burton, S.H., *Exmoor* 3rd ed. (London: Robert Hale Ltd, 1978).

Chadwyck Healy, Charles E.H., *The History of the Part of West Somerset comprising the Parishes of Luccombe, Selworthy, Stoke Pero, Porlock, Culbone and Oare* (London: Henry Southeran and Company, 1901)

Clay, C., 'Landlords and Estate Management in England' in Joan Thirsk, ed.,*The Agrarian History of England and Wales V 1640–1750* (Cambridge: Cambridge University Press, 1985).

Collinson, Rev. John, *The History of Somersetshire in Three Volumes* (Bath: R. Cruttwell, 1791); microprint edition (Trowbridge: Alan Sutton Publishing Limited, 1983).

Couldridge, Christopher, John Coldridge of Exeter, Land Surveyor, unpublished PhD thesis (Oxford, Brookes University).

Delano-Smith, Catherine and Roger J.P. Kain, *English Maps: A History* (London: British Library, 1999).

Dixon, Janet with Edward F. Williams, *Parish Surveys in Somerset 3 Carhampton* (Taunton: Somerset Archaeological & Natural History Society, 1980).

Dunning, R.W., ed., *The Victoria County History of the County of Somerset, volume VI (Bridgwater and neighbouring Parishes)* (London and Oxford: University of London Institute of Historical Research, printed by OUP, 1992).

Exeter Flying Post.

Fortescue, Hugh, 4th Earl, *A Chronicle of Castle Hill* (Privately printed, 1929).

Fraser, Robert, *General View of the County of Devon* (London: C. Macrae, 1794).

Gover, J.E.B., A. Mawer and F.M. Stenton, *The Place-Names of Devon* Parts I & II (Cambridge: The University Press, 1969).

Gray, Todd, *The Garden History of Devon* (Exeter: University of Exeter Press, 1995).

Hadfield, Charles, *The Canals of South West England* (Newton Abbot: David & Charles, 1967, 2nd ed., 1985).

Hainsworth, D. R., 'The Estate Steward' in Wilfred Prest, ed., *The Professions in Early Modern England* (London, New York and Sydney: Croom Helm, 1987).

Harley, J.B. and Yolande O'Donoghue, *The Old Series Ordnance Survey Maps of Englanf and Wales* Vol. II Devon, Cornwall and West Somerset (Harry Margary, Lympne Castle, Kent, 1977).

Harley, J.B., *Maps for the Local Historian* (Leicester: Blackfriars Press, 1972).

Harris, Helen and Monica Ellis, *The Bude Canal* (Newton Abbot: David & Charles, 1972).

Harris, J. Delpratt, *The Royal Devon and Exeter Hospital* (Exeter: Eland Brothers, 1922).

Heriz-Smith, Shirley, *The House of Veitch A Horticultural Record* (Diss, 2002).

Hughes, E., 'The Eighteenth-Century Estate Agent' in H.A. Cronne, T.W. Moody & D.B. Quinn, eds, *Essays in British and Irish History* (London: Frederick Muller Ltd, 1949).

Leybourn, William, *The Compleat Surveyor...* (London, 1653).

Lysons, Daniel and Samuel Lysons, *Magna Britannia Volume The Third containing Cornwall* (London: Thomas Cadell and W. Davies, 1814).

Lysons, Daniel and Samuel Lysons, *Magna Britannia Volume the Sixth containing Devonshire Parts I & II* (London: Thomas Cadell,1822).

Maxwell Lyte, Sir H.C., *A History of Dunster and the Families of Mohun and Luttrell* 2 vols (London: The St Catherine's Press, 1909).

The National Trust, *Killerton House* (National Trust Enterprises Ltd, 2000).

The National Trust, *Trerice Cornwall* (London, 1970 and 1981).

O.E.D., *The Oxford English Dictionary*.

Oliver, Richard, *Ordnance Survey Maps a concise guide for historians* (London: The Charles Close Society, 1993).

Porter, J.H., 'The Development of Rural Society' in G.E. Mingay, ed., *The Agrarian History of England and Wales, 1750–1850* (Cambridge: Cambridge University Press, 1989).

Ravenhill, Mary R. and Margery M. Rowe, eds, *Devon Maps and Map-Makers: Manuscript Maps before 1840* (Exeter: DCRS, 2000, 2002).

Ravenhill, Mary R. and Margery M. Rowe, *Maps of Georgian Devon* (Exeter: Friends of Devon's Archives, 2002).

Ravenhill, W.L.D., *A Map of the County of Devon* (Exeter: DCRS and University of Exeter, 1965).

Richards, John, *The Gentleman's Steward and Tenants of Manors Instructed* (London, 1730), reprinted with *Annuities on Lives* (London, 1739), – copy in WCL.

Savage, James, *History of the Hundred of Carhampton in the County of Somerset* 3 vols (Bristol: William Strang and London: Longman etc, 1830).

Shephard, Sue, *Seeds of Fortune* (London: Bloomsbury Publishing Plc, 2002).

Sherborne Mercury.

Thompson, F.M.L., 'Landowners and the Rural Community', in *The Victorian Countryside* G.E. Mingay, ed., (London: Routledge Kegan & Paul, 1981).

Vancouver, Charles, *General View of the Agriculture of the County of Devon* (London:1808).

Vivian, J.L., *The Visitations of Cornwall* (Exeter: William Pollard, 1887).

Vivian, J.L., *The Visitations of the County of Devon* (Exeter: William Pollard, 1895).

Worgan, G.B., *A General View of the Agriculture of the County of Cornwall* Published by the Board of Agriculture and Internal Improvement (London: G. & W. Nichol, 1811).

THE DEVON AND CORNWALL RECORD SOCIETY

7 The Close, Exeter EX1 1EZ
(founded 1904)

Officers (2006–7)

President:
Professor R.J.P. Kain CBE, BA, PhD, DLitt, FBA, FSA

Chairman of Council:
Professor C.J. Holdsworth MA, PhD, FSA, FRHistS

Hon. Secretary:
vacant

Hon. Treasurer:
R.A. Erskine BA

Hon. Editor:
Professor A. J. Thorpe BA, PhD, FRHistS

General Editor for Volume 49:
C.L. Todd Gray BA, PhD, FRHistS

The Devon and Cornwall Record Society promotes the study of history in the South West of England through publishing and transcribing original records. In return for the annual subscription members receive the volumes as published (normally annually) and the use of the Society's library, housed in the Westcountry Studies Library, Exeter. The library includes transcripts of parish registers relating to Devon and Cornwall as well as useful genealogical works.

Applications to join the Society or to purchase volumes should be sent to the Administrator, Devon and Cornwall Record Society, c/o The Devon and Exeter Institution, 7 The Close, Exeter EX1 1EZ.

DEVON & CORNWALL RECORD SOCIETY PUBLICATIONS

Obtainable from the Administrator, Devon and Cornwall Record Society, 7 The Close, Exeter EX1 1EZ

§ No longer available.   * Restricted availability: please enquire

ISSN/ISBN 0 901853

New Series

1§   *Devon Monastic Lands: Calendar of Particulars for Grants, 1536–1558*, ed. Joyce Youings, 1955   **04 6**

2   *Exeter in the Seventeenth Century: Tax and Rate Assessments, 1602–1699*, ed. W. G. Hoskins, 1957   **05 4**

3§   *The Diocese of Exeter in 1821: Bishop Carey's Replies to Queries before Visitation*, vol. I, Cornwall, ed. Michael Cook, 1958   **06 2**

4*   *The Diocese of Exeter in 1821: Bishop Carey's Replies to Queries before Visitation*, vol. II, Devon, ed. Michael Cook, 1960   **07 0**

5§   *The Cartulary of St Michael's Mount*, ed. P. L. Hull, 1962   **08 9**

6   *The Exeter Assembly: The Minutes of the Assemblies of the United Brethren of Devon and Cornwall, 1691–1717*, as Transcribed by the Reverend Isaac Gilling, ed. Allan Brockett, 1963   **09 7**

7*, 10*, 13*, 16*, 18*   *The Register of Edmund Lacy, Bishop of Exeter, 1420–1455*. Five volumes, ed. G. R. Dunstan, 1963–1972   **10 0**   **12 7**   **15 1**   **02 X**   **17 8**

8§   *The Cartulary of Canonsleigh Abbey*, calendared & ed. Vera London, 1965 **16 X**

9§   *Benjamin Donn's Map of Devon, 1765*. Introduction by W. L. D. Ravenhill, 1965 **11 9**

11§   *Devon Inventories of the Sixteenth and Seventeenth Centuries*, ed. Margaret Cash, 1966   **13 5**

12   *Plymouth Building Accounts of the Sixteenth and Seventeenth Centuries*, ed. Edwin Welch, 1967 **14 3**

14   *The Devonshire Lay Subsidy of 1332*, ed. Audrey M. Erskine, 1969   **00 3**

15   *Churchwardens' Accounts of Ashburton, 1479–1580*, ed. Alison Hanham, 1970   **01 1**

17§   *The Caption of Seisin of the Duchy of Cornwall (1377)*, ed. P. L. Hull, 1971   **03 8**

19   *A Calendar of Cornish Glebe Terriers, 1673–1735*, ed. Richard Potts, 1974 **19 4**

20   *John Lydford's Book: the Fourteenth Century Formulary of the Archdeacon of Totnes*, ed. Dorothy M. Owen, 1975 (with Historical Manuscripts Commission) **011 440046 6**

21   *A Calendar of Early Chancery Proceedings relating to West Country Shipping, 1388–1493*, ed. Dorothy A. Gardiner, 1976   **20 8**

22   *Tudor Exeter: Tax Assessments 1489–1595*, ed. Margery M. Rowe, 1977   **21 6**

23   *The Devon Cloth Industry in the Eighteenth Century: Sun Fire Office Inventories, 1726–1770*, ed. Stanley D. Chapman, 1978   **22 4**

24, 26   *The Accounts of the Fabric of Exeter Cathedral, 1279–1353*, Parts I & II, ed. Audrey M. Erskine, 1981 & 1983   **24 0**   **26 7**

25, 27   *The Parliamentary Survey of the Duchy of Cornwall*, Parts I & II, ed. Norman J. G. Pounds, 1982 & 1984   **25 2**   **27 5**

28   *Crown Pleas of the Devon Eyre of 1238*, ed. Henry Summerson, 1985   **28 3**

29   *Georgian Tiverton: the Political Memoranda of Beavis Wood, 1768–98*, ed. John Bourne, 1986   **29 1**

30   *The Cartulary of Launceston Priory* (Lambeth Palace MS.719): A Calendar, ed. P. L. Hull, 1987   **30 5**

31   *Shipbuilding on the Exe: the Memoranda Book of Daniel Bishop Davy (1799–1874) of Topsham, Devon*, ed. Clive N. Ponsford, 1988   **31 3**

32   *The Receivers' Accounts of the City of Exeter, 1304–1353*, ed. Margery M. Rowe and John M. Draisey, 1989   **32 1**

33   *Early-Stuart Mariners and Shipping: the Maritime Surveys of Devon and Cornwall, 1619–35*, ed. Todd Gray, 1990   **33 X**

34   *Joel Gascoyne's Map of Cornwall 1699*. Introduction by W. L. D Ravenhill and Oliver Padel, 1991   **34 8**

35   *Nicholas Roscarrock's 'Lives of the Saints': Cornwall and Devon*, ed. Nicholas Orme, 1992   **35 6**

36   *The Local Port Customs Accounts of Exeter, 1266–1321*, ed. Maryanne Kowaleski, 1993   **36 4**

37   *Charters of the Redvers Family and the Earldom of Devon, 1090–1217*, ed. Robert Bearman, 1994   **37 2**

38   *Devon Household Accounts, 1627–59, Part I: Sir Richard and Lady Lucy Reynell of Forde House, 1627–43, John Willoughby of Leyhill, 1644–6, and Sir Edward Wise of Sydenham, 1656–9*, ed. Todd Gray, 1995   **38 0**

39   *Devon Household Accounts 1627–59, Part II: Henry, Earl of Bath, and Rachel, Countess of Bath, of Tawstock and London, 1639–54*, ed. Todd Gray, 1996   **39 9**

40   *The Uffculme Wills and Inventories, 16th to 18th Centuries*, ed. Peter Wyatt, with an introduction by Robin Stanes, 1997   **40 2**

41   *Cornish Rentals and Surveys of the Arundell Family of Lanherne, Fourteenth to Sixteenth Centuries*, ed. H. S. A. Fox and Oliver Padel, 1998   **41 0**

42   *Liberalism in West Cornwall: The 1868 Election Papers of A. Pendarves Vivian MP*, ed. Edwin Jaggard, 1999   **42 9**

43, 45   *Devon Maps and Map-makers: Manuscript Maps before 1840*, ed. with introduction Mary R. Ravenhill and Margery M. Rowe, 2000 & 2002 **43 7   45 3**

44   *Havener's Accounts of the Earldom and Duchy of Cornwall, 1301–1356*, ed. Maryanne Kowaleski, 2001   **44 5**

46   *Death and Memory in Medieval Exeter*, ed. David Lepine and Nicholas Orme, 2003   **46 1**

47   *The Survey of Cornwall by Richard Carew,* ed. John Chynoweth, Nicholas Orme, and Alexandra Walsham, 2004   **47 X**

48   *Killerton, Camborne and Westminster. The Political Correspondence of Sir Francis and Lady Acland, 1910–29*, ed. Garry Tregidga, 2006   **48 8**

Extra Series

1   *Exeter Freemen 1266–1967*, edited by Margery M. Rowe and Andrew M. Jackson, 1973   **18 6**

2   *Guide to the Parish and Non-Parochial Registers of Devon and Cornwall 1538–1837*, compiled by Hugh Peskett, 1979; supplement 1983   **23 2**

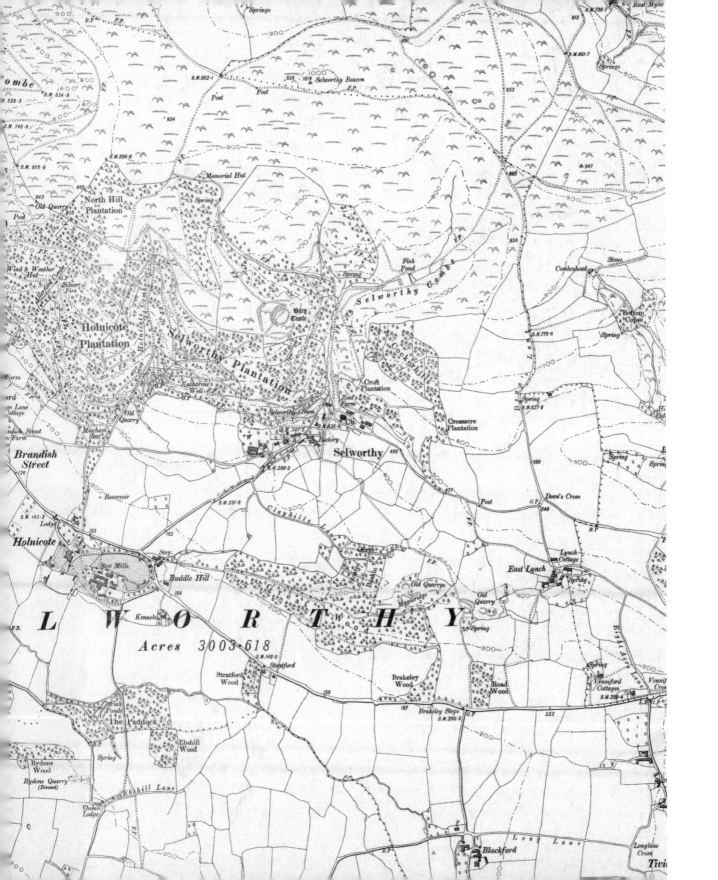